TRANSCULTURAL TEENS

New Directions in Ethnography is a series of contemporary, original works. Each title has been selected and developed to meet the needs of readers seeking finely grained ethnographies that treat key areas of anthropological study. What sets these books apart from other ethnographies is their form and style. They have been written with care to allow both specialists and non-specialists to delve into theoretically sophisticated work. This objective is achieved by structuring each book so that one portion of the text is ethnographic narrative while another portion unpacks the theoretical arguments and offers some basic intellectual genealogy for the theories underpinning the work.

Each volume in *New Directions in Ethnography* aims to immerse readers in fundamental anthropological ideas, as well as to illuminate and engage more advanced concepts. Inasmuch, these volumes are designed to serve not only as scholarly texts, but also as teaching tools and as vibrant, innovative ethnographies that showcase some of the best that contemporary anthropology has to offer.

Published Volumes

1. *Turf Wars: Discourse, Diversity, and the Politics of Place*
By Gabriella Gahlia Modan

2. *Homegirls: Language and Cultural Practice among Latina Youth Gangs*
By Norma Mendoza-Denton

3. *Allah Made Us: Sexual Outlaws in an Islamic African City*
By Rudolf Pell Gaudio

4. *Political Oratory and Cartooning: An Ethnography of Democratic Processes in Madagascar*
By Jennifer Jackson

5. *Transcultural Teens: Performing Youth Identities in French Cités*
By Chantal Tetreault

TRANSCULTURAL TEENS

Performing Youth Identities in French *Cités*

Chantal Tetreault

WILEY Blackwell

This edition first published 2015
© 2015 John Wiley & Sons, Inc.

Registered Office
John Wiley & Sons, Ltd, The Atrium, Southern Gate, Chichester, West Sussex, PO19 8SQ, UK

Editorial Offices
350 Main Street, Malden, MA 02148-5020, USA
9600 Garsington Road, Oxford, OX4 2DQ, UK
The Atrium, Southern Gate, Chichester, West Sussex, PO19 8SQ, UK

For details of our global editorial offices, for customer services, and for information about how to apply for permission to reuse the copyright material in this book, please see our website at www.wiley.com/wiley-blackwell.

The right of Chantal Tetreault to be identified as the author of this work has been asserted in accordance with the UK Copyright, Designs and Patents Act 1988.

Wiley also publishes its books in a variety of electronic formats. Some content that appears in print may not be available in electronic books.

Designations used by companies to distinguish their products are often claimed as trademarks. All brand names and product names used in this book are trade names, service marks, trademarks or registered trademarks of their respective owners. The publisher is not associated with any product or vendor mentioned in this book.

Limit of Liability/Disclaimer of Warranty: While the publisher and author have used their best efforts in preparing this book, they make no representations or warranties with respect to the accuracy or completeness of the contents of this book and specifically disclaim any implied warranties of merchantability or fitness for a particular purpose. It is sold on the understanding that the publisher is not engaged in rendering professional services and neither the publisher nor the author shall be liable for damages arising herefrom. If professional advice or other expert assistance is required, the services of a competent professional should be sought.

Library of Congress Cataloging-in-Publication data applied for.

Hardback 9781118388112
Paperback 9781119044154

A catalogue record for this book is available from the British Library.

Cover image: French and Libyan flags painted on the face of a protester during a demonstration in support of coalition air strikes in Libya, Benghazi, March 2011. © SUHAIB SALEM/Reuters/ Corbis

Set in 11/13pt Bembo by SPi Publisher Services, Pondicherry, India
Printed and bound in Malaysia by Vivar Printing Sdn Bhd

1   2015

CONTENTS

ACKNOWLEDGMENTS

This book would not exist without the help of many others, for which I am very grateful.

My thanks first go to the teens, parents, and tutors in Chemin de l'Ile who generously let me into their lives and who were so patient with my many questions. Thank you. I hope that I have done justice to your words, stories, and experiences.

My family has been a constant source of emotional, intellectual, and economic support over the many years that I have worked on this project— thank you so much, Elijah, Stuart, Mary Kay, and Marc.

I have been lucky to have many teachers who have believed in this project and in me. My heartfelt thanks go to my advisors, Elizabeth Keating and Joel Sherzer, and to Bob Fernea, Deborah Kapchan, Pauline Turner-Strong, and Keith Walters.

To my editors and series editors at Wiley-Blackwell, Norma Mendoza-Denton and Galey Modan, as well as the anonymous reviewers of the man-uscript—I am so fortunate to have worked with you. Your suggestions and generous contributions have very much improved this book.

The list of colleagues who have supported me throughout this process is long. Thank you for help in conceptualizing, writing, and revising this work: Azouz Begag, Brahim Chakrani, Elaine Chun, Susan Frekko, Pilar Garcés-Conejos Blitvich, Erika Hoffmann-Dilloway, Tony Jackson, Michèle Koven, Elizabeth R. Miller, Mindy Morgan, Valentina Pagliai, Jennifer Reynolds, Paul Silverstein, Gregg Starrett, and the Working Group on Gender and Childhood at the Rutgers Center for Historical Analysis.

I also owe thanks to the various institutions and entities that have funded my research and writing: the Chateaubriand Fellowship Program, Michigan

State University, Rutgers Center for Historical Analysis, University of North Carolina at Charlotte, and the University of Texas at Austin.

To my dear friends who sustained me over many years intellectually, emotionally, and, perhaps most important, gastronomically, I send my love and gratitude: Vânia Cardoso, Scott Head, Liz Lilliott, Dana Maya, Erica Windler, and Elana Zilberg.

Thank you! I could not have done this without you!

The author gratefully acknowledges that permission was granted to include portions of the following journal articles:

Tetreault, Chantal. 2013. Cultural Citizenship in France and le Bled among Teens of Pan-southern Immigrant Heritage. Language and Communication. Volume 33, pp. 532–543.

Tetreault, Chantal. 2010. Collaborative Conflicts: Teens Performing Aggression and Intimacy in a French Cité. Journal of Linguistic Anthropology. Volume 20, Number 1, pp. 72–86.

Tetreault, Chantal. 2009. Cité Teens Entextualizing French TV Host Register: Crossing, Voicing, and Participation Frameworks. Language in Society. Volume 38, Issue 2, pp. 201–231.

Tetreault, Chantal. 2009. Reflecting Respect: Transcultural Communicative Practices of Muslim French Youth. Pragmatics. Volume 19, Issue 1, pp. 65–83.

Tetreault, Chantal. 2008. La Racaille: Figuring Gender, Generation, and Stigmatized Space in a French Cité. Gender and Language. Volume 2, Issue 2, pp. 141–170.

INTRODUCTION: PERFORMING TRANSCULTURAL YOUTH IDENTITIES

MIRIAM[1]:	*Ḥashak!*
MOHAMMAD:	*Star Trek!*
MIRIAM:	*Double-échec!*
	(epic failure, literally "double failure")
MOHAMMAD:	*Bifteck!*
	(steak)
MIRIAM:	*Toulouse-Lautrec!*

(Miriam, a female teenager, and her 20-something male tutor, Mohammad, break into laughter.)

In the preceding exchange, Miriam and Mohammad, both young French citizens of North African descent, play a word game that is always initiated with the word *ḥashak*,[2] an Arabic politeness formula. Normally used to create deference in North African Arabic, here the term is used to initiate a stream of spontaneously uttered non-sequiturs, ranging from "steak" (*bifteck*) to the Post-Impressionist French artist Toulouse-Lautrec. Participants play by pairing the word's Arabic phonology with terms that share the same distinctive sound which is quite rare in French: an ending that sounds to American ears like "ek." By stringing together odd-sounding terms to rhyme with *ḥashak*, opponents create a fun, bizarre-sounding blitz of nonsense; the person uttering the last word ending in "ek" wins the round. The fun of the game lies in its absurdity, in the incongruity of multiple cultural and linguistic references from North Africa, France, and the United States.

Transcultural Teens: Performing Youth Identities in French Cités, First Edition. Chantal Tetreault.
© 2015 John Wiley & Sons, Inc. Published 2015 by John Wiley & Sons, Inc.

Other than the rhyming endings, what do the American TV show *Star Trek*, the French Post-Impressionist painter Toulouse-Lautrec, and the Arabic politeness formula *ḥashak* have in common? They are all points of reference that are meaningful to these speakers, who share the cultural attachments that they represent. As with the other participants in my study, Miriam and Mohammad share a connection to North African culture and language, especially the rituals of politeness such as *ḥashak* that are so important in diaspora. Within Chemin de l'Ile, the largely North African community located 15 kilometers west of Paris where I conducted my research, young people might not actually speak Arabic, but will know the formulaic language of greetings, well-wishing, and politeness, including the usage of *ḥashak*. Furthermore, participants in the study were French-born and attending middle school, and thus not only fluent in the French language but also *la culture générale*—general European culture that encompasses the Post-Impressionist artist Toulouse-Lautrec. In addition, they are young and intimately familiar with American popular culture, including *Star Trek*, because they watch TV and movies imported from *les states*, as they call it.

The *ḥashak* word game is thus a transcultural moment that demonstrates the multiple connections shared between these participants—they are young, French, and of North African Arab heritage—connections they establish by voicing these incongruous but shared cultural references and by the humor resulting from their juxtaposition. The meaning of the *ḥashak* word game is thus found *between*—between individuals from similar backgrounds sharing an inside joke through word play; between two transculturally situated speakers for whom this seemingly incongruous talk makes perfect sense; and between the gaps created by the cultural and linguistic referents uttered.

Yet, simultaneously occupying these identities—young, French, and Arab of North African descent—is not all fun and games. In addition to their knowledge of *la culture générale*, French teens of North African background have an intimate understanding of the negative and widely circulating stereotypical discourses regarding them. Within mainstream French politics and media, "French" and "Arab Muslim" are often constructed as mutually exclusive, even incompatible categories. As children of predominantly Algerian Muslim immigrants living in state-subsidized, low-income housing projects called *les cités*, these adolescents occupy multiple stigmatized positions in relation to dominant French national discourses and cultural ideologies.

To address these issues, I analyze forms of discourse and everyday language practices to examine how Arab French *cité* teens translate these experiences into communicative displays of social agency.[3] The adolescents who participated in this study were generally located between what the French call second and third generations, in that they tended to have one parent of

North African descent who had grown up in France and another who had migrated as an adult from North Africa, usually Algeria. Because of their varied competence in Arabic—there were very few Kabyle (Algerian Berber or Amazigh) speakers in the neighborhood—adolescents tended to speak French with one another while incorporating Arabic loan words. In their everyday speech, these adolescents used non-standard French grammar and the pronunciation and prosody typical of the working class, or as Gadet (1996) calls it, *le français ordinaire* ("ordinary French"). Rather than code-switching into Arabic, innovative language practices such as the *ḥashak* game constitute a primary means for Arab–French teens in Chemin de l'Ile to express their transcultural affiliations.

In general, language practices provide a discerning tool for studying processes of identity construction and their enactment in everyday interactions. In this regard, naming (assigning group names) is one way that language is central to the construction of social difference and identities, both self-ascribed and other-ascribed. Shifting name ascription regarding the North African immigrant community in France is a prime example of both the centrality of language to identity construction and the dynamic relationship between dominant French discourses and discursive practices within North African communities.

During the oil crisis of the 1970s, French media and politicians conducted highly negative coverage of North African immigrants in which the word *arabe* ("Arab") was repeatedly associated with the growing problem of unemployment in France. Then, in 1983, *le mouvement beur* ("*beur* movement") was launched by a protest march across France that began 100,000 strong in Paris, to redress police violence against North Africans and to decry a host of economic and political injustices including job and housing discrimination. Similar to the socially consequential wordplay discussed at the beginning of this chapter, activists' strategic use of the term *beur* in this political movement demonstrated their attempt to redefine their status in France, not only economically and politically, but also socially and symbolically. Forgoing the stigmatized term *arabe*, activists used the popular vernacular term *beur* to indicate that they were the grown children of North Africans, derived from the French word game *verlan* that inverts syllables or phonemes of words.[4]

However, in the 1990s, the word *beur* became widely used in mainstream media and political discourse, and often in a stigmatizing way. French people of North African descent once again renamed themselves by performing *verlan* on the word *beur* another time—called *double-verlan*—thus creating the word *rebeu*. This term was preferred among adult informants in this study, most likely because it was both agentive and non-stigmatizing. The centrality of naming to the process of identity construction and the ways that names take on different meanings in different contexts show the importance of studying these issues through everyday language practices. The case of North African communities in France repeatedly renaming themselves in response and resistance to popular stereotypes demonstrates the dynamic relationship between dominant representations of stigmatized groups and their own collective performances of identity through self-naming, among other practices.

I analyze such creative verbal play and naming strategies along with other emergent language practices of French teenagers of North African descent through a theoretical lens that I call *transculturality*.[5] Here, "transculturality" refers to how French teens of North African descent experience and express migration and diaspora in ways that are related to the experiences of their parents, but that are also innovative, bifurcated, and differential. Teens' discursive performances of identity thus hinge upon brokering cultural difference as well as continuity. In this way, Arab French teens' transcultural experiences are forged in practices that evidence movement and connection between multiple social norms, cultural systems, and linguistic forms. The social and spatial identifications of Arab French youth in *les cités* are articulated and negotiated across sets of shifting relationships, including *self* and *other*, *here* and *there, feminine* and *masculine, French* and *immigrant*, as well as *teen* and *parent.* The experiences of these teens are thus characterized by the negotiation of multiple social identities that are, by turns, disparate, overlapping, and conflicting.

In the chapters to come, I explore these issues through a variety of types of discourse, including that which widely circulates and which involves intimate peer interactions. I pay particular attention to points where these two types of discourse intersect, for the ways that they evidence how everyday performances of social identity are imbued with and sometimes transform large-scale discursive forms. In addition to providing historical and ethnographic background, Chapter 1 analyzes particular patterns and effects of spatial stigmatization in France in order to contextualize teens' performances and politics of identity within the context of *les cités*. The centrality of *cités* to the history of North African immigration and the marginalization of these spaces have contributed to the formation of new communicative styles, including language, dress, and music. Chapter 2 takes a close look at such *"cité styles"* through analysis of various practices that encompass their cultural and linguistic production in Chemin de l'Ile and other *cités* across France.

Along with spatial identifications and dis-identifications, racialized and gendered categories constitute a central resource for the creative production of teenaged identities in Chemin de l'Ile. Chapter 3 considers the ways that adolescents reproduce and subvert dominant French discourses about Arab Muslims by rearticulating and challenging stereotypes in peer interactions. The linguistic and cultural resources by which these teens perform their youth are saturated with larger, hegemonic discourses that they alternately reject, reproduce, and transform. I argue that, through such practices, teens construct and express their emergent identities as simultaneously Arab Muslims and as French citizens.

The relationships that I articulate in this book between processes of stigmatization and identification with respect to gender, "race," space, and socioeconomic class are symbolically distilled in the image of *la racaille* (literally, "trash," or figuratively, "male street toughs").[6] Chapter 4 analyzes how dominant French discourses that stigmatize *la racaille* are transformed and re-circulated in adolescent girls' narratives. Further developing the relationships articulated here between gender and space, Chapter 5 examines girls' use of "masculine" verbal styles and social behaviors associated with their *cité*, as a way to identify with the local neighborhood and as an alternative way to gain a positive reputation among their peers. I argue that such gendered style shifting constitutes one way that adolescent girls of Algerian descent perform their transcultural identities as French teenagers living in *cités* and as Arab Muslims attempting to fulfill the cultural requirements of *le respect* ("respect") in their community.

Both teenaged boys and girls in Chemin de l'Ile negotiate transcultural attachments through the verbal performances that I describe in Chapter 6. Adolescents transform a traditional North African Arabic name taboo into the irreverent, peer-based verbal practice "parental name-calling." I argue that parental name-calling constitutes a particularly important discursive genre for adolescents to articulate cultural ties to both their parents' North African origins and their own emergent French adolescent subculture. In these performances, personal names and other information about parents and kin are used to evoke these absent persons as foils for the adolescent self, in talk that conflates the voices of parents and children, as well as immigrants and French-born citizens.

Just as adolescents reinterpret North African language practices by subverting a name taboo in Chapter 6, they also reinvent French discursive practices, as I show in Chapter 7. Teens re-imagine French social personas, such as TV hosts, in order to playfully mock their peers in public performances. By adopting the voices of these socially recognizable "Others," adolescents momentarily de-stabilize recognizable identity categories and thereby create a transcultural discourse in order to negotiate moral and social orders for their peer groups.

The multiple relationships that are evidenced here between widely circulating French and North African discourses and local performances of social identities form the core subject of this book. The ethnographic and linguistic research that I explore here demonstrates the interplay among transnational migration, cultural changes in French *cités*, and subcultural youth styles. Teens' communicative practices, including recycling dominant stereotypes, strategic self-naming using *verlan*, and repurposing the Arabic politeness formula *ḥashak* for wordplay, are all evidence of the multiple ways that young people in Chemin de l'Ile are creating continuity and cultural change in their everyday interactions.

Notes

1 All personal names that appear in the book are pseudonyms.
2 In general, I follow Kapchan's (1996) system for the transliteration of Moroccan Arabic, which is highly similar to the Arabic spoken in Chemin d'Ile. For example, I transliterate short Arabic vowels as a schwa (ə), as Kapchan does. However, my system of transliteration is influenced by the following factors. In cases in which the Arabic word is a common loan word in French and used widely among monolingual French speakers, I tend to use the conventional French spelling, as in, for example, "wallah" ("by God" or "I swear to it"). In cases in which the Arabic word is a common loan word among American English speakers, I tend to use the conventional English spelling, as in "sheikh." Finally, my transliteration of teens' use of Arabic words is also influenced by their pronunciation of them, which was highly influenced by French phonology. Many teens in the study were not fluent in Arabic and their pronunciation of Arabic loan words reflects this.
3 Throughout this book, I alternate among *teens*, *adolescents*, and, less frequently, *youth*. In doing so, I recognize adolescence as a life stage and youth as an analytic category, after Bucholtz's distinction (2002; but see also Amit-Talai 1995: 223–225; Durham 2000). Both notions, adolescence and youth, are important to my research, in that I analyze communicative practices among my consultants as both integral to how they experience adolescence as a life stage in ways typical of other teens and, simultaneously, to how they produce youthful cultural forms contingent upon their positioning as Arab French youth living in a *cité*.
4 The term *verlan* is derived from the French word *l'envers* ("reverse") by "reversing" the syllables. *Verlan* is a word game that predates the *beur* movement and comprises part of "traditional slang" in France (Goudaillier 1997: 18). Many *verlan* terms are now conventionalized elements of mainstream French, such as *meuf*, the inverted form of the word *femme* ("woman"). *Verlan* did not originate in *cités* and is a very old French word game that can be verified as a form of

spoken jargon as early as the late nineteenth century, although evidence of it as a literary device exists as early as the twelfth century (Lefkowitz 1991: 50–51). Nonetheless, the use of *verlan* lends a casual, youthful tone to conversation, and has become emblematic of *cités* in France, and specifically in the Parisian region (ibid: 18).

5   See also Bucholtz (2002: 543) on transcultural youth practices, and Pratt (2008/1992: 7) for a discussion of transculturation as the process whereby subordinated peoples reinvent cultural forms transmitted by a dominant, colonizing culture.

6   By placing the word "race" in quote marks, I follow Gilroy (1991) in thereby indicating that the concept fails to encompass a viable biological model for humans. Rather, as Gilroy asserts, "race" is "socially and politicaly constructed and elaborate ideological work is done to secure and maintain the different forms of 'racialization' which have characterized capitalist development" (ibid: 38).

CHAPTER 1

ETHNOGRAPHY IN *LES CITÉS*

Stigmatizing Labels: ZEP, HLM, and *Cité*

My arrival in October 1998 to Chemin de l'Ile occurred just after a decisive communal and political event: the successful strike to retain the neighborhood's status as a ZEP or *zone d'éducation prioritaire* ("priority education zone"). Created in 1981 by Minister of Education Alain Savary, the ZEP designation ensured that local schools would be granted additional resources such as higher teacher salaries and smaller class sizes. The strike had mobilized a variety of populations in the neighborhood, all of whom had different interests in whether the neighborhood continued to be classified as such.[1]

Teachers at the local middle and grade schools had mobilized in order to keep their salaries at a higher rate as well as to secure the lower student-to-teacher ratio that the ZEP classification guaranteed. *Educateurs*—French civil servants who combine social work with education—participated because of the higher municipal funding granted to areas designated as ZEPs, ensuring their continued employment at local associations working on a variety of issues such as school retention and anti-criminality among adolescents.[2] Students were encouraged by their teachers and educators to participate in a march, and local schools posted pro-ZEP slogans. School itself was cancelled for several days in order to persuade local legislators to

Transcultural Teens: Performing Youth Identities in French Cités, First Edition. Chantal Tetreault.
© 2015 John Wiley & Sons, Inc. Published 2015 by John Wiley & Sons, Inc.

retain the ZEP status and, even though some parents grumbled that students would be behind for the year, many participated in the march as well.

A few days after the strike had ended, I arrived at *Cerise* (or "Cherry"), the association where I volunteered as an English tutor for middle-school students, only to find that all the educators were off making visits to parents' houses, and that the children were still in school. I decided to walk the neighborhood to look for remnants of the strike and to get a better sense of the place where I would conduct an initial 18 months of fieldwork, with subsequent visits over the next dozen years. My self-led tour revealed a jumble of buildings, the vast majority of which consisted of various forms of rent-subsidized housing. On the perimeter of the neighborhood were mostly run-down single-family homes or *pavillons*; farther in were several early-model HLM or *habitation à loyer modéré*, rent-subsidized apartment complexes standing four stories and built in the early 1970s. Finally, in the core of the neighborhood stood nine buildings built in the 1980s that towered over the rest of the area, over 10 stories high, that included seven *cités* (state subsidized high-rise apartment complexes) and two *foyers d'immigrés* or all-male immigrant workers' apartments, also state-supported.

On my walking tour, I retraced the route of the ZEP protest march, down the now mostly deserted main boulevard. In the local middle school (*collège*), slogans were painted in the windows, such as *Gardons la ZEP!* ("Keep the ZEP!"). Graffiti, usually rare in the neighborhood, also commemorated the success of the strike with spray-painted catchphrases on the train station wall: *On a gagné!* or "We won!"[3] As I walked around the gray and desolate assembly of largely concrete, state-subsidized buildings, I began to wonder seriously about the complicated mix of "winning" and "losing" that such "priority" status would entail for a community such as Chemin de l'Ile. As a newcomer to the neighborhood just before the aforementioned strike, I was surprised at the readiness and enthusiasm that many people displayed in attempting to retain the ZEP classification.

Today, densely populated neighborhoods with a high proportion of such housing that are located outside of major towns are called *les cités*. In American English, "suburban" has the connotation of a safe, dull, middle-class lifestyle. In France, however, *les banlieues* or "suburbs" tends to connote economically poor, socially marginalized, and racially stigmatized spaces, consisting often of government-subsidized housing projects called *les cités*. Moreover, whereas *bidonvilles* (shantytowns), *cités de transit* (temporary housing), and early HLMs have historically been located near manufacturing and mining industries—that is, near jobs—France's current post-industrial economy has left most *cités* isolated and far from both employers and mass transit.

Often erected in the same or a nearby location as early *bidonvilles, les cités* are stigmatized, suburban spaces that provide a rich and timely ethnographic site because they reside, culturally and representationally, at the intersection of a number of related and contested French social issues: state-sponsored housing, immigration, emergent ethnic identities, changing gender norms, and youth subcultures. The history of how *cités* arose in France demonstrates the legacy of exclusion and racism that immigrants and their children still face today.

The strike to maintain ZEP status in Chemin de l'Ile illustrates a complex picture of the ways that *cités* figure in larger representational, social, and political landscapes of France. Despite their support for the strike, adolescents I worked with often expressed anxiety about the negative reputation of the neighborhood. They feared that using their home address would lessen their chances of getting jobs or internships.[4] Several high school students mentioned that they planned to use a non-local relative's address on their resume in order to avoid spatial stereotyping. At the time, Chemin de l'Ile hardly deserved the negative reputation, as it was relatively calm; in the late 1990s and early 2000s, it had one of the lowest crime rates in Nanterre, the town in which Chemin de l'Ile is located. Yet, the neighborhood had experienced a very turbulent past, including heroin dealing and the incineration by local inhabitants of a police station built at the bottom of a residential complex.[5]

By using their relatives' home addresses and in other ways, the young people at the center of this study, predominantly of Algerian parentage, demonstrate their sophisticated understanding of how labels such as "ZEP" or "*les cités*" contribute to negative stereotypes about the spaces and styles of Chemin de l'Ile and other similar low-income, suburban neighborhoods. Unlike their immigrant parents and grandparents for whom *cités* provided relatively affordable and safe living conditions after often dreadful experiences in shantytowns, successive French generations of suburban inhabitants have faced the overwhelmingly negative effects of growing up there. Adding spatial prejudice to racial prejudice, the young people in this study encounter stigma that marks "who they are" as Arab youth, and also "where they are from" as *jeunes de la cité* ("*cité* youth").

The immigrant parents and grandparents of these young people have also clearly experienced discrimination in France. However, racism and discrimination may have played less of a role in their parents' and grandparents' experience of work in France because they (the men at least) were recruited specifically for manual labor after World War II, and so their immigrant status was closely related to their function as workers to rebuild France. In contrast, due to the economic crash in the 1970s and their improved access to education, children of North African immigrants have been both less able and less willing to find the low-paying, manual labor jobs that their parents came to France to obtain. At the same time, high rates of scholastic failure, a poor economy, and racist hiring practices often impede these French citizens from attaining economic security.

Along with other official designations, such as *zone urbaine précaire* or ZUP (precarious urban zone), *habitation à loyer modéré* or HLM (moderated rent housing), and *les cités* (high-rise subsidized housing), *zones d'éducation prioritaire* (ZEPs) have been stigmatized in the French media since the early 1980s. Much as the terms ZEP, ZUP, and HLM constitute official categories with which to describe (and attempt to redress) the social and economic marginality experienced in such areas, they may also serve to stigmatize them. Economically, these spaces have become increasingly marginal in relation to manufacturing jobs, as France has largely shifted away from an industrial economy. Representationally, low-income suburban neighborhoods have been repeatedly associated with negative journalistic topics such as crime, immigration, drugs, and scholastic failure. In a finding in line with the problem of stigma inherent to such categories, an official French census study conducted from 1981 to 1992 by the National Institute of Statistics and Economic Studies or INSEE (Bénabou et al. 2005) found no significant benefit of the ZEP designation to the students themselves. Teachers benefitted from higher salaries in these areas, whereas student performances and schools failed to improve, in part due to decreased enrollment in the face of parental fears regarding the designation.

In another pattern that illustrates the social force of stigma, Gross, McMurray, and Swedenburg (1994) describe representations of nocturnal *rodéos* during the early 1980s as a powerfully negative way that HLMs were depicted in the French press. These urban battles with the police involved young men stealing cars and racing them, only to later set them on fire so that any evidence would be destroyed. The so-called *rodéos* were highly publicized in the French press, giving HLMs a reputation for lawlessness and violence. In the 1990s, both right-wing and left-wing newspapers such as *Libération* and *Le Figaro* focused on *la banlieue chaude* ("the hot suburb"), a category that conflated negative stereotypes by repeatedly linking civil disturbances and violence with North African migration in general and disaffected Algerian youth in particular, in conjunction with representations of crime, scholastic failure, and drug addiction (Tetreault 1992).[6]

Most recently, the civil uprisings in low-income suburban areas across France in 2005 and 2010, both of which began following civilian deaths after police intervention, have been characterized in political rhetoric and media coverage as the fault of *la racaille*, a racialized, violent image of *cité* street toughs (Silverstein and Tetreault 2006). While the left-wing has tended to depict this population as social victims, the French political right-wing has blamed *cité* dwellers for a purported rise in crime and *l'insécurité* ("insecurity"), a term that emerged in post-9/11 French politics, often serving as a code word for "terrorism" and forming the basis for the newest version of anti-immigrant sentiment. Thus, for close to 40 years, low-income suburban areas and their inhabitants have been stigmatized by shifting labels that belie an insidious semiotic stability in French media representations and political rhetoric.

In Chemin de l'Ile, adolescents were aware that the successful strike to retain ZEP classification would function in part to keep many such stereotypes about them and their neighborhood intact. "Winning" ZEP status (or, in this case, maintaining it) meant that the stigma of need and poverty would be officially recognized, but only partially rectified, since unemployment for young people within the neighborhood would likely remain at roughly 20%, or almost twice the national average.[7] And a large number of the immigrant and working-class parents in the neighborhood would likely remain poor and possibly illiterate—both negative predictors of their children's success in school.

As I will explore further in Chapter 2, adolescents' awareness of the neighborhood's stigmatized status coincided with their understanding of it as an "Arab" space—that is, a space predominated by inhabitants of North African background. As such, Chemin de l'Ile offered a density of community, extended kinship, and social networks that often afforded teens a strong sense of belonging and "home." At the same time, adolescents were aware of popular negative representations of *cités* as "Arab" spaces, and recycled such stereotypes in everyday conversation—for example, by mentioning to me frequently that there were "lots of Arabs" in Chemin de l'Ile.

Although increasing numbers of North African immigrants have stayed in France and produced children who are considered French by nationality, the categories "French" and "Arab" are still too often counterposed as mutually exclusive.[8] As French journalist Sylvain Cypel noted in 2014, in France, a "diffuse populism is stirring … [with] a nostalgic mindset that everything 'was better before' … [and] a palpable conviction that everything bad comes from the outside: Brussels, globalization, immigration" (*The New York Times*, January 23). Cypel goes on to cite the 2013 desecration of Muslim French soldiers' tombstones in Carpentras as evidence for the ways that, in France, "racism and xenophobia" are often expressed as "anti-Arab, anti-Muslim, or anti-black." In this case, symbolic violence against deceased French soldiers casts them as "Muslims" only, rather than simultaneously as national French heroes who lost their lives for their country, and is thus indicative of the pervasive tendency to treat "French" and "Muslim–Arab" as incompatible or non-overlapping categories.

Moreover, popular anti-immigrant discourses that specifically target North Africans essentialize "French" and "Arab" "cultures" as embodying traits that purportedly exist outside of historical context. Justin E. H. Smith, in a 2014 op-ed piece in *The New York Times*, takes issue with popular French philosopher Alain Finkielkraut and argues instead for a historicized understanding of diversity and multiculturalism in France:

> ... his recent popular book "L'identité malheureuse" ("The Unhappy Identity"), proclaims, in effect, that immigration is destroying French cultural identity. He bemoans the "métissage" of France, a term one often sees in the slogans of the far right, which translates roughly as "mongrelization." [...] Immigration in Europe, as in, say, the Southwestern United States or within the former Soviet Union, is determined by deep historical links and patterns of circulation between the immigrants' countries of origin—in France's case, particularly North Africa and sub-Saharan Françafrique—and the places of destination. (*The New York Times*, January 5)

Popular anti-immigrant discourses as that of Finkielkraut serve to erase the fact that French and North African cultures have been irrevocably mixed and relationally defined for centuries, due to French colonization of the Maghreb and its attendant historical, political, and cultural proximity to France. Along these lines, Etienne Balibar (1991) has argued that the commonly voiced essentialist position that "French" and "Arab" cultures are too different to be successfully compatible represents a "neo-racism" that substitutes "culture" for "race." Low-income suburban neighborhoods such as Chemin de l'Ile are at the frontlines of these struggles over spatial and symbolic territory, both within the French popular imagination and within *cités* themselves, as I show in my following description of the conflict that arose at the ZEP strike celebration.

After-Party—Spatialized Conflicts within the *Cité*

While representational and political struggles over who is to be included within the imagined "French" national community (Anderson 1991) are often waged in popular media with respect to neighborhoods such as Chemin de l'Ile, similar struggles arise within the *cités* themselves in people's everyday discourse (Essed 1991; VanDijk 1987). Some of these conflicts emerge, for example, as "culture wars" over the linguistic, musical, and dress styles emerging in French *cités*, including Chemin de l'Ile. After the success-ful ZEP strike, I attended a celebratory potluck that teachers and educators working in the neighborhood had organized, held in a local community center. Neighborhood parents and children of a variety of national origins attended the party and enjoyed the food and music together. By the time dancing began, however, the convivial exterior had begun to erode in a conflict about which type of music to play: "French" or "Arab." The young, hip assemblage of educators and teachers of various backgrounds (often, but not exclusively, North African) who had organized the party decided to play "Arab" music, such as Algerian *raï* stars Khaled and Cheb Mami as well as Arabic-influenced French pop bands such as *Zebda*.[9]

Farouk, father of three grade-school children and who had been very active in the strike, confided in me that night that a "French" parent (of non-immigrant descent) had complained pointedly to him about the music, implying the country's "takeover" by Arabs: "This is France, after all!" (*C'est la France, quand même!*). Being originally from Algeria, Farouk took her comment personally and responded with a sexist (and typically "French") insult, claiming that she was *mal baisée* ("badly fucked," i.e., "needing to get laid"). The two refused to speak to each other afterward. This seemingly banal conflict over what constitutes appropriate music for a neighborhood party demonstrates the tensions inherent in Chemin de l'Ile's ambivalent positioning between "French" and "Arab" identities, which are by and large posed as mutually exclusive categories in popular representations of the French national community.[10]

Theorizing Style and Stigma through *Transculturality*

This book addresses the multiple relationships between local performances of social identities and widely circulating discourses. "Discourse" refers to spoken or written communication as well as more formal discussion or debate of a topic. This book brings together the two, in that it addresses how teens' everyday interactions intersect with broadly circulating formu-lations regarding social identities in France. As Sherzer (1987) notes, discourse resides at the nexus of culture and language, and thus exists as a way to access shared knowledge among cultural members. Also central to my approach is the idea that "culture is localized in concrete, publicly acces-sible signs, the most important of which are actually occurring instances of discourse" (Urban 1991: 1). In that sense, forms of discourse, such as myths, rituals, or, in this study, genres of teasing and verbal play, are publicly accessible, but this does not mean that they are shared in a monologic way; rather, through performance, instances of discourse emerge as dynamic expressions of cultural experience (ibid: 2).

Language practices, including recycling dominant stereotypes ("there are lots of Arabs here"), strategic self-naming using *verlan*, and repurposing the Arabic politeness formula *ḥashak* for wordplay, are all evidence of the multiple ways that young people create continuity and cultural change in their everyday interactions. I use a theoretical framework of *transculturality* to analyze such everyday verbal performances of social identities as creative responses to widely circulating discourses that often stigmatize and sometimes valorize *les arabes* and *les cités*. By theorizing such linguistic and cultural innovations as *transcultural* practices, this book demonstrates how symbolic forms come to take on ideological social meanings, as well as how these meanings are transformed in interaction. In *les cités*, French adolescents of North African descent combine cultural and linguistic referents in their communicative styles in ways that serve to both deconstruct and re-imagine the ideological underpinnings of their multiple social identities. Teenagers' language and cultural production in Chemin de l'Ile thereby challenge naturalized assumptions about the link between identity and language, contributing to a new scholarship that rejects the previously common pattern of equating ethnic groups and particular language styles.

I extend Cuban anthropologist and ethnomusicologist Fernando Ortiz's notion of "transculturation" to describe how cultures converge (1947). Ortiz argued that cultures, such as Spanish and African in the Cuban context, surmount differences and even conflicts to forge something new and transcendent. My use of *transculturality* differs from Ortiz's in that rather than a transcendent combination of practices or beliefs from two groups, I focus on the ways that French teens of Algerian descent forge transcultural identities through the *simultaneous* creation and counter-opposition of Frenchness and Arabness. The example of the *ḥashak* game that begins this book illustrates this different approach. *Ḥashak* exists in contradistinction to Toulouse-Lautrec, and the meaning of the game is found in between the two terms rather than in a synthesis of the two. Speakers are thus expressing, creating, and simultaneously holding onto (in the sense of symbolic placeholders) at least two culturally informed positions.

Although W. E. B. Du Bois (1903) emphasized multiple internal psychological states of African Americans rather than linguistic performances, my use of transculturality is not wholly unlike his concept of double consciousness in its emphasis on two or more simultaneously held perspectives. Double consciousness refers to African Americans' experience of simultaneously occupying cultural insider and cultural outsider status in the

United States, an experience that was presumably much more acute when Du Bois theorized this concept at the start of the twentieth century. In contrast, intercultural communication literature often posits that communicators reside in one "camp" or culture, and that communication occurs "across" these camps rather than through speakers' simultaneous positioning within two or more cultures.[11]

Through its potential to articulate dynamic intersections among complex social relationships and discourses, my use of *transculturality* also differs from notions of transnationalism and diaspora. Transnationalism often describes the transplantation of people or symbolic forms into a new national context—someone or something "is transnational" due to movement from "there" to "here"—that is, from "sending" nation to "receiving" nation (Kearney 1995: 548).[12] As Kearney notes, "Transnationalism overlaps globalization but typically has a more limited purview. Whereas global processes are largely decentered from specific national territories and take place in a global space, transnational processes are anchored in and transcend one or more nation-states" (1995: 548). Diaspora often emphasizes a "homeland" that links the present to a mythic past or place, in symbolic movement from "here" to "there" (Koven 2013: 325). And yet, as Sandhya Shukla (2001: 551) notes, "Diaspora, by definition, is dispersion, which effectively compresses time and space such that it enables the experiences of many places at what would appear to be one moment. And today such multiplicity and simultaneity have become particularly pronounced."

This book attempts to address such multiplicity and simultaneity through the concept of transculturality. Rather than emphasizing a projected movement in one direction from "old country" to "new" (as in much literature on transnationalism), or from "new country" to "old" (as in much literature on diaspora), transcultural processes and discourses involve the simultaneous positioning *between* social categories and semiotic referents.[13] In this sense, my work draws much from semiotics, the study of relationships among social signs (Ochs 2012; Peirce 1931–1958; Urban 1991), as well as theories that challenge the possibility of singular or unified linguistic meaning (Bakhtin 1981; Hoffmann–Dilloway 2008; Ochs 2012; Woolard 1998).

In the communicative practices of French teens of North African descent, the relevant semiotic categories are often dictated or at least shaped by operative power relations within France. For example, the discursive distinction—"French or Arab"—lies at the heart of the ongoing controversy about the roles of second and third generations of North African descent with respect to the French Republic, a controversy that is played out in political rhetoric, everyday experiences of racism, and everyday expressions of social identity. In particular, the polarity between "French" and "Arab" is at the center of elaborate debates and policies surrounding *intégration*, a set of French discourses and legislation designed to facilitate the cultural and economic assimilation of immigrants that includes the 2004 ban of the Muslim headscarf in French schools and official state contexts (Bowen 2007). Moreover, the negative representations of *les arabes* in popular French discourse frequently coincide with stigmatized interpretations of *les cités*, a fact that emerges through adolescents' complex and contradictory processes of identification and dis-identifications with these spaces as well as with the social category *les arabes*.

That said, it would be a mistake to consider the teens in this study as "neither" French "nor" North African; rather, they are more accurately described as "both/and" (Barrett 1999). Yet, I must emphasize that the teens I worked with were born in France, and few expressed a desire to move "back" to North Africa—for the most part, they like France and they certainly *are* French, both born and raised. In this sense, they are not truly "transnational," nor are they migrants, but rather children and grandchildren of immigrants.[14] Neither are they true cosmopolitans or "global citizens," for they are physically, culturally, and economically bound to the local spaces of their low-income housing projects, *les cités*. All the same, my teenaged consultants often expressed to me their feelings of exclusion from French society, as not being considered acceptably or "truly French." It is their experiences and expressions of in-between-ness, both in terms of social relationships and discursive categories (e.g., "French" and "immigrant"), that I attempt to encapsulate and describe with *transculturality*.

My notion of transculturality also differs from the popular and largely apolitical American concept of "multiculturalism" due to my attention to the roles of stigma and power relations that are operative and central to teens' transcultural experiences and forms of expression. As I conceive of it here, transculturality is a model for cultural and linguistic identities forged through intersections among social relationships and discursive forms that are not neutral, but rather (over)loaded with historical and political meanings.[15] The teens in this study are simultaneously negotiating multiple, complex, and sometimes conflicting social relationships with their immigrant parents and French-born peers, as well as engaging with and transforming multiple, often stigmatizing, and even conflicting local, national, and transnational discourses regarding Muslim Arabs living in *les cités* and their contested "place" in relation to France.

I am not the first to write about these issues with respect to immigrants and their descendants in France. Paul Silverstein's (2004) work on *transpolitics* has been a major influence because he argues that immigration politics and policies in France have been constitutive of how the nation has been imagined, both externally, in its relationship to Europe, and internally, in the construction of the urban spaces of les cités. Whereas Silverstein's (2004) model looks at French identity struggles through the grass-roots politics of Amazigh (Berber/Kabyle) activists within colonial and post-colonial France, Pierre Bourdieu's reflexive sociology addresses the conundrum of post-colonial France by juxtaposing narratives of people who occupy polarized subject positions, for instance, white union factory workers and unskilled immigrant laborers (Bourdieu et al. 1999: 3). Still others, such as Alec Hargreaves, have attended to similar issues of transcultural identities in post-colonial France largely through literature and other forms of popular cultural expression (see Hargreaves and McKinney 1997). In addition, many French scholars explore relationships among identity formation, citizenship, and migration histories with respect to North African communities in France.[16] Yet, the study of language in ethnographic context is often missing in such scholarship dealing with immigrant communities in les cités.[17]

Although relatively few scholars have addressed everyday language use among French youth of North African descent, Koven documents the inherent contradictions of occupying both "modern" French and "backward" Portuguese social personas in narratives by Luso-descendant French speakers (2001, 2013). At the core of this work are concerns that are akin to my own—that is, to analyze how citizens of immigrant descent within post-colonial France re-imagine belonging and membership in a Republican political system that recognizes only individual membership as the basis of civic participation (to the exclusion of community politics), despite the fact that racism and exclusion are pervasive elements of French society (Beriss 2004; Chapman and Frader 2004).

In addition to the wide array of scholarship addressing notions of belonging and exclusion in post-colonial France, this book builds upon the tradition of scholarship on verbal art and performance (Bauman 2004, 1977; Sherzer 2002, 1990), by analyzing how heightened moments from everyday communicative practices, such as ritualized teasing and speech play, allow us to understand how teenagers articulate and re-negotiate social identities through collaborative performances. While the study of youth has a long history in the social sciences, only recently has research addressed the linguistic expression of identity among adolescents (Androutsopoulos and Georgakopoulou 2003; Bailey 2000; Bucholtz 1999; Chun 2009; Coates 1999; Eckert 1989; Heller 1999; Lo 1999; McElhinny 2007; Mendoza-Denton 2008; Pujolar, 2001; Reyes 2006).

In this regard, a discourse-centered approach (Sherzer 1987) offers a particularly fruitful perspective from which to study social identity among adolescents. A focus on the collective uses of discourse facilitates the study of social identity as emergent in social interactional practices, rather than as static, predetermined social categories (Bucholtz 2002; Eckert and McConnell-Ginet 1992). At the same time, speakers engage with social categories and discourses that pre-exist the moment of interaction and that are available for teens' use as publicly accessible semiotic forms. This book explores the tensions, collusions, and transformations that occur at the emergent intersections between large-scale discursive forces in the media and politics and the local discourses of adolescents.

Historical Contexts: Colonial to Post-colonial

French histories of state-subsidized housing and immigration policy are highly intertwined, a fact evidenced in Chemin de l'Ile as well as Nanterre, the town where the neighborhood is located. The low-income housing projects that are typical of Chemin de l'Ile are most often located near where immigrant laborers were originally housed when they were recruited to help rebuild France after World War II and to re-launch industrial production in the 1950s and 1960s. Central to France's industrial boom during this period, Nanterre has had a long history with immigration generally, and with Algerian immigration in particular. Male Algerian workers, among them several grandfathers of the adolescents in this study, were recruited by factories in Nanterre and lived in *bidonvilles* ("shantytowns"), located about a mile away from Chemin de l'Ile.

In Nanterre, as elsewhere in France post-World War II, *bidonvilles* arose near factories and coal mines outside of major French cities where (initially usually male) immigrant workers lived without water, plumbing, and heat. Inhabitants were legally prohibited from building homes or improving these veritable shacks.[18] Facing public outcry over the living conditions of immigrant workers and, by the late 1960s, some of their families, the French government built temporary housing called *cités de transit* while it pursued building permanent state-subsidized housing. By the 1970s, immigrant workers and their families were forcibly relocated into *les grands ensembles* ("high rises"), or subsidized low-income housing called *habitation à loyer modéré* or HLM (Sayad and Dupuy 2008).

After a moratorium on economic immigration was passed in France in 1974, the familial resettlement law allowed migrants currently living in France to relocate their families to France. For some, *les HLM* were a clear improvement in terms of basic living conditions because, prior to relocation, most immigrant workers and families were restricted to either *bidonvilles* or the worst of private housing in run-down inner-city tenements, for example, in *La Goutte d'Or* in Paris or *Le Panier* in Marseille.

Due to a lack of other housing options because of low incomes and ongoing housing discrimination in the private sector, immigrants and their descendants are often "stuck" in HLMs. Within the Paris region (Ile-de-France), by 1975, roughly 30% of Algerians were living in HLMs, and this figure continued to rise through the 1980s (Schain 1985: 170–171). Although exclusionary housing practices limit the total number of immigrant and "foreign" occupants in *les cités* (cf. MacMaster 1997), these areas nonetheless continue to be among the only available housing choices for the low-income families that generally comprise these social groups in France. As a result, *les cités* are marked as spaces that immigrants and their descendants inhabit, creating a representational conflation between negative depictions of these stigmatized spaces and negative depictions of immigrants, Arabs, and blacks as stigmatized groups.

Algerians have migrated to France more than any other group, due to the long history of Algerian colonialism and owing to the various labor recruitment programs before and after de-colonization in 1962. France colonized Algeria for 132 years, creating both a kind of cultural intimacy and protracted conflict between the two countries and their citizens, which lasts to this day. Algerians' centrality to French immigration policies and debates can thus be traced to the French colonial legacy in North Africa. Throughout the colonial period, which lasted for Algeria from 1830 through the start of the war with France in 1954, "migration" for Algerians consisted of the relocation of colonized subjects to work in the metropole, a process that inversely mimicked the relocation of French settlers into colonial territories.

Algerians' presence and the related controversy in France predates de-colonization and thus "immigration" in the traditional sense. In 1946, the migrant population in France totaled 1.7 million, a figure that would double to 3.4 million by 1975 (Blatt 1997: 41). Although the post-World War II government's policies favored "culturally compatible" immigrants from Europe, competition over these groups meant that immigrants from former colonies and developing nations such as Algeria necessarily filled the labor gap (Blatt 1997: 41). MacMaster notes, for example, the "push and pull" factors that brought in Algerians, more than Tunisians and Moroccans, long before World War II—the "push" of the economic destruction from colonialism, and the "pull" of France's labor shortage brought on by World War I casualties and falling birth rates beginning in 1900 (1997: 3). While North Africans only constituted 3.5% of the overall total foreign population in 1930, France was, at that time, the country with the highest per capita foreign population in the world (MacMaster 1997: 4). Furthermore,

Algerians then, as now, were represented as the most problematic group to French society, according to publications of the time, which referred to the "Arab problem" (MacMaster 1997: 4).

MacMaster attributes the social "panic" over Arab migration in the first third of the twentieth century (and, to a degree, in the present) to the troubling effect of seeing the mass migration of colonized subjects moving into the space and cultural realm of the colonizers (1997: 5). According to MacMaster, due to the large rotation of migrant workers from Algeria in the early 1900s, one in five men of working age (some 500,000 people) had some experience living and laboring in the metropole (1997: 5). Anxieties about the mobility of colonized subjects were expressed most vehemently by colonial settlers, who complained not only of rising labor prices in the colonies but also of migrants becoming accustomed to the more liberal political atmosphere of continental France, including labor unions, communism, and the growing Algerian nationalist movement. Of course, this is, generally speaking, what did indeed occur, galvanizing the Algerian struggle for independence (see Silverstein 2004).

The Algerian–French war (1954–1962) holds another key role in the dynamic of anti-immigrant sentiment directed toward Algerians in France. Provocatively known as *la Guerre Sans Nom* ("the War without a Name") because of its taboo status, the Algerian war holds a place in French history not unlike that of Vietnam in American history. After long 8 years of battle, the French lost much more than the war; France lost status as an imperial power and 3 million French soldiers. As Hargreaves and McKinney note, almost an entire generation of French citizens experienced the violence and destruction of war (1997: 18). Furthermore, re-constructing "French" nationhood after the colonial period in Algeria was a project that was intimately related to defining which Algerians were "citizens" according to the changing boundaries of "France." For example, the phrase *les avant '62* ("those before 1962") refers to those Algerians who were born prior to decolonization at the end of the Algerian–French war. This group of individuals was automatically granted French citizenship and the right to vote on the principle that current territories of Algeria were under French rule. The classification of Algerian natives as French citizens further highlights the permeability of national boundaries with respect to the two countries.

Throughout the most recent media and political "crisis" which casts immigration as a challenge to French sovereignty, Algerians have figured centrally in anti-immigrant French political rhetoric and negative media representations. Because of the French government's recruitment and general support of short-term immigration to stem the labor shortage, immigration as a politicized "problem" did not discursively emerge until the late 1960s

(Blatt 1997: 41). However, immigration became politicized after 1968, when governments under Pompidou and Giscard d'Estaing restricted migration (and forced unemployed foreigners to leave) in response to an economic downturn and "social conflict arising from the settlement of North African immigrants" (ibid.: 42). Political response by immigrants included widespread, "militant protest campaigns against restrictive government policies, squalid housing arrangements, discriminatory workplace conditions, and widespread racial violence against Arab immigrants in particular" (ibid.: 42). Then, as now, however, the most striking element to the construction of Algerians in discourse and politics is their strategic use by French politicians as scapegoats to further personal and national political aims.

North Africans and Algerians in particular have been particularly prone to anti-immigrant sentiment with respect to the economic downturn in France, beginning with the oil crisis in the early 1970s. While French census rules prohibit asking for respondents' ethnicity, parents' country of origin, and religion, Michèle Tribalat (2009), researcher at INED (National Institute of Demographic Research), estimates that there are 3.5 million people of North African heritage currently living in France with at least one grandparent from Algeria, Morocco, or Tunisia, corresponding to 5.8% of the total French population. High rates of migration from the Maghreb continue today; according to the national French census in 2008 (INED), the largest percentage of immigrants came from Algeria (11.2%) and the second largest group from Morocco (11.1%). Despite these large numbers and the longevity of high migration trends, Algerians have never enjoyed the facility with which earlier European immigrants, such as those coming from Italy and Poland, were considered "French" in one generation. Rather, adult children of Algerians have continued to mistakenly be referred to as *étrangers* ("foreigners") in popular French media.

Further, stereotypes that conflate these and other categories have emerged in conjunction with political and public discussion over immigration's role in the construction of citizenship and national identity in France and across Europe. While migration itself is depicted as the "cause" of French conflict over national identity, fostering contentious public "debates" about *l'immigration* has provided political opportunities and rhetorical fodder for many a public figure and would-be policymaker in France. Anti-immigrant policies and rhetoric became common after the oil crisis in the 1970s and the subsequent moratorium on economic immigration in 1974. However, on both political and symbolic levels, French politicians of every ilk took to blaming immigrants in public discourses for a variety of social ills, including crime, drug sales, and violence, starting in the 1980s.[19] Prior to this time, socialist and communist politicians had supported policies geared toward the inclusion of immigrants in French civic society, such as the proposed legislation allowing immigrants to vote in municipal elections if they had lived in France over 5 years. By the mid-1980s, however, reacting to political pressure exerted by the anti-immigrant party *Le Front National* ("The National Front"), even pro-immigrant socialist President François Mitterrand had changed his stance on the immigrant vote, as well as on a variety of other policies relating to migration.

In the political rhetoric of founder Jean-Marie Le Pen and now his daughter Marine Le Pen (current head of *Le Front National*), hegemonic discourses about *l'immigration* have taken the most extreme form, and, in themselves, are touted as a platform to justify the political aspirations of the party leaders. Jean-Marie Le Pen garnered both infamy and a devout following by making anti-immigrant political proposals such as returning all "foreigners" (including immigrants and their descendants) to "their" countries of origin and by questioning the historical validity of the Holocaust. Although Le Pen was active in politics in the 1970s, his emergence as a prominent political figure occurred only after 1980, when *Le Front National* was recognized as an official national organization and allowed to participate in elections.

Unfortunately, the aftermath of 9/11 has unleashed a new wave of anti-immigrant rhetoric and increased *Le Front National*'s popularity. In 2002, Jean-Marie Le Pen was one of two successful candidates for the presidential run-off elections, winning a larger percentage of the French vote than former Prime Minister Lionel Jospin, and beating many more moderate candidates. This time around, Le Pen's platform consisted primarily of discourse of fear regarding growing "insecurity" (*l'insécurité*) in France, the new code word for the supposedly rising rates of criminality and domestic terrorism and thus a way to implicate, once again, Arab immigrants and their children as national scapegoats. In the end, although the other finalist Jacques Chirac won by a landslide victory, some French voters chose the pro-nationalist, anti-immigrant platform of Le Pen to express their dissatisfaction with current politics in France. Such dissatisfaction was furthermore expressed in pro-Chirac slogans that highlighted the economic and moral corruption of each candidate, respectively: "Votez escroc, pas facho!" ("Vote for the Crook, not the Fascist").

Jacques Chirac's own involvement in anti-immigrant policies and political rhetoric dates back to his tenure as the mayor of Paris. For example, in the early 1990s, Chirac crafted a very aggressive urban gentrification project in Paris to forcibly relocate poor and homeless families outside of the city in subsidized housing, rather than provide this service for them in the center of it. Neighborhoods such as La Goutte d'Or, which have been traditionally inhabited by immigrants from North and sub-Saharan Africa, were renovated and reconstructed for the consumption of middle-class and upper-middle-class French buyers. Also during his tenure as mayor, in a highly controversial speech in June 1994, Chirac decried the predicament experienced by the "average" Frenchman ("*le français moyen*") living in subsidized housing, supposedly frustrated by the disturbing "noise and smell" (*le bruit et l'odeur*) of his immigrant neighbors, purportedly living with several wives and many children in a cramped apartment (Guyotat 1994).

Underlying Chirac's statement are racialized and cultural assumptions about the hypothetical "uncivilized" immigrant neighbor, namely that "he" is of sub-Saharan-African or Arab origin, and thus necessarily polygamous, noisy, and smelly. Further, Chirac's underlying claim is that only "average" French citizens (i.e., working-class, European-descent, male, monogamous) can rightfully claim ownership of French *cités*. This scenario of competition existing between "average French" citizens and non-white foreigners has been reproduced in right-leaning newspapers such as *Le Figaro* and *France-Soir* and popular magazines such as *l'Evénement*, depicting brown and black *cité* inhabitants as the victimizers of nearby "French" inhabitants, rather than the other way around. Statistically, though, there has been far more gratuitous violence committed by European-descent French citizens and police against Arabs than the reverse.[20]

Ethnographic Contexts: Marsh to *Cité*

The teenagers in this study are descendants of mostly Algerian immigrants, and are marginalized inhabitants of French *cités* who occupy physical spaces and institutions owned or financed by the state: low-income housing, associations, and schools. As such, these teens are under constant threat of removal by immigration "reform," eviction, incarceration, and political exclusion. French political and journalistic discourses that stigmatize *les cités* serve to construct youth of immigrant descent as trespassers in their own neighborhoods, as illegitimate users of public space. This book delves into the heart of these issues with a look at how French Arab teens use everyday forms of communication to create transcultural expressions of identity with respect to (sub-)urban space, ethnicity, gender, and generation.

Chemin de l'Ile was not always a neighborhood of migration, nor was it originally an impoverished place; until fairly recently, it was uninhabitable due to its location on the banks of the Seine. Literally "Road of the Island," the neighborhood is named for its nineteenth-century life as a road leading to the marshy edge of the Seine river, where partygoers would take small boats out to L'Ile Fleurie; the so-called "flowered island" provided them with a place to dance and drink at open-air clubs called *les guinguettes*. In addition to achieving local fame as an outpost for nineteenth-century Parisian partygoers, Chemin de l'Ile became an early destination on one of the first locomotive passenger train lines in the world, which brought visitors from Paris to the fashionable and formerly royal town of Saint-Germain-en-Laye, starting in 1837. Located further west than Chemin de l'Ile from Paris, Saint-Germain-en-Laye was a popular tourist destination due to its château of the same name.

The last vestige from this legacy can be seen in the fading grandeur of the nineteenth-century brick homes built by early entrepreneurs in the Chemin de l'Ile tourist trade—now mostly occupied by regional governmental offices—that line one side of the main road entering the neighborhood. On the other side of the road is a run-down strip mall that, despite its dated appearance, displays the entrepreneurial spirit of the neighborhood's inhabitants. Aside from a post office and discount national grocery store ("ED"), its businesses include two ḥalal (ritually pure) butcher shops, a ḥalal restaurant "Chicken Spot," a North-African-inspired wedding and dress shop, a dry-goods store featuring products from the Middle East, and an Internet café complete with phone booths for calling *le bled* or "home country." Avenue Général Leclerc, originally a raised wooden platform that led from the tracks of that first passenger train to the banks of the Seine, now travels from the RER (*Réseau Express Régional*) commuter train and across the six-lane national freeway that together completely isolate the neighborhood from the center of the town, called Vieille ("old") Nanterre. On three other sides, Chemin de l'Ile is completely enclosed by an industrial park, the Seine, and a military base.

Farther down the road, the insularity of Chemin de l'Ile is compounded by the combination of one main thoroughfare and centrally located high-rise *cités* that provide their inhabitants bird's-eye views of the comings and goings of the neighborhood's roughly 11,000 inhabitants. Chemin de l'Ile grew exponentially after the shantytowns in Nanterre were dismantled and families were re-housed in early *cité de transit*, first located where the early HLMs now stand, and later in the permanent buildings that still stand in the neighborhood today. The relatively late development of the neighborhood, due in large part to its original marshy location, created a community in which the majority of residents are poor and live over several generations in subsidized housing; a significant portion of families currently living there are descended from the original migrants who lived in *bidonvilles* down the road. The intense communal spirit that many residents of Chemin de l'Ile enjoy has been tempered by poverty, as well as attendant insularity and stigma.

Similar to immigration patterns throughout the world, migration to Chemin de l'Ile created diasporic communities at a highly localized level. Families in Chemin de l'Ile often have ties to one another because many migrated from the same two medium-sized Algerian towns: Maghnia, with a population 95,000 and located on the Moroccan border, and El Oued, an oasis town of 135,000 located near the Tunisian border. Since relatives and neighbors often provide newcomers with the sponsorship necessary for obtaining migration papers and other networks of support, communities of neighbors and kin from the "home" country (*le bled*) extend to the local context.

Similar to other *cités*, Chemin de l'Ile is an ethnically mixed space, but it is quite difficult to obtain accurate information about the ethnic composition of the neighborhood. Officially, in the 1999 local mayor's annual report, North African immigrants comprised roughly 20% of neighborhood inhabitants. This figure includes immigrants, but excludes French citizens who are of North African (and mostly Algerian) heritage, so the percentage of Arab Muslims in the neighborhood is certainly much higher than the official figure.

Although Arab residents are by no means the exclusive inhabitants of Chemin de l'Ile, dominant representations of *cités* both within and outside them cast these spaces as being predominantly North African, and, to a lesser degree, sub-Saharan African. There are several reasons for this common conflation. Despite admonitions from many parents for young women to avoid "the street" (*la rue*), Arab residents in Chemin de l'Ile tended to use outdoor, public spaces, including playgrounds, front stoops, parks, and parking lots, more often than their non-Arab neighbors. Similarly, women and men of North African descent tended to frequent the bi-weekly neighborhood open-air market, which features mostly North African vendors. Also, Chemin de l'Ile, as with other *cités*, has a dense network of state-subsidized neighborhood associations, many of which are managed and utilized by North African Arab residents. Highlighting the struggle over ownership of public space in *cités*, one of my adolescent female consultants who is herself of Algerian descent claims that North Africans are simply "more visible" in Chemin de l'Ile because they have "appropriated the territory" within the neighborhood. Such statements indicate the representational slippage that occurs when dominant stereotypes are re-appropriated by the group in question to achieve new political ends—in this case, to legitimate and valorize the use of public space in *les cités* by Arabs themselves.

My Own Transcultural Journey

I came to the issues of belonging and exclusion in France from the perspective of my own initial search for a "French" identity as a college student and then a graduate student. Despite my French-sounding name, I am a third generation American of French–Canadian descent on my father's side only, and I speak English-influenced French that I learned at school rather than at home. To the teens in Chemin de l'Ile and to all French people, I was clearly *not* French, although I initially tried to be. Convinced that I was "French" before embarking upon a yearlong college study-abroad program in Paris, I was quickly disabused of this idea due to my imperfect French as well as my supposedly "typical" American views on politics and history. Occurring mostly over heated dinner conversations (in French) with my host family, my reorientation toward myself as emphatically *not* French was coupled with the sense that "the French" were not whom I expected either.

I had the great fortune to spend a year with a couple, Madame and Monsieur Degrand, who, along with several of their grown children, had dedicated their lives to understanding and rectifying the many social problems of modern France. Monsieur Degrand, although he had originally been an engineer who had obtained his first job working in the (then) North African colonies, had shifted his emphasis to the intertwined contemporary French problems of unemployment, scholastic failure, and immigration. Madame Degrand, although not working for paid employment, dedicated her working life to rehousing immigrant workers who were either squatting or homeless in Paris. Nightly, at their dinner table, I was introduced to people who educated me about contemporary France and the webs of social, economic, political, and intellectual influence brokered through post-colonial relations.

Whereas I lived inside the apartment with Monsieur and Madame Degrand, above us, in the "maids' chambers" (*chambres de bonnes*), was a young woman who had been repudiated by her Algerian-born parents due to her outspoken beliefs and open dating practices. Across the hall from her was a young man displaced by the civil war in Lebanon (yes, this was long ago!). Neither was charged rent. Not only did they regularly attend dinner, so did international scholars working on immigration such as Alec Hargreaves, who has written extensively about *beur* literature. In short, the France that I found was far more heterogeneous and multiple than the culturally monolithic country I had expected to find.

Motivated to understand the ethnic, cultural, and political complexity of France, during a follow-up year-long stay after graduating from college,

I decided to conduct research on a journalistic category that was popular at that time (the early 1990s): *les banlieues chaudes*, or "the hot suburbs," a derogatory term coined during that period to indicate *les cités*. In coverage (both left-wing and right-wing) that naturalized a connection among immigration, crime, scholastic failure, and drug addiction, French newspapers frequently targeted North Africans, and particularly Algerians, in conjunction with such representations. By choosing this topic for a thesis that I conducted as part of a French master's (*maîtrise*) program at the University of Paris 7 (Jussieu), I embarked on a journey to understand and critically assess the conflation of certain social problems with certain "problematic" groups in dominant French public discourse.

Later, in graduate school at the University of Texas at Austin, I decided to attempt to understand these processes from the perspective of the young people most centrally concerned by them. Thus, my interests in belonging and social exclusion in France began both with my own understanding that I was not French and that "the French" encompassed many people whom I had previously not considered. Surprisingly, being considered a cultural and linguistic outsider by my teenaged consultants during fieldwork was ideal. That is, it helped me enormously that I was not French, did not work for the state, nor was employed as a French journalist or sociologist, who have at times engaged in aggressive interviewing and research tactics in Chemin de l'Ile and in *les cités* elsewhere.

My introduction to Chemin de l'Ile was as serendipitous as my placement as a junior year student abroad. Although I knew that I wanted to work with teenagers of North African descent living in *les cités*, I initially had difficulty finding an introduction to such a community. While deliberating about how to make this happen during initial fieldwork, I enrolled in a college-level class at *Ecole des Hautes Etudes en Sciences Sociales* (School for Advanced Study in Social Science). The course dealt with a political and social understanding of French Republicanism, and was taught by a famous political scientist. Repeatedly using the United States as a counter-example, the professor excoriated multiculturalism, including bilingual education and affirmative action. Feeling that many of my core beliefs in a pluralistic society were being trampled, I tried, in my unrefined French, to argue with the professor in favor of an American model of inclusion. Only one other person in the room agreed with me: part-time graduate student Akil Yacine, an adult son of Algerian immigrants who had previously worked in a factory and who had marched in *le mouvement beur*. He had returned to school and was currently the director of a state-supported neighborhood association, *Cerise*. He and I not only had a meeting of the minds with respect to our professor; Akil invited me to tutor at his association and to begin discussing my project with local families. If parents and kids were interested in participating, he would let me begin my project in his association.

After a few months of tutoring at *Cerise*, I was lucky to be accepted by middle-school students both as tutor and researcher and was granted their and their parents' consent to audio record tutoring sessions. The kinds of data I collected over the next 16 months of fieldwork represent my focus on adolescents' agency to create contexts for the expression of social identity through everyday talk. While I occasionally visited the local middle school where the adolescents in this study were enrolled, I decided to focus my energies on adolescent-centered social networks and activities as often as possible. For example, although much of my time in Chemin de l'Ile was spent in the semi-institutional setting of neighborhood associations (including *Cerise*, and eventually others as well), most of the data that I analyze here represent casual interactions among peers and between peers and adult mentors. These impromptu exchanges often took the form of highly creative group performances, wedged in between more structured tutoring activities or ongoing throughout a tutoring session.

In addition to the data that I collected in more institutional contexts such as the neighborhood association *Cerise*, I audio-recorded in a local park with a core group of adolescents as frequently as possible. It was the habit of small groups of some of these 13–16-year-old girls (and a few boys) to gather in a local park after school to chat, weather permitting. These groups shifted and changed depending on the day and included roughly a dozen teens. I became a group member of sorts, since these were adolescents with whom I had worked at *Cerise* and who were accustomed to my audio recorder and persistent questions. These teens were also solicitous of my company because my presence sometimes provided them the adult chaperoning needed for forays into *cités* in other neighborhoods. The many roles that I assumed in relation to these adolescents afforded me both rich insight into their daily lives and a difficult line to walk between the responsible adult and participant–observer. For example, on some occasions, I had to refuse to act as chaperone outside of the confines of local associations because to facilitate girls' outings to the mall or other *cités* after school might abuse the trust that their parents placed in me. As adults often quite marginalized from their children's experiences of school, some parents mistook me for a "official" (institutional) adult chaperone because of my role as a tutor at the neighborhood association *Cerise*.

The multiple and sometimes conflicting roles that I occupied as ethnographer, tutor, mentor, chaperone, and friend were further enriched and complicated when, after roughly a year of fieldwork, I was invited to live with a family in the neighborhood. When I shifted from commuting to

Chemin de l'Ile to living there, both my standing in the community and my own view of it changed. I lived with the Hamdani family, who numbered seven people, including mother, father, two daughters, and three sons, aged 2–18 years. From this experience, I enjoyed much closer relationships not only with the people I lived with but also with other neighbors who, I believe, took my move as a sign of my acceptance of them and my commitment to them. Also, my own (shifting) social identity became more relevant to my research and more complex once I was attached to a particular family, in that I ceased to be "just" the American ethnographer, and was recognized as someone with enduring ties to a local family and to local social networks more generally.

Consequently, my collection and analysis of data were enhanced by a more complex understanding of my consultants, their families, and the local community. In addition to a better understanding of social identity categories on the ground, this increased ethnographic complexity afforded me better and more informal contexts for data collection, as when I was able to record teens' interactions outside of *Cerise* and in local playgrounds or on outings. The research was greatly enhanced through my experience of daily rhythms and quotidian spaces of Chemin de l'Ile in particular and *les cités* more generally. Living with the Hamdani family meant that I was privy to everyday interactions that helped me address how categories and discourses of identity that widely circulate in France are apprehended and transformed in local interactions—as, for example, with the notion of *mec de la cité* ("guy from the *cité*") that is addressed in the next chapter.

Notes

1 Although the term still persists in common French parlance to this day, the ZEP designation has not existed since the 2006–2007 school year, when it was replaced by other initiatives, such as the ÉCLAIR program (*écoles, collèges, et lycées pour l'ambition, l'innovation et la réussite* or "grade, middle, and high schools for ambition, innovation, and success"). Originally, ZEP schools were designated by the minister of education according to a set of criteria, such as percentage of foreign-born parents, dropout rates, and median income for the neighborhood.

2 I discuss the central role played by state-supported associations in establishing services and daily life within immigrant communities in Chapter 2.

3 The rumor in Chemin de l'Ile about the lack of graffiti was that the "older brothers" or *grands frères* had told younger community members not to *tagger* ("tag"). I will return to the archetype of the "big brother" later in Chapter 4, but, loosely defined, it means the older, unmarried young men who are most

active in "business" (illegal sale and trade of stolen goods and drugs). While these young men don't yet have access to the respect accorded fathers and family heads, they still have a significant measure of status and respect in the neighborhood by virtue of their age and financial success. In contrast, "little brothers" or *petits frères* refer to the younger set of up-and-coming male adolescents who usually train for big brother status by working informally for *grands frères* by selling goods, running errands, etc. The system of "big" and "little brothers" is not specific to Chemin de l'Ile, and has been documented in other *cités* by Pascal Duret (1996).

4   Willis (1977: 5–6) reported a similar practice among the working-class "lads" of industrial Hammertown who would use the neighboring city's postal code when describing where they lived to girls from other areas. However, the adolescents with whom Willis worked were so disenchanted with school and the working world that they reserved this practice for personal purposes, unlike adolescents in Chemin de l'Ile.

5   Personal communication, Michel Guirao, neighborhood coordinator, Mayor's Office, Chemin de l'Ile.

6   These negative associations existed both in the right-wing newspaper *Le Figaro* and left-wing *Libération*, except that the causality was framed in slightly different terms. *Le Figaro* implied that North African immigration and Algerians in particular were responsible for bringing crime and drug sales into "French" communities, and hence creating *les banlieues chaudes*. On the other hand, *Libération* implied that immigrants and their descendants were only indirectly responsible for creating *les banlieues chaudes*, since the French society was responsible for discriminating against immigrants and their children, neglecting their poverty, and thus pushing them toward feelings of alienation (*"ennui," "la haine"*) that, in turn, caused them to be violent and reject civil French society. The more reticent and intellectual newspaper *Le Monde*, however, refused to participate in this journalistic category, and would only discuss specific suburbs and neighborhoods, rather than *la banlieue chaude* (the "hot suburb") or even *la banlieue* ("the suburb"). Bonnafous (1991) notes a similar pattern of amalgamation of negative stereotypes and immigration in French media.

7   Tribalat (1995) notes that adult children of Algerian immigrants are more frequently unemployed after finishing school, even though their levels of education are comparable to those of other adult children of immigrants. For example, Tribalat's 1995 unofficial census of 13,000 respondents found that 53% of adult males and 47% of adult females whose parents are of Algerian origin experience at least 1 year of unemployment between the ages of 20 and 29 years, as compared to 23% of adult males and 33% of adult females of Portuguese parentage (1995: 177). Tribalat notes that this discrepancy probably indicates discrimination on the part of prospective employers toward Algerians, a pattern that holds generally in her data in relation to French citizens of African origin (North and sub-Saharan). More recently, two 2012 studies by INSEE (French National Institute for Statistics and Economic Studies) and DARES (Direction for the

Organization of Research, Studies, and Statistics) have found that unemployment rates are higher in adult, active French children of immigrants than for immigrants themselves, the former representing 18% of unemployed workers over 18 years, and the latter 17%. These same studies show that adult children having one or both parents from Algeria represent the highest percentage of unemployment from a non-European Union background, and roughly half of the unemployed in this group (see Fiches thématiques: Populations immigrées, 2012 and Emploi et chômage des immigrés en 2011, 2012).

8   As well, "French" and "Muslim" are often constructed as mutually exclusive categories of identity; Fernando, for example, demonstrates "the ambiguity between racial and religious visibility and invisibility in dominant conceptions of Frenchness by analyzing the difficulty of being Muslim French when those two terms—Muslim, French—are considered incommensurable" (2014: 6).

9   *Raï* is a form of popular Algerian music that dates back to the early part of the twentieth century. Its tendency to openly discuss matters of sex and romantic love have threatened the careers and physical safety of many Algerian *raï* singers, many of whom have immigrated to France in order to perform there (Schade-Poulsen 1999).

10   The French culture wars with respect to popular art forms has not been limited to *cités*, but has evolved as a national conflict. Throughout the 1980s, censorship on French radios was institutionalized; French radio announcers' motto was *pas de rap, ni d'arabe* ("no rap, and no Arabic music"). The French music scene has since exploded with a new fusion of influences, including American-styled rap, popular North African *raï*, and traditional music styles from North and sub-Saharan Africa. African–French rap artist MC Solaar is largely regarded as the vanguard of this movement, whose intellectual, poetic lyrics paved way for the widespread popularity of French rap that followed.

11   See Singh, Lele, and Martohardjono (1988) for their critique of intercultural or "interethnic" communication scholarship.

12   At the same time, a growing body of literature, including that which deals with language, is attempting to theorize transnationalism from a multi-centered perspective (Blommaert 2010; Dick 2010; Duranti 1997; Koven 2004, 2013; Mendoza-Denton 2008; Park 2009; Reynolds 2013a & 2013b; Rouse 1991; Wagner 2008; Zentella 1990).

13   This is akin to Blommaert's (2010) notion of polycentrism, that is, that speakers orient to multiple sociolinguistic "centers" of language authority or ideology, as well as to Koven's (2013) analysis of how Luso-descendant French adults orient to two contrasting language ideological models for transnationalism when telling narratives. At the same time, the analysis that I present in this book is distinct from both of these approaches, in that I describe how speakers simultaneously orient to multiple social categories, discourses, and language forms, rather than to language ideologies/centers (Blommaert 2010), or to models for language and personhood (Koven 2013). In other words, whereas Blommaert and Koven describe similar processes at the level of language

ideology, I address speakers' invocation and transformation of ideological categories for identity that reside in discourse, such as "Arab" and "French."

14 And, although some teens did return to Algeria in the summers, many did not with regularity, often due to economic reasons. For these reasons, this book does not address transnational movement for vacations and the identity work involved (but see Wagner 2008).

15 Along these lines, Marjorie Faulstich Orellana's very important work on the language experiences and forms of expression among immigrant-descent child translators builds upon the notion of transculturation (2009). Her work differs from my own, in that Orellana's deals with translating children's in-the-moment experiences of in-betweenness rather than ideological representations of in-betweenness through performances of identity, as my work emphasizes. Also, Orellana's work does not emphasize that these processes are born out of stigma, as my work does.

16 While not a comprehensive list, the following are notable contributors to this scholarship: Begag and Rossini 1999; Bloul 1996; Bouamama 1993; Boucherit 2008; Costa-Lascoux 1989; Dabène 1990; Douville 2012; Feldblum 1993; Grillo 2006; Jazouli 1992; Muxel 1988; Noiriel 2007; Poinsot 1991; Rosello and Bjornson 1993; Taleb Ibrahimi 1985; Wihtol de Wenden 1988; Wihtol de Wenden and Daoud 1993.

17 However, the following are examples of a growing French sociolinguistic literature regarding young people living in *les cités* and those from immigrant backgrounds: Abu-Haidar 1995; Basier and Bachmann 1984; Billiez 1985; Boucherit 2008; Boyer 1994; Dabène 1991; Dabène and Billiez 1987; Dannequin 1999; Goudaillier 2012; Moïse 2003.

18 The conditions of *les bidonvilles* are documented in Azouz Begag's novel *Le Gone du Chaâba* ("The kid from Chaâba"), and in the film *Vivre au Paradis* ("To Live in Paradise") by Yemina Benguigui.

19 Of course, the use of immigrants as a foil for national identity is not particular to France, but part of a wider process of externalization whereby nationalist politics are generally asserted.

20 As Hargreaves notes, drawing from evidence reported by the National Commission on Human Rights, "Almost 80 percent of violent acts officially classed as racist and more than 90 percent of racist murders in France are committed against Maghrebis" (1997: 19).

CHAPTER 2

SPEECH IN THE *CITÉ*: STYLE AND STIGMA

My first exposure to the notion of *mec de la cité* ("guy from the *cité*") occurred on a day when I was spending time outdoors with a group of adolescent girls in a playground at the base of an early-model HLM. As I sat chatting with the girls while younger children played on a structure nearby, I noticed an adult woman who was pulling a young adolescent boy of roughly 14 aside to scold him. As I learned later, this woman was the boy's aunt. As she stood over him, she asked in a large penetrating voice that bordered on yelling, *"Pourquoi tu te comportes comme un mec de la cité?!"* or "Why are you acting like a guy from the *cité*?!" Although I was not able to discern at the time what the boy had done to receive the scolding by his aunt, her question puzzled me. Was not the teen, after all, de facto a *"mec de la cité,"* in that he clearly was male and living in one? And, since the boy very literally was a "guy from the *cité*," how and why was he supposed to not act like one?

This conundrum reveals ethnographic and theoretical information central to this chapter and the rest of the book. As I eventually understood through continued fieldwork, this boy's aunt was able to scold him because *un mec de la cité* has solidified into what Eckert (2004) would call a type of "social persona" and Koven (2001) a "locally imaginable persona." In other words, the aunt could entreat her nephew not to embody "the guy from the *cité*" because this entity evokes a particular set of behavioral and stylistic characteristics. The notion of a "guy from the *cité*" entails assumptions that such a

Transcultural Teens: Performing Youth Identities in French Cités, First Edition. Chantal Tetreault.
© 2015 John Wiley & Sons, Inc. Published 2015 by John Wiley & Sons, Inc.

person engages in aggressive verbal and physical behavior, spends too much time *dehors* (outside), may conduct small-time drug dealing or sell stolen goods, and wears certain styles of clothing, usually designer tracksuits, unlaced sneakers, and baseball caps.

In theoretical terms, the notion of "a guy from the *cité*" is evidence for how people interpret stylistic difference in everyday interaction, including linguistic variation, but other kinds as well: behavioral and stylistic choices that exist alongside of language such as dress, hair, and makeup.[1] To a degree, linguistic styles, similar to styles of dress or make-up, can be taken on and off by users to perform identifications with or against particular social groups (LePage and Tabouret-Keller 1985; Rampton 1995b). For example, the young boy being scolded by his aunt may "act" or "talk" like a "*mec de la cité*" but may not inherently or always "be" one. Accordingly, I take into account a variety of practices, such as music, everyday speech, and dress, as integral to teens' stylistic performances of recognizable social identities. Linguistic, musical, and embodied styles (e.g., dress, hair, and gesture) are not only central to the ways that French *cités* are represented in popular French culture and media, but also in everyday identity practices among *cité* inhabitants themselves.

The centrality of *cités* to the history of North African immigration and the marginalization of these spaces have contributed to the formation of new linguistic, dress, and musical styles. Adolescents' enactments of these verbal and embodied styles are important to my larger discussion of teens' identity practices because performances of self-presentation in Chemin de l'Ile often revolved around their use. That is, as in other *cités* across France, crafting a personal identity in Chemin de l'Ile was achieved through the use of speech, dress, and musical styles that embodied the aesthetic of the urban space and subculture of *les cités*.

Theorists of adolescent culture note that linguistic and subcultural styles are central, organizing features of adolescent peer groups because they provide a way to express, reproduce, and sometimes subvert social hierarchies of class, age, "race," and gender (Bucholtz 1999; Eckert 1989; Mendoza-Denton 2008; Willis 1977). Although individually expressed and achieved, adolescents managed their personal reputations in part through the adoption, elaboration, or rejection of a code of behavior that was referred to as *se comporter comme une fille ou un mec de la cité* ("to act like a girl or guy from the *cité*"). Self-identifying or being labeled as a *fille* or *mec de la cité* ("girl or guy from the *cité*") involved identifying with stigmatized or even "deviant" identities as they were represented and produced in mainstream French discourses as well as in everyday discourses in Chemin de l'Ile. In these ways, youth in Chemin de l'Ile used material and linguistic stylistic choices to negotiate the often competing constructs of stigma and empowerment.

Goffman has described "stigma" as the process whereby social identities become negatively marked as deviant, or as falling outside the range of "normal" (1963:4–5). With regard to the notion of the "girl" or "guy from the *cité*," stigma is operative in that, as in the example discussed earlier, older people and sometimes peers in the community entreated youth to avoid personifying these identities. Here, stigma is being read not in face-to-face interactions between stigmatized individuals and "normals," as Goffman argued, but is a perspective that is inherent in everyday behavioral and stylistic choices within the *cité* itself. With respect to styles associated with *les cités*, stigma acts as an interpretive filter for categories of persons and behaviors. As such, teens' stylistic choices and attendant processes of identification and dis-identification with *les cités* evidence complex connections among representations of space, types of persons, and categories of behaviors and styles.

This chapter focuses upon performances of adolescent styles in Chemin de l'Ile from a transcultural perspective: teens' personal empowerment in the neighborhood is, in large part, dependent upon stylistic choices that serve to affiliate them with the local *cité*, and yet these styles, as well as the neighborhood, are stigmatized in the broader national French community and even locally. Through their material (dress, hairstyle) and linguistic choices, teens demonstrate a connection with the space and subculture of their *cité* but are also routinely made aware that these choices may compromise their individual and communal reputations on a larger scale. Consequently, adolescents manage their personal reputations through not only the adoption and elaboration but also the rejection of communicative styles that indicate affiliation with *les cités*. Through examining teens' shifting orientations to such stylistic choices, this chapter demonstrates the complexity and centrality of the stigmatized spaces of *les cités* to adolescents' emergent identities.

Embodied Stylistic Practices: Global Meets Local

The following ethnographic moment illustrates how styles become ideologically attached to social persons who, due to their affiliation with *les cités*, are stigmatized. The social connections that speakers draw between styles and types of people often lead adolescents to broker a complicated positioning between valorizing and rejecting such styles.

At *Cerise* one day, Samira, a younger girl of about 12, Mohammad, a 25-year-old adult male tutor, and I were casually talking in the kitchen.

Samira, who was generally very shy and a very dedicated student, had been one of the first middle school students to show up that day for tutoring, and was sitting in the outermost room, quietly doing her homework while we chatted. I noticed she was wearing a Nike ring and I could not help but say "*Toi aussi?*" ("You too?") in an incredulous tone. My astonishment stemmed in part from the sheer ubiquity of the Nike "swoosh" in Chemin de l'Ile. Furthermore, many of these purportedly "Nike" products were counterfeit, demonstrating the ways that, despite strong ties to corporate entities, *cité* styles often depend upon a parallel economy that includes production and distribution, as well as consumption.

However, my surprise also involved a sense of moral and aesthetic disconnect. After all, Samira's best friend was Habiba, the only girl in the association (and one of the few in the neighborhood) who chose to wear the *foulard* or Muslim headscarf. Also, the "good girl" behavior of these younger (roughly 12 years of age) middle school students was quite different from that of some of the older girls (aged 15–16 years) who had formed a friendship group at *Cerise* that reveled in troublemaking at school. Samira was not the "type" I associated with these styles, a response that also emerged in Mohammad's reaction.

After I registered my surprise at Samira's ring, Mohammad jokingly interjected an explanatory statement for her possession of the Nike ring: "*Parce que t'es une caillera*" ("Because you're a *caillera*")—thereby transforming the word *racaille* by using *verlan*, the practice of inverting syllables of words that constitutes a prevalent form of vernacular speech in France. The roughly synonymous words *caillera* and *racaille* constitute the most extreme and negative representational version of *mec de la cité*.[2] As noted in Chapter 1, the hyper-masculine, racialized, and violent figure of *la racaille* or "street trash" is a stereotype that has been reproduced in popular French media as well as in political discourse. Such a pattern was evident, for example, when former French President Sarkozy blamed *la racaille*, rather than police brutality or social injustice, for the 2005 civil disturbances in *les cités* that arose after the death of two teens while being pursued by the police (Ridet 2005).

When accused of being a *caillera*, Samira initially laughed, indicating that she understood that Mohammad was teasing her. Yet, Samira quickly qualified her reason for wearing the ring, "No, it's because it's my birthday and a girl gave it to me." Mohammad asked, "Today?," and when Samira answered "Yes," Mohammad and I wished her "Happy birthday." Teasing aside, Mohammad and my pinpointing of the Nike ring as *caillera* style shows the ways that we, along with other speakers in Chemin de l'Ile, evaluated markers of style in terms of social behaviors and by organizing them according to stigmatized social persons. Mohammad's ironic commentary that Samira was a *caillera* functioned to associate a style marker (the Nike "swoosh" ring) with this social persona, along with the attendant characteristics such as toughness and masculinity.

Just as Mohammad and I were jokingly commenting on the apparent disjuncture between Samira's "good girl" status and her wearing a Nike ring, Samira also found it necessary to deny her attachment to the ring, seemingly to reject a *racaille* identity for herself. She was only wearing the ring, Samira justified, because a girl had given it to her, thereby implying that not to wear it would be rude. In her explanation for why she wore the ring, Samira evidenced that she, too, associated the "swoosh" ring with behaviors linked to the stigmatized figure of *la racaille*, which she rejected by rejecting the ring. Thus, all three of us were reproducing ideologically motivated connections about who would likely wear such a ring and what such a ring would indicate about their social behavior.

In addition to showing how style markers such as the Nike swoosh get attached to locally recognizable persons, uses of this symbol also illustrate the connections that style brokers between globalizing and localizing processes. As in many places in the current global economy, adolescents in Chemin de l'Ile consume styles of music and dress that exist within a global "capitalist culture"—involving both what is available on the "market" and patterns of consumption—that is often dominated by American and international corporations such as Nike and Levi's (Foley 1990). Many styles of clothing, jewelry, and sneakers that are identified within Chemin de l'Ile and elsewhere as part of a localized, *cité* stylistic repertoire were appropriated from the circulation of transnational goods and styles emanating from multinational conglomerations.

The Nike "swoosh" offers a particularly rich example of how global styles are reinterpreted for local consumption. The "swoosh" appeared on everything in Chemin de l'Ile from jewelry to *henna* markings on hands during Ramadan, the month-long Muslim holiday. Whereas *henna* (a traditional temporary tattoo) is used across North Africa to ritually mark participants in marriages and religious holidays, its use to perpetuate the already ubiquitous Nike sign was becoming a new tradition among adolescents in the neighborhood. The semiotics of such stylistic practices indicate teens' innovation and creativity in the ways that they blend a mass-produced icon of capitalism with a traditional practice usually reserved for cultural and religious rituals. Whether we interpret such a practice as a case of secularizing sacred tradition, as the strategic use of capitalist icons for cultural and religious maintenance in diaspora, or both, such practices demonstrate lived transcultural experience and creative expression among children of Algerian immigrants growing up in French *cités*.[3] In this way, adolescents in Chemin de l'Ile and other *cités* appropriated status symbols of transnational capitalism and used them for their own cultural and communal purposes.

Adolescents living in the stigmatized spaces of French *cités* are not alone in the practices of co-optation and re-valuation of symbolic capital. Hebdige (1979) borrowed anthropologist Claude Lévi-Strauss' concept of *bricoleur* ("handyman") to describe the mix-and-match stylistic creativity of British youth—a notion that resonates with how adolescents in Chemin de l'Ile appropriated mainstream and mass-produced brands and icons and transformed them for their own purposes of identity construction. In France, examples of strategic stylistic appropriation and re-signification abound. Similar to the mainstream borrowing of African-American styles of speech and music by the white, middle-class teenagers in the United States (Bucholtz 2011), popular French media has expressed a national fascination with North African music, such as *raï*, and *cité* styles of dress and speech. For example, Albert (2001) has documented that French, middle-class, white adolescents appropriate *cité* styles of speech and dress to craft tough, "authentic" identities from *la rue* ("the street"). On the whole, however, French media, politics, and scholarship have consistently fueled a "moral panic" (Hall et al. 1978) about violence and crime in French *cités* and have either censured or demonized musical, dress, and linguistic styles popular in *cités* (Terrio 1999). For example, the 2004 ban on Muslim headscarves in French state schools also effectively banned jewelry styles typical in *les cités*. The law banned all "conspicuous signs of religion" (Bowen 2007), and, under the guise of "fairness," potentially also all oversized gold and silver hands of Fatima, crosses, and stars of David. The law thus simultaneously censors both practicing Muslim girls and the "bling" of *la racaille*.

And yet, emulating styles and behaviors associated with the stigmatized spaces and stigmatized personas that typify *la cité* provide a source of creative self-expression for teens. In Chemin de l'Ile, adolescents paid detailed attention to bodily practices, including clothing styles and brands, hair, and jewelry styles, and such practices are considered significant for how they marked the spatial affiliation as well as personal style of the wearer. As Bourdieu (1987) notes, style or "taste" (*le goût*) is intimately tied to patterns of consumption and social stratification. In particular, Bourdieu surveyed consumption of food, music, and leisure activities as "an economy of cultural goods" that "corresponds to a social hierarchy of the consumers" (ibid: 1). According to Bourdieu, this hierarchy of taste favors a modern, middle-class "cultural nobility" (the *bourgeois*) that has replaced the social nobility of pre-Revolutionary France. Namely, bourgeois tastes and affinities are shaped by the process of "distinction" that neatly separates them from working-class patterns of material and cultural consumption. For example, small, "classy," or more *bourgeois* necklaces bearing a hand of Fatima or cross are not banned under the 2004 law, mostly likely because they fail to incite a strong reaction among *bourgeois* French lawmakers.

Although Bourdieu focuses mostly on the social construction of *bourgeois* taste, his theory can aptly be applied to working classes in France and elsewhere. For, not only *bourgeois*, but all social classes are defined and reproduced through practices relating to taste and style: "Consumption is, in this case, a stage in a process of communication, that is, an act of deciphering, decoding, which presupposes practical or explicit mastery of a cipher or code" (ibid: 2). Just as everyday consumption practices can exemplify a *bourgeois* aesthetic, adolescents' identification with urban styles from *les cités* demonstrate how expressions of social class, ethnicity, and age status emerge through everyday consumption and production of popular culture.[4]

Insiders/Outsiders: Shifting Spatial Affiliations, Styles, and Group Membership

Teens' notions of style are forged through their contact with and social understandings of "outsiders." Further, these interactions demonstrate complex relationships between style and stigma. Part of the manner in which stylistic identifications and dis-identifications function is to help establish shifting insider and outsider categories that teens use to negotiate group membership. Because styles affiliated with *les cités* are often interpreted through a filter of stigma, the stakes of negotiating who is "us" and who is "them" are high and involve figuring out which groups are or are not "marked" by difference. The notion of marking—that is, the process whereby a society decides who or what is outside of "neutral" or "normal"— fits well with Bourdieu's ideas of taste and distinction because styles function to mark social difference. The teens included in my study were still in the process of learning which styles were marked and for whom—for example, who "had an accent" and who "did not." Of course, as Lippi-Green (1997) notes, everyone who speaks has an accent; yet, the widespread perception that some speakers do not is evidence that, due to power relations, some accents are considered neutral and some accents are marked *as accents*, as in a "southern accent" in the United States.

Neighborhood associations such as *Cerise* are central to introducing *cité* teens to outsiders, through field trips and cultural activities designed to take them out of their neighborhoods. In the process, adolescents from Chemin de l'Ile and elsewhere are "educated" about their place—in terms of spatial, racialized, and classed locations—within the French society.[5] As mentioned in Chapter 1, historically and currently, neighborhood associations have played a very important role in the lives of immigrants and their children in France. In 1981, immigrants were given the right to form federally recognized associations, and special funding was made available for this purpose, called the "Social Action Fund" or FAS (Silverstein 2004:163). In Chemin de l'Ile, as in other *cités*, neighborhood associations have had deeply empowering effects for materially and representationally disempowered people in France—for example, by offering free or low-cost tutoring, literacy programs, and legal, employment, and housing services.

At the same time, due to a client-based relationship to the French state, which acts as patron, associations sometimes reproduce a neo-colonial power imbalance. An ethnographic moment that made this dynamic clear to me occurred during one of the routinely scheduled fieldtrips for middle school students to Paris. *Cerise*, as with other neighborhood associations that provided after-school tutoring, also provided programs designed to enhance *la prévention* that is, the prevention of young people's activity in delinquency, drugs, and membership in *les bandes* (similar to American "gangs" but less formally organized). Previous to my stint conducting fieldwork at the association, *la prev* (as *les éducateurs* call it) had focused almost exclusively on teenaged boys since they were deemed to be most at risk. Around the time that I started to volunteer, *Cerise* hired a new *éducatrice* Shakira. Until she fled Algeria in the 1990s after religious extremists tried to murder her with a machete for showing films during Ramadan, Shakira had been a professional journalist and was (and is currently) a grass-roots political activist. Upon beginning her contract with *Cerise*, Shakira set about creating parity in services to girls as well as boys. One of the first things that she worked on was creating cultural outings that were tailored to girls' interests and needs.

One such outing involved Shakira and I taking a group of teenaged girls to Paris to visit the Louvre. The museum portion of the trip seemed to function much in the way that it was intended. Despite some groaning and foot-dragging, Shakira successfully and generally incited enthusiasm in the teens for works of art as well as for the newly exposed archaeological foundations beneath the museum. The trip's aim hit a snag, however, when we happened to walk through some of Paris' more posh shopping streets and when we passed by a store selling one of the teens' favorite brands, Lacoste. The girls begged Shakira to enter the extremely expensive designer Lacoste store, complete with a security guard at the door. Shakira eventually acquiesced, but the guard did not.

The guard refused entry to the group of roughly 12 girls, aged 13–16 years, purportedly due to a store policy that prohibited large groups, assumedly to prevent shoplifting. Therefore, groups of three girls were allowed to enter to view the merchandise, which was far too expensive for them to buy. Upon exiting the shop, the first group complained to those of us standing in front of the store that there was a group of 20 or more Japanese tourists who had supposedly been allowed to enter together. Bit by bit, the cultural outing turned sourly toward an experience of perceived racism and social exclusion. Although black, the guard was deemed a "racist" by the girls present, and many a derogatory thing was said about "racist" Paris as well by the teenaged suburbanites. Strikingly, socioeconomic class per se did not emerge in the girls' conversations about the event; however, claims that the guard could tell that they were "*de la cité*" or "from the *cité*" did. The girls claimed, and with some accuracy I think, that the guard had refused them entry because of their racialized appearance ("that they looked Arab" in their words) and because their styles of dress, in their own estimation and apparently also on the part of the guard, revealed their provenance from *les cités*.

This exchange illuminates the ways that, despite admirable intentions, when state-subsidized associations orchestrate events to "expose" *cité* teens to bourgeois French culture, they often also simultaneously teach teens the dominant society's rejection of working-class Arab youth, particularly those from the *cité*. Other outcomes may be more positive, such as fostering a love of art or cultivating a general appreciation for learning. Yet, some of the lessons learned on the trip were clearly stigmatizing to teens and evidenced strong links among styles of dress and speech, spatial affiliation, and stigma. Its intended cultural "edification" ended with an experience of intense alienation for the teenaged girls who participated.

Their perceived experiences of "racism" and rejection by bourgeois Parisian circles continued as we walked through the streets of Paris after our visit to the Lacoste store. Paris is increasingly a city for the rich, and the group's morale was quite low by the time we headed home to Chemin de l'Ile on our RER commuter train. The girls on the trip felt that they stood out on the streets of Paris (which they did, especially since we were such a large group), and were demoralized by the large number of shops in which they could afford to buy nothing and, in the case of Lacoste, were not even allowed free entry to look.

In addition to the difficult position that educators and associations must occupy when attempting to "expand the horizons" of disadvantaged youth, the incident at Lacoste points to some other important issues regarding style and stigma. The girls on this outing, as with other teens from Chemin de l'Ile, were fascinated by expensive and even "designer" goods. Style within French *cités*, from the point of view of clothing and other forms of adornment, was understandably part and parcel of the larger French and global fashion industry. That is, working-class Arab teens craved the luxury goods that other French teens wanted, and perhaps even more so, given their stigmatized position in French society. However, their access to these goods was frustrated by poverty as well as alienation and exclusion.

At the same time, the girls' fascination with Lacoste demonstrates the creative malleability of style. For, unlike the largely female group of Japanese tourists at Lacoste who were examining scarves and dresses, the girls from Chemin de l'Ile were interested in men's wear and particularly men's leisurewear such as expensive track suits. Much like their male teenaged counterparts, teenaged girls' taste was aligned with styles of dress typical of *les cités*, where, at that time, designer jogging ensembles and sneakers constituted the coin of the realm. Thus, while brand affiliation on the part of these teens reproduced a kind of hegemony by propping up an exploitative fashion industry, the way that these brands were used to create styles remained malleable and multiple. A simple example resided in the designer tennis shoes that were *de rigueur* for teens in Chemin de l'Ile. They might have been Nike, as with practically everyone else in France at that time, but were worn with tongues hanging out and laces untied in *les cités*. At the same time, as the preceding example illustrates, there were costs to being the bearers of such stylistic markers when teens stepped outside their *cité*, due to their connection with this stigmatized space.

Ongoing negotiations of insider and outsider categories were also relevant between suburban neighborhoods of *les cités*. Teens' own outings usually entailed visits to nearby *cités* rather than Paris, and provided them the opportunity to meet and visit dating partners and friends, sometimes trade and sell illicit goods, and occasionally participate in conflict through verbal or physical fighting. While visiting other *cités* was perhaps more common among adolescent boys due to their relative freedom of mobility, girls also participated in this practice. On some outings to other housing projects, I was co-opted as a semi-official chaperone, given permission by parents, but not by *éducateurs* in local associations who would have preferred to be included.

Ranging in age from 14 to 16, the group of girls with whom I was closest traveled to other *cités* for a variety of adventures, including checking out other teenagers, male and female. In this regard, checking out the styles and brands that other adolescents wore constituted a central function of these outings. Conversations on the way home would invariably turn to "did you see the girl who was wearing the Diesel jeans, Nike Air Max, etc.?" The girls I worked with were also on the lookout for boys to date, partly because it was considered "safer" (more secret) to date someone from another neighborhood, away from what the girls viewed as the prying eyes of peers in their *cité*. Some adolescent girls were also fascinated with illicit activity in other *cités* and could spot the lookout posted while *le business* (drug dealing) occurred. The adolescent girls I worked with claimed that boys from

Chemin de l'Ile knew guys from other *cités* through economic activity, not only through *le business* but also through the sale of goods (e.g., clothing, cell phones, perfume, etc.). In addition to the economic aspect of these networks and exchanges, there was a territorial aspect to these visits—fights would sometimes occur between *les mecs* ("the guys") from one *cité* and those from another, in a symbolic show of defending local territory.

Girls, too, sometimes showed such spatial affiliation through aggression, although of a less organized kind. In my presence, Mina and some other adolescents once almost picked a fight with a group of girls at Pablo Picasso, another *cité* that was reputed to be "tougher" than Chemin de l'Ile. Expectations for physical conflict seemed to increase when adolescent boys traveled to other *cités*. On another occasion, I went to Pablo Picasso with a large group of girls and one boy of Turkish descent, Kader, one of the few who regularly hung out with adolescent girls. Eight of us, including Mina, Hamida, Sarah, Cécile, Rashida, Béatrice, and the lone boy Kader, traveled by RER to Pablo and walked through the art deco concrete gardens and rounded buildings. As we wandered through the paved footpaths of the *cité*, two younger boys, roughly 10, walked up to Kader and snatched his Polo cap off his head and walked off with it, sneering.

Although a bit frightening, their aggression demonstrated that the boys from Pablo understood that we were from outside their *cité* and took our presence there as an aggressive act in itself. On a personal level, I was upset by this close brush with violence on an outing "led" by me. I felt I needed to take action, and was confident that I could, probably because of the small size, age, and number of these aggressors. Kader himself showed no sign of responding to the theft of his cap. So, I walked back to the group of boys, who were playing catch with the cap, and asked them to give it back. When they refused, I used a commonly translated expression from Arabic that commands respect for "guests": "I come from far away" (*Je viens de loin*) and asked again for the cap. The irony of this statement did not strike me at the time—I was using the logic that they should be polite to me because I was a "guest" in their neighborhood, but the aggression toward us seem to be based on the fact of our being outsiders. However, I was apparently foreign enough to be granted special rules for participation; likely thanks to my accent and adult status, the two boys seemed to consider my request sympathetically. After saying that it was a miserable excuse for a cap because the brim was broken, they tossed it back to me. When I returned it to Kader, the others claimed that what I had done was dangerous, but also brave. A more central point is that, through shifting affiliations and distinctions that are linked to style and space, adolescents negotiate insider and outsider categories that are tied to local, national, and international entities.

Language Styles in Establishing Insider and Outsider Categories

As with other embodied practices such as clothing, language encompasses one parameter of stylistic expression that is central to teens' daily identity performances. Embodied styles such as language, hair, jewelry, and clothing are uniquely valued by adolescents in *cités* as the most important types of creative expression in their everyday production and consumption of popular culture. Also, these forms of expression have come under the most public and political scrutiny in the ongoing processes of stigmatizing and othering spaces of French *cités* and their inhabitants.

Similarly, studies of youth language in these contexts have often taken the form of slang dictionaries that propose to translate this mysterious new "language" to a middle-class white audience (Pierre-Adolphe et al. 1995; Seguin and Teillard 1996; Goudaillier 1998). These texts tend to construct French youth in *cités* as speakers who are un-assimilated or "foreign" (Boyer 1997; Tetreault 2007). In contrast, French anthropologist David LePoutre (1997) has conducted one of the few in-depth ethnographic studies of language practices within a *cité*. This work is innovative for its description of adolescent speech genres and linguistic rituals. However, LePoutre's emphasis on obscenities and physical aggression, combined with his near-exclusive focus on male, non-white adolescents, serves to reinforce a dominant image of *cité* youth as socially dangerous.

The frequent emphasis on adolescent males' use of vernacular and competitive interactional genres in early French language research is strikingly similar to how early American sociolinguists constructed "language varieties of adolescent male gangs as authentic or core" in African-American communities in the 1960s (Morgan 1999). Much early linguistic research on French *cités* thus reaffirms popular stereotypes that what distinguishes the speech of teenagers in *cités* is "linguistic deviance" (Boyer 1997). Such depictions are also notable for the recurrent claims they make that a monolithic style has emerged in *cités*. In the late 1990s, this style was embodied in the TV character Joey Star, a "real-life" rapper whose likeness appeared as a puppet on the *Bébête Show*, along with Jacques Chirac. This style consists of a guttural accent, aggressive speech, punctuated by *verlan* and the word *quoi* (meaning "what"— used much as "like" is in English).

More and more, however, scholarship in France and elsewhere shows an increased appreciation of the multiple factors that influence language practices among young people of both genders in *les cités*. Emanating from Canada, France, the United Kingdom, as well as the United States, such research is notable for its attention to the relationships among language attitudes, identity formation, and ideology or representation (Abu-Haidar 1995;

Tlatli 2012), and for dramatically increased attention to the effects of gender to language practices and experiences of migration (Basier and Bachmann 1984; Bordet 1998; Keaton 2006; Moïse 2003; Selby 2012). Furthermore, rather than reproduce stigmatizing discourses, scholarship is increasingly dealing with identity production among French citizens of North African descent in ways that are critical of how this population has been represented both within social science research and in the media (Boyer 1994, 1997; Laronde 1988; McMurray 1997; Seux 1997). For example, although research on racialization of and racism toward these populations has been fairly sparse, particularly in France, there are some notable exceptions to this (Beriss 2004; Chapman and Frader 2004; DeRudder 1980; Ben Jelloun 1984; Koven 2013; Terrio 1999; Fong 2008; Silverman 1991 & 1992; Silverstein 2004 & 2005).

Also particularly exciting are the ways that current research that attempts to link language and identity production among Arab French youth is increasingly attentive to globalization and the circulation of styles across national boundaries (Bensignor 2012; Bentahila and Davies 2002; Goodman 2005; Silverstein 2004). This research dovetails particularly well with new scholarship (in France and elsewhere) on linguistic "crossing" (Rampton 2005b), which challenges the assumed link between ethnic groups and linguistic styles (Alim 2009; Androutsopoulos 2007; Rampton 2006; Rampton and Charalambous 2010; Goudaillier 2012; Jaspers 2005; Pennycook 2003; Tlatli 2012; Vermeij 2004).

While select, stylistic markers (such as ending sentences with *quoi* or "what") are popularized as typical of *cités* in the French media, there is no strong evidence that a uniform or authentic *cité* "language" or uniform style exists (cf. Bucholtz's 2003 critique of "authentic" speech). Rather, the variety of speech styles and even slang collected by these researchers points to the diversity of language practices within French *cités*. Most adolescents in Chemin de l'Ile can emulate the popular stereotype of *cité* language by ironically performing this linguistic and social identity. However, the linguistic styles in the neighborhood that adolescents themselves associate with a local *cité* identity are stylistically and pragmatically more complex.

Uses of Arabic Loan Words as Emblematic Identity Work

Unlike representations of *cité* speech in mainstream French media and scholarship, what was often most important to adolescents in this study was proficiency with particular Arabic loan words. This emphasis on particular Arabic loan words was true even for adolescents who were not of Arab descent, who showed proficiency in comprehension of certain loan words even if they were sometimes reluctant to verbally produce these terms because of fears of being teased for their mispronunciation of them. In the following ethnographic example, for instance, competence with key loan words in Arabic is held up as evidence of insider status, among Arab and non-Arab teens.

One day at *Cerise*, the association at which I conducted tutoring, a group of adolescent girls, a Tunisian-born *éducateur* of about 40 named Kamel, and I sat talking in the kitchen. During our conversation, one of the girls present used the word "kahəl," which in colloquial Arabic intermixed with French is used to mean "to get the better of someone" (*obtenir le meilleur de quelqu'un*). When Kamel asked what the term meant, one of the girls present exclaimed, "*Mais t'es pas un vrai arabe ou quoi?!*" ("Hey, you're not a real Arab, or what?!"). The adolescents present had identified the Arabic loan word as a marker of in-group status.

This example demonstrates that such highly localized uses of Arabic loan terms are typical in French *cités*, but *not* among native Arabic speakers from North African like Kamel. Yet, such loan terms are associated with "Arabness" among adolescents in Chemin de l'Ile. The accusation that Kamel was not a "real" Arab was an effective way to shame him for not knowing words central to these adolescents' daily expression. Thus, the fact of being a native Arabic speaker and growing up in a predominantly Arab country did not guarantee Kamel an insider status for these teens, who conflated highly localized styles of speech from the *cité* with "Arabness." This exchange shows that, despite varied fluency in Arabic, adolescents in Chemin de l'Ile are creating in-group definitions of belonging based upon a local construction of linguistic competence that is largely focused upon Arabic loan word use.

Teens' expectation that North African-born *éducateurs* and tutors would be culturally and linguistically similar to them constituted a poignant conflation of spatial, ethnic, and linguistic identities. A similar conflation occurred when adolescents interacted with adult mentors who were French-born of North African descent, but who did not grow up in *les cités*. Sherazade was a tutor who lived with her parents and brothers in non-subsidized housing in a nearby neighborhood of Nanterre. As with many of the adolescents in this study, Sherazade's parents migrated to France from North Africa (Tunisia) and were not formally educated. Yet, perhaps because she grew up in a neighborhood that was economically and culturally mixed rather than in a *cité*, Sherazade spoke standard French. As well, against all odds, she had successfully obtained a university degree and currently taught French language and literature for a living.

Sherazade and I often worked on transcribing my audio recordings together, and, during an informal conversation with her, I asked her if, in her eyes, the kids at *Cerise* used a lot of Arabic in their speech. She hesitated, but then replied, "Yes, a lot." She claimed that, among her *Maghrébin* (North African descent) friends, people used less Arabic loan words when speaking French. She used the example of her younger brothers, and said that, although fluent in North African Arabic, they only interspersed a few Arabic terms into French occasionally, and not nearly as much as the children and adolescents who she tutored at *Cerise*, who were often not fluent in Arabic. My question reminded Sherazade of an anecdote that she thought was relevant to my study. When Sherazade first arrived to tutor at *Cerise*, the children she worked with were astounded that her name was Sherazade, an Arabic name common among North Africans. Because she did not speak like them, they assumed that she was not an Arab. They informed her that she spoke with an accent: "*Mais tu parles pas comme nous—t'as un accent*" ("You don't talk like us. You have an accent.").

Sherazade explained it differently, of course. She told me that she did not have the "*accent maghrébin*" ("North African accent") when she spoke French, which is basically non-standard (i.e., working-class) French with some phonological similarities to Arabic. Of particular relevance here to the relationship between style and stigma is that *cité* speech patterns and Arabness were conflated among adolescents in Chemin de l'Ile. That is, the "real" linguistic effects of the concentration of children of Arab immigrants and pejorative stereotypes existed side by side and informed one another.

In their stylistic performances, linguistic and otherwise, adolescents were often actively conscious of stigmatizing discourses about *les arabes* and *les cités*, and sometimes participated in them even though they were also critical of them. For instance, adolescents' treatment of both Kamel and Sherazade as cultural and linguistic outsiders demonstrates that teens' conflation of Arabness with *cité* styles is similar to the most stigmatizing of Jean-Marie Le Pen's anti-immigrant rhetoric—that *cités* have become "taken over" by Arabs. In the next chapter, I will further explore teens' notions of Arabness. When considering the previous examples, what emerges is how young people in Chemin de l'Ile come to understand their own stylistic practices in relation to outsiders, such as linguistic outsiders in the case of Kamel and Sherazade. In these cases, teens' understandings of their tutors as culturally and ethnically similar (i.e., as "Arabs") clashed with an expectation for their speaking styles to conform to local *cité* speech norms.

Style, Stigma, and Spatial Affiliation in Interaction:
Solidarity and Competition

At the same time that stigma is operative in how adolescents interpret local styles, ways of speaking also confer teens the chance to establish solidarity and to have fun with peers, even when these verbal styles are competitive or aggressive (cf. Pagliai 2010). Fourteen-year-old Hannah allowed me to read her yearbook and proudly showed me where it was written, "*Merci pour toutes tes vannes qui nous cassent!—Mona*" or "Thank you for all your humorous insults (*vannes*) that "crack" us!—Mona." Here, *casser* or "to crack" was used in the sense of both humorously "cracking up" and "cracking" or devastating the audience through insult. Mona thus validated her female peer's mastery of this genre of ritualized insult (*les vannes*), which has been widely documented as emanating from *les cités* (Goudaillier 1997; Seguin and Teillard 1996).

Competitive, interactive genres such as *les vannes* that are popular in many *cités*, but not necessarily exclusive to them, are used in Chemin de l'Ile by girls and boys alike to build both peer solidarity and personal reputations. In daily interactions, adolescents in Chemin de l'Ile use competitive bragging, slang, and ritualized insults associated with the *cité* for a variety of purposes, demonstrating the multiple ways in which linguistic styles can be appropriated and thus symbolically transformed. For example, competitive verbal exchanges among peers were a main way that teens socialized younger children and each other into locally valued speech styles affiliated with *les cités*.[6] The following exchange demonstrates the centrality of competitive verbal exchanges to girls' as well as boys' peer socialization into communicative practices in Chemin de l'Ile.

"Putting on the Pressure": Competitive Bragging Routines

One sunny spring day, at around 4 o'clock in the afternoon, I happened upon Naima sitting alone on the low wall on the side of the playground where older girls would usually sit to talk. A girl of about 12, Naima greeted me warmly, and I stopped to talk. As with many of her peers, Naima was fascinated with my being American, and told me about the clothing and shoes that her older brother had brought her and her family back from *les States*. Her enthusiasm for comparing the price and quality of brands of clothing continued to be central to our discussion when two older girls, Béatrice (15) and Sarah (14), stopped by. Soon all three girls were comparing brands and competitively bragging about the quality of their clothing and shoes, citing the country that produced each product. For example, in the exchange that follows, "Décathlon" is a popular French brand of sporting wear, "Sloggi" a popular brand of underwear, and "Air Max" a popular type of Nike sneakers. Much as these girls and other adolescents in Chemin de l'Ile used brands of clothing as resources to construct a local system of social distinction, they used competitive verbal genres to construct their individual reputations as competent performers of local speech styles.

Béatrice and Sarah were close friends, but their relationship with Naima was limited to being neighbors and attending the same school. However, because the two older girls knew Naima's older brothers, Béatrice and Sarah enjoyed pre-established teasing rights with her. In the playful bragging and ritualized insults about clothing and brand names that followed, Naima and the older girls turned their keen interest in these status markers into a motif for verbal competition. Naima's efforts to out-brag these older girls might also be viewed as a bid for their attention and an attempt to craft a verbal performance that would earn their respect.

Featured in the following example is a genre of competitive bragging then popular in *les cités, mettre un coup de pression*, which literally means "to make a blow of pressure" or, more figuratively, "putting on the pressure." Successfully achieving *mettre un coup de pression* entailed out-bragging or out-insulting a peer in a competitive verbal exchange. As is the case in the following exchange, an evaluation of a speaker's verbal performance was usually embedded within the performance itself in that adolescent peers would judge each other's attempts to insult and brag. In the transcription of the interaction, words spoken in Arabic are shown in bold type, not only to distinguish them from French, but to emphasize the prevalence of Arabic loan words in verbal performances among these adolescents.[7]

Performing "Mettre Un Coup De Pression"

1	Sarah	*Moi, mon pull c'est un Décathlon et mon slip c'est un Sloggi, alors hein, ta gueule!*	Me, my sweater is a Décathlon and my underwear's a Sloggi, so huh, shut up!
2	Naima	*Hé Décathlon, Décathlon, Décathlon et k- et et Air Max. Alors s'il te plaît ta bouche maintenant et **ka'b** chez toi don- **druk**!*	[Pointing to the other girls' sweatpants and then her own] Hey Décathlon, Décathlon, Décathlon and k- and and Air Max. So please shut your mouth now and **go** home no- **now**!
3	Béatrice	*Hé Naima elle met des coups de pression en ce moment. Chais pas ce qu'elle a dans le cul!*	Hey Naima's putting on the pressure lately. Dunno what she has up her ass!

The preceding exchange demonstrates how these girls used competitive verbal styles common to this and other *cités* to distinguish themselves among their peers. The act of instigating a bragging session was a means for adolescents in Chemin de l'Ile, boys and girls alike, to build positive individual reputations for themselves through self-aggrandizement. At the same time, these performances provided the opportunity to engage a peer in interaction that was both challenging and inclusive, in that they gave the other speaker the chance to also construct her own reputation as a competent verbal performer. The particular performance represented here incorporated both playful and challenging qualities, showing that the girls were using this interaction to create a feeling of familiarity, but also to compete with one another individually.

Verbal genres such as *coup de pression* thus contributed to both a shared stylistic aesthetic for everyday interaction within the neighborhood and to the individual reputations of adolescents who verbally challenged one another. In a pattern common to many of these verbal competitions, here two of the girls, Sarah and Naima, exchanged bragging and insults while a third, Béatrice, evaluated the interaction. Initially, Sarah verbally challenged the other girls by bragging about her sweater and underwear and by adding the insult "shut up." Naima responded to this challenge by bragging about her own and the other girls' clothing, implying that Sarah's clothes were no more prestigious than their own. Naima also completed her bragging by insulting Sarah, "so please shut your mouth now, and go home now."

The older girls' willingness to engage in such an interaction with a younger girl shows how older adolescents socialized their younger peers through ritualized performances of local speech styles. A younger girl, Naima's response was hesitant—she corrected herself and repeated "and," then initially mispronounced the Arabic word **druk** ("now"). Her hesitancy seemed indicative of Naima's status as a less experienced verbal challenger, who lost her nerve when responding to the older girl, Sarah. Similarly, Béatrice's assessment of Naima's performance—"Hey Naima's putting on the pressure lately. Dunno what she has up her ass"—seemed significant in that Béatrice chose to comment about Naima's performance rather than directly respond to her challenge. Thus, while the older girls overtly recognized Naima's response to Sarah as a type of verbal challenge, neither Sarah nor Béatrice chose to respond to it— perhaps because it was not skillful enough to warrant their engagement. Nonetheless, the exchange demonstrates the collective valuing of competitive verbal styles by these girls in that they collaboratively performed, named, and critiqued this instance of *mettre un coup de pression*.

The preceding example shows that, despite the local association of such competitive verbal styles with toughness and masculinity, they were important to how girls constructed personal reputations among their peers. Such performances can thus be viewed as attempts on the part of both adolescent girls and boys to construct personal authority within a larger context that encodes *cité* styles and genres of interaction as central to individual self-expression.

La Fête du Quartier

Affiliations with local space and verbal competition both come to the fore in an annual event in Chemin de l'Ile, *la Fête du Quartier* ("Neighborhood Party"), when neighborhood associations and official entities throw an outdoor, community-wide fair and fundraiser. As noted earlier, state-subsidized associations constitute the very fabric of local social relations in low-income neighborhoods across France. Legal, political, leisure, networking, scholastic, and adult educational activities all figured centrally within associative life in Chemin de l'Ile. All of these activities come together at one time and in one place during the *Fête du Quartier*.

Hosted each June, this public event is common to other *cités* and neighborhoods within Nanterre and across France generally, and provides the occasion for local residents and those from nearby *cités* to participate in a variety of public activities, including games and sports activities for children, but also political and legal forums for adults. In more rural areas of France, *Fêtes* or agricultural *Foires* ("fairs") are touristic events designed not only to entice nearby visitors but tourists from major French cities and abroad who are vacationing in the region. In these less urban contexts, the sale of local gourmet foods and artisanal products are a way to ensure attendance. Being a low-income urban neighborhood of predominantly public housing projects, Chemin de l'Ile's *Fête du Quartier* is characterized by a high degree of participation by local public administration and associations. Each year at this bazaar-like fair, local associations set up booths that promote both public relations and organizational fund raising. *Cerise*, the primary association I worked with, sold a couscous dinner and sweets homemade by mothers of the students we tutored. In addition to raising money for the association, the director used the opportunity to engage parents in an organized debate about the state of the French educational system in which he included experts from the nearby University of Nanterre.

Besides its civic and fund-raising functions, the annual *Fête du Quartier* constitutes an important site for the local production of styles in Chemin de l'Ile. By drawing teens from other nearby *cités*, Chemin de l'Ile's *Fête du Quartier* provided the opportunity for young people, children and adolescents, to participate in organized activities. And, as with other *Fêtes du*

Quartier in nearby *cités*, the event provided an opportunity for adolescents from other nearby low-income neighborhoods to come "check each other out" and compete at events such as the singing contest and deejayed dance at the local *SMJ* or *Salle Municipale de Jeunesse* ("Municipal Youth Center").

In my second year of initial fieldwork, several singers and rappers from other neighborhoods competed in this annual singing contest, including a group of girl rappers from a *cité* outside of Chemin de l'Ile. While the female vocalists from other towns were greatly appreciated by the audience, several girls and boys from Chemin de l'Ile told me later that they thought it "wasn't good" for girls to rap, implying that it was unfeminine or unseemly. In this instance, girls who were publicly participating in rap—a verbal style central to *cité* life and identity in France—were considered to behave in gender-inappropriate ways. The judgment of adolescent girls who rap and do other "masculine" things is another way that aesthetic choices are infused with social distinctions; here, stylistic expectations fall along gender lines. (I explore the conflicts and complexities around adolescent girls' relationship to *cité* styles and the stigmatized spaces of the *cité* in Chapters 4 and 5.)

At the same contest, two local teenaged male rappers, Ahmed and Ali, formed a duo to perform their original composition entitled "Rap SMJ," named for the Municipal Youth Center (*Salle Municipale de Jeunesse*) in which it was performed. Judging from the appreciative screams of female teens in the audience and the general cheering afterward, the performance was a great success. I include in the following table the text of this rap and an analysis to further explore the ways that adolescents participate in creative performances of *cité* styles that foreground their experiences as *cité* inhabitants as well as stigmatizing discourses about these spaces. In the following table, *Zilinas* and *Casbah Zilinas* refer to the names of the housing project where one of the rappers lived in Chemin de l'Ile.

Rap SMJ

1	Même le Préfet Bônnet	Even the Prefect Bônnet
2	a dû se faire serrer, incarcérer	had to be locked up, incarcerated
3	par ces putains de kisdé	by these whores of cops
4	Moi j'ai fait moité	Me, I did it half way
5	j'ai lâché passer le BEP	I dropped out of high school
6	23 ans, 4 enfants	23 years old, 4 kids
7	Mama Mia	Mama Mia

8	Mais n'oublie pas	But don't forget
9	Casbah Zilinas	Casbah Zilinas
10	Fracasse-moi Paris de coups bas	I hit Paris below the belt
11	Resté mythique-tik	Stayed mythic-tik
12	Emmerder la polémique	Screw the controversy
13	et faire de moi un homme chic	and make me a chic man
14	**Wash bik, sheikh?**	**What's your problem, sheikh?**
15	J'suis dans le move **khuya**	I'm in the groove **brother**
16	Mais t'inquiète pas	But don't worry
17	pour les mecs des Zilinas	for the guys from Zilinas
18	Partout où je passe passe	Everywhere I go go
19	les méchants trépassent	the tough types flee
20	je glisse sur la glace	I slide on the ice
21	car je suis l'as des as	because I'm the ace of aces
22	Mais n'oublie pas	But don't forget
23	Nanterre chaud, quartier chaud	"hot" Nanterre, "hot" neighborhood
24	Reputé chaud, archi-chaud	Reputed "hot," super-hot
25	Fais gaffe à ta peau	Watch out for your skin
26	Mama mia	Mama mia
27	Y'a ta reunda	There's your mom
28	aux Zilinas	in Zilinas
29	en **djellaba** Coste-La	wearing a Lacoste **djellaba**
30	rends d'la **zetla**	selling **drugs**
31	Nanterre chaud, quartier chaud	"hot" Nanterre, "hot" neighborhood
32	Reputé chaud, chaud l'artichaut	Reputed to be "hot," hot artichoke

This creative performance encompasses many of the styles of speech and social discourses that I have addressed throughout this chapter. The rap, and conceivably all rap, as noted by Morgan (1996), evokes affiliations with local space, in this case in the form of a particular *cité* through multiple references to "Zilinas" (lines 9, 17, and 28)—including *Casbah Zilinas*, after the Arabic word for a North African "city" or "citadel," and *les mecs des Zilinas* ("guys from Zilinas"), which can be considered a correlate to *les mecs de la cité* ("guys from the *cité*") discussed earlier in the chapter. Also, more general references to Nanterre and *le quartier* ("the neighborhood") are paired with *chaud* ("hot"), meaning dangerous, in line 23, and then repeated at the end of the song as a refrain.

Through these repeated references to the local neighborhood and its purportedly tough and dangerous reputation, Ahmed and Ali attempt to craft an identity for themselves and the neighborhood as tough and authentically from *les cités*. Their claimed identity as tough rappers from a tough *cité* is counterposed against a bourgeois Paris through the boast, "I hit Paris below the belt" (line 10), meaning that they are both tougher than Parisians and better rappers than Parisians. By evoking the "hot," violent suburb, Ahmed and Ali are co-opting widely circulating, negative discourses regarding les cités that have repeatedly appeared in French media. In so doing, they adopt these stigmatizing discourses and adapt them to their interactional needs at the moment: to appear as authentically tough cité rappers. At the same time, humor and fun are clearly present here too, as in the last line of the rap, where Ahmed and Ali playfully insert "hot artichoke" (artichaut) to replace "super-hot" due to its being a near homonym to archi-chaud.

Stereotypical themes of urban decay and social exclusion abound throughout the rap, in the form of references to prison (lines 1–3), scholastic failure (lines 4–5), struggling families with young parents and (by French standards) large numbers of children (line 6–7), allusions to tough guys and dangerous neighborhoods (lines 16–19 and 23–25), and the sale of illegal drugs (line 30). The last reference to illegal drugs is particularly interesting for its form and for the cultural references that it provocatively mixes. The claim that the rapper saw the audience's mother selling drugs constitutes an embedded verbal challenge in the form of a ritualized mother insult to the audience: "There's your mom … selling drugs" (lines 26–30). Here, "your mother" in line 27 is achieved with the word reunda, which is verlan (inverted slang) for daronne, a slang word originating from the Romani ("Gypsy") language that has gained popularity in cité styles of speech (Goudaillier 1997). Furthermore, the audience's mom is described as wearing a Lacoste djellaba, a humorous, clever image since it mixes neighborhood teens' favorite designer brand with North African traditional dress style. (Djellabas are long-flowing robes worn either alone or over Western clothing. Needless to say, Lacoste does not manufacture them.) In this way, a tough urban cité style is achieved here through innovative transcultural mixing, but also playful and aggressive humor; the rappers insult their audience's mother while making them laugh at the absurdity of the insult.

Finally, gender ideologies inform the entirety of this performance, in form, style, and content. As I mentioned earlier, rap was constructed in the neighborhood and in France more generally at that time as a masculine speech genre, which often excluded "nice girls" from participating in its performance. The tough, violent reputation that Ahmed and Ali evoke throughout their rap was generally more indicative of normative social values for masculinity. Along these lines, the theme of "respect" that emerges in the final mother insult, "There's your mom … selling drugs," is typical of the ways that adolescents in Chemin de l'Ile evoke the importance of the cultural value of *le respect* through the public undermining of their inter-locutor's female kin, a point to which I will return in subsequent chapters. More generally, the SMJ event at the *Fête du Quartier* provided an important social event for adolescents to exhibit and engage with verbal and dress styles, both within their own *cité* and across *cités* generally. As I mentioned earlier, these events were attended by adolescents from nearby neighborhoods who competed in the contest and came to socialize in a mixed-gender setting. Thus, in addition to forging ties with other adolescents in the local *cité*, an important aspect of adolescent sociability is forming a mix of alliances and competition with adolescents from other nearby *cités*.

These examples illustrate the multiple relationships among style, space, and stigma that pervade the everyday lives of adolescents in Chemin de l'Ile. Style is inherently connected to spatial and social entities, in that certain styles come to stand in for stigmatized social personas such as *mec de la cité* and *la racaille*. Accordingly, styles provide teens in Chemin de l'Ile a way to negotiate and (re-)interpret stigma within the broader French political and social landscape. At the same time, stylistic performances are a central way that teens have fun and create solidarity among peers, particularly through competitive genres such as *mettre un coup de pression*. Such performances can therefore be considered transcultural, in that localized interpretations of these styles serve to filter stigmatizing outsider discourses as well as to broker insider affiliation and belonging. Teens' alternating affiliation and dis-affiliation with *les cités* and the styles and personas evocative of these spaces are evidence of this dual dynamic of affiliation and dis-affiliation. The next chapter explores a similar dual dynamic in how teens employ transcultural stances to reproduce and transform widely circulating French stereotypes about *les arabes* or "Arabs."

Notes

1   Traditionally in sociolinguistic literature, the term "style" has exclusively indi-cated a level of formality of speech, for example, "casual" or "careful" talk (Labov 1972). Current linguistic anthropological and sociolinguistic research on style is "driven by an explosion and rearticulation of its definition" (Mendoza-Denton 2001:235). Such literature deals largely with naturally occurring language and takes into account other aspects "style" than formality or informality of speech, to include other symbolic practices such as verbal per-formances, leisure activities, and embodied practices, such as dress and make-up (Bucholtz 1999; Eckert 1989; Mendoza-Denton 2008). Recent scholarship also theorizes the relationship between styles (or registers) and spatial distinctions (Mendoza-Denton 2008; Roth-Gordon 2009).

2   I did not encounter a significant difference between *racaille* and *caillera* while conducting fieldwork. However, as is apparent in the preceding example, *caillera* can be used as a singular, countable noun, "Because you are a *caillera*," whereas *la racaille* is similar to its literal translation "trash," in that it is a non-countable noun in French. Hence, using *"caillera"* instead of *"racaille"* facilitates Mohammad calling Samira "a" *caillera*—rather than the more formal and damning sounding *"elle est de la racaille"* or "she's (of the) racaille."

3   In a somewhat different process, Metcalf discusses the increasing overlap between Muslim religious expression and mass-produced iconography, noting "the ever-increasing array of objects distributed by Islamic shops and catalogues: posters, hangings, mugs, bumper stickers, key chains, jewelry, and so forth..." (1996: 3). She argues that such representations and objectifications reflect Islam's temporal and spatial shift toward post-modernity and diaspora. Thus, being Muslim in both the Middle East and "the West" (Europe and North America) increasingly "entails self-examination, judging others, and judging oneself" (ibid.: 7).

4   Here, the work of both Penny Eckert (1989, 2000) and Paul Willis (1977) is of central importance because it specifically analyzes the relationship between the stylistic production and patterns of consumption among working-class youth with their subsequent reproduction of working-class economic status.

5   In the United States, Arabs have historically been classified as Caucasian and have been included in this category on the US Census since 1997. In France, successive colonial administrations racialized Arabs as comprising a distinct *ethnie* ("ethnic group") from Europeans. Although currently "ethnicity," "race," and even racism are taboo subjects in France, discrimination against Arab and black citizens has been widely documented in the forms of housing and job discrimination (Beriss 2004; Chapman and Frader 2004; Hargreaves and McKinney 1997; Koven 2013; Silverstein 2004; Terrio 2009).

6   See Kyratzis (2004) for an extensive discussion of the multiple ways that children and teens socialize each other into forms of interaction and thereby elaborate peer culture.

7   Transcription conventions are as follows: An exclamation point is used to indicate combined stress and loudness; a question mark indicates rising intonation. Periods and commas are used to indicate pauses, the first within a phrase and the second at the end of a phrase. Longer pauses appear in brackets in numbers of seconds. A dash indicates speech interrupted mid-sound. Brackets indicate author's comments. Arabic words are indicated by bold font. Double brackets indicate overlapping speech.

CHAPTER 3

"SANS PROBLÈME" OR "CENT PROBLÈMES"? REVOICING STEREOTYPES ABOUT LES ARABES

I was sitting with Abdel, Madame Hamdani's brother, in the kitchen, drinking coffee one afternoon when, in the hallway, a heated argument broke out between Madame Hamdani and her eldest son, Ahmed. In addition to five children, aged 2–18 years, the Hamdanis' five-bedroom subsidized apartment also accommodated Abdel, who had recently arrived from Algeria and who hoped to immigrate to France permanently. The hallway quarrel had arisen because Madame Hamdani was concerned and frustrated that her 16-year-old son, Ahmed, a very bright teen, was failing out of high school due to poor attendance and grades.

Hearing the tense yelling between his sister and his nephew in the hallway, Abdel leaned in to me and said quietly with a grin, "You know, Chantal, when a French person is asked how he's doing, he responds 'sans problème' or 'no problem'. When an Arab is asked how he's doing, he also responds 'cent problèmes', but what he's really saying is that he's experiencing '100 problems' at that moment." Abdel's pun—based on near-homophones "sans problème" and "cent problèmes"—seemed to perfectly illuminate the combination of gratitude and frustration often experienced among members of extended North African families in diaspora. Grateful that his sister was trying to help him permanently immigrate to France, Abdel was expected to demonstrate that the social obligations and tensions he experienced living with his sister's family were "no problem," although, in reality,

Transcultural Teens: Performing Youth Identities in French Cités, First Edition. Chantal Tetreault.
© 2015 John Wiley & Sons, Inc. Published 2015 by John Wiley & Sons, Inc.

the situation posed "100 problems" to him and to Madame Hamdani's family. More centrally for the focus of this chapter on racializing discourse, the preceding pun—*sans problème* "no problem" or *cent problèmes* "one hundred problems"—is indicative of the double-voiced, transcultural utterances of stereotypes about "Arabs" by "Arabs" themselves.

This chapter considers the ways that French adolescents of Arab Muslim heritage reproduce, reinforce, and subvert stereotypical discourses about "Arabs," "Muslims," and "the French." Dominant French representations of national identity, "race," immigration, and cultural difference are central to how adolescents of Algerian descent experience and perform their own social identities. In their everyday talk, adolescents bring together nationally circulating representations in locally achieved performances of identity that appropriate and sometimes subvert hegemonic discourses—that is, discourses that are widely reproduced and that seem like "common sense" but serve to reinforce the dominant group's social advantage. For example, Abdel's commentary that "Arabs have lots of problems" might serve to locate these problems with "Arabs," and thus may reinforce a widely circulated discourse in France that serves to blame *les arabes* for the endemic *French* problems of racism, unemployment, immigration inequities, and housing shortages.

In everyday interactions, stereotypes provide a powerful, if highly imperfect, explanatory logic to teens. As in Abdel's joking comment, the complexity of everyday problems and challenges involving work, school, and family are often crystallized in one simplifying paradigm of "the French vs. Arabs." At the same time that this paradigm is obviously reductive, it is also helpful for explaining the deep structural inequities and obstacles that immigrants and French citizens who are Arab often face in France. Such creative, interactional uses of stereotypes about "the French" and "Arabs" reproduce reductive categories of identity, but also transform the meaning of stereotypical discourse through a pointed critique of the structural inequality inherent to these categories or "classes" of people.

To contextualize Abdel's pun, his problems extended far beyond family obligations. As a recent arrival to France on a tourist visa, his desire to remain in the country was continually threatened by immigration requirements and a lack of work. In constructing the categories "French" and "Arab" as distinct social identities, Abdel simultaneously critiques and normalizes their social positions in relation to everyday experience: there are those who have "no problems" (the "French") and those who have "100 problems" (the "Arabs"). By contrasting the purported "French" and "Arab" perspectives, Abdel is drawing his audience's attention to the gap between his own experience and the perceived ease with which "the French" navigate life's challenges.

Through voicing his contrastive pun, Abdel simultaneously occupies idealized "French" and "Arab" subject positions. His transcultural utterance is thus akin to the double-voiced or "dialogic" speech that Bakhtin discusses (1981), and reminiscent of the experiences of double-consciousness (Du Bois 1903; Gilroy 1993) described in Chapter 1. Abdel's double-voiced and self-ethnicizing utterance is further enhanced by the fact that it is couched as a joke. Ethnic or racialized joking, as with other forms of joking, potentially "provides a frame that invites critical reflection on communicative processes" as well as social processes (Bauman and Briggs 1990: 60). That is, joking allows the joker to say what is otherwise either unsayable or only said with difficulty. Moreover, a joking "frame" or humorous mode can allow the joker to engage in a critical stance toward the immediate interactional situation as well as the larger social situation. Similar to Apache Indians' jokes about "the white man" (Basso 1979) that simultaneously critique present participants and our racialized American society, Abdel's pun illustrates both the personal relationships at hand—here, the difficulties that he was experiencing living in his sister's house amid ongoing conflict—and the structurally determined social relationships at large: "Arab" versus "French."[1]

In Chemin de l'Ile, French adolescents who are also Arab Muslims engage with circulating discourses about les musulmans, les français, and les arabes. In so doing, they respond with their own interpretations of what it means to occupy all of these subject positions even when they are often depicted as mutually exclusive in dominant discourse and within teens' everyday talk. As children of primarily Algerian immigrants living in low-income housing projects, the adolescents described here have a relationship and access to "Frenchness" that is complicated by socioeconomic exclusion and pervasive forms of new cultural racism, which posit that "French" and "Arab" cultures are too different to be compatible (Balibar and Wallerstein 1991; Gilroy 1991). Among my consultants, adolescence is verbally and symbolically performed through other complex social identities, which are over-determined (inordinately influenced) by dominant French ideologies regarding race/ethnicity, class, culture, religion, and gender. That is, the linguistic and cultural resources by which adolescents perform their "youth" are saturated with larger, stereotypical discourses that they alternately reject, reproduce, and elaborate. Central to this process is the transformation of dominant, structural relationships between idealized "types" (e.g., "Arab," "French," "immigrant"), through the expression and elaboration of interpersonal relationships in interaction.

"Arabs Got Nothing": Recycling Stereotypes for Interactional Goals

Not only do adolescents use widely circulating stereotypes about *les arabes* to interpret everyday experiences as noted in the preceding text, they also use stereotypes to "do" (enact) everyday interactions with their peers and mentors. This can have both empowering and dis-empowering effects for teens at the level of social interaction. Using stereotypes in interaction can be a powerful means of exerting social control, as well as a way to have fun and even play. However, evoking stereotypes in interaction can be risky in that the speaker may garner criticism for their use (Chun 2009). And, more generally, although re-voicing stereotypes can be a powerful way to get things done in interactions, their larger critical power remains ambiguous, in that they can naturalize experiences of racism and prejudice, even while condemning them.

The Arab teenagers in this study often evoked stereotypes that entailed negative depictions of Arabs. I observed the rare use of a positive "Arab" stereotype during tutoring at *Cerise*, the neighborhood association where I conducted much of my research and audio recording. In an effort to get a student to work independently, Mohammad, an adult mentor of Moroccan parentage, said, "Work a bit there instead of calling me over. That's how it is with Arabs. Are you an Arab or not?" (*Travaille, toi un peu là au lieu de m'appeler. C'est ça avec les arabes. T'es une arabe ou pas?*) Here, the dominant French stereotype that "Arabs are lazy" was countered with a positive in-group construction of Arabs as hardworking—a "real" Arab would work harder. Nonetheless, Mohammad still used this positive stereotype to negatively assess the student's behavior (that she was asking for help too quickly), demonstrating the normative powers inherent to racial and ethnic stereotyping generally (Williams 1991: 127–128). In this way, interactional uses of *les arabes*, among other social labels, are central to formulating and expressing moralizing social criticism (such as "you should work harder" earlier), both within the immediate interpersonal exchange and broader contexts.

The vast majority of participants in my research were non-Amazigh (non-Berber) teens of North African descent, generally of Algerian parentage, and so would be considered *arabe* in dominant French parlance. However, adolescents rarely used the term *arabe* to refer to themselves. Rather, adolescents generally used their parents' national origin to describe their social identity even to non-Arabs—for example, "I'm Algerian." Alternatively, for cultural insiders, including children of North

African descent and other neighborhood kids, adolescents would indicate their parents' and/or grandparents' hometown to indicate social identity, for example, *"je suis Maghnaoui"* ("I'm from Maghnia," a town in Algeria).

Rather than a self-descriptor, *arabe* was often used to describe others, and, as mentioned earlier, to critique others, including peers. In the following example, several adolescent girls are doing homework together in the association *Cerise* when Samira asks her classmates for correction fluid or "white-out." When she finds none, Samira jokingly teases her fellow classmates by voicing a pejorative stereotype about *les arabes*. It should be noted that, being of Algerian parentage and non-Amazigh, Samira is as "Arab" as the other girls present.

"Arabs Got Nothing"

1	Samira	*Attends, je te prends un tippex.*	[Looking inside Mounia's pencil bag] Wait, I'm borrowing your white-out.
2	Mounia	*J'en ai pas.*	I don't got any.
3	Samira	*Hé, hé, ah, ah Hourriya, t'as un tippex?*	Hey, hey, ah, ah Hourriya, you got white-out?
4	Hourriya		[Shakes her head "no"]
5	Samira	*Les arabes, ils ont rien!*	Arabs got nothing! [Samira laughs]

In this exchange, Samira twice requests white-out from her classmates, but is twice refused. Her response, "Arabs got nothing!" shows Samira using a negative depiction of Arabs to serve as a criticism of her peers for not having the desired white-out. By invoking the social label *arabes* as a way to tease individual peers, Samira strategically voices a social category and attendant stereotype to convey a personalized message in a face-to-face context. Here, a stereotype is a vehicle for both constructing shared group membership (i.e., "we are Arab") and to engage in social critique ("you/we got nothing").

Because Samira is a member of the group she categorizes, her comment seems to be voiced with irony. Specifically, her use of the non-inclusive pronoun *ils* ("they") to refer to "Arabs" indicates that Samira is likely re-voicing here. That is, she is using speech that is reminiscent of previously voiced utterances, for example, in the anti-Arab rhetoric of French politician Jean-Marie Le Pen. The singsong quality of Samira's voice seems to indicate that she is ironically quoting another speaker, a prior utterance. Furthermore, the brief, matter-of-fact quality of the statement paired with her playful voicing makes this comment sound like a slogan—a summary of a longer message that encodes meaning through a form of semantic shorthand. Samira thus appears to be acting as an ironic mouthpiece for the anti-Arab rhetoric that is ubiquitous in dominant French discourse. That is, similar to the the racist slogans of Jean-Marie Le Pen (e.g., "France for the French"), Samira's glib statement stands for something more: a system of power relations between "Arab" and "French" and a shorthand for expressing one's position in an ongoing racialized conflict.

At the same time, unlike Le Pen's rhetoric, stereotyping about *les arabes* is used here to evoke and explain the experience of occupying an underprivileged economic and social position—of "having nothing." In the process, Samira posits that experiences of poverty and discrimination are contingent upon occupying the racialized position of *les arabes*. At a discursive rather than interactional level then, Samira is providing an account for why there is no "white-out" that extends well beyond a mere critique of her friends. In other words, her comment serves to normalize the connection between "having nothing" and being "Arab." It is in these mundane, routinized experiences, of asking for white-out and finding none, that such racializing stereotypes emerge. Interactional contexts that are not ostensibly about "race" or ethnicity get encoded as such because the teens in question are grappling with their own racialization in French society. This example, as with the others that follow, shows speakers strategically using social labels and stereotypes to speak not only to those present but also to larger discourses and systems of racialized difference and inequality in national and global contexts (cf. Reynolds 2013b).

The next example of teens' racializing talk is drawn from a particular event at *Cerise*, namely, the return of former adult mentors Mohammad and Djamel one evening to the association. Both men had just completed studies in math and computer science at French universities and were in their mid-twenties. Although born and raised in France like the adolescents they tutored, Mohammad's parents were originally from Morocco and Djamel's from Tunisia. The two men were good friends and had attended high school and college together. Their return visit to *Cerise* was an exciting event for the children present that night. Mohammad, having worked full time for over a year at the association, was close to the children, and Samira, who figures frequently in the examples, was among his favorites. Samira was 13 at the time of the recording and is French of Algerian descent, as is the other girl, Mounia.

Their exchange involves a more elaborate teasing routine between students and mentors just after the white-out exchange. Here, the motif for joking deals with stereotypes about Arabs and education. The exchange begins with Samira asking Mohammad if he passed his final high school exam, the *bac* or *baccalauréat*. This question is significant for locating Mohammad's place in the two-tiered French educational system, comprised of academic high school, culminating in the *bac* and university study, and trade school, culminating in a specialized trade degree, the "BEP" or *Brevet d'Etudes Professionelles* (called "Professional Studies Certificate," but akin to a degree from trade school). Academic high school presents several advantages, including the symbolic value that the *bac* confers and the material benefit of gaining access to university study that normally leads to higher paid, professional careers. In contrast, trade school (BEP) students receive highly specialized training (e.g., carpentry, secretarial skills, electronics) that normally culminates in working immediately at 18 years of age. Whereas a BEP once practically guaranteed its recipients a career in a given trade, the current market produces more trade school graduates than it can accommodate. The French economy has struggled on and off since *les trente glorieuses*, or "the glorious 30," in reference to the 30 years after World War II during which France experienced unprecedented growth.

At the time of Mohammad and Djamel's visit, both Samira and Mounia were attending middle school, the stage at which students are evaluated for their potential to enroll in either academic or trade high school. As both girls were still at the initial stage of their middle school years, neither had her high school curriculum defined at the time, and so was likely interested in situating herself and others in relation to the French school system. Typical of other low-income neighborhoods, Chemin de l'Ile has a low percentage of students who go on to academic high school in relation to the national average. The following exchange is thus, in part, an effort by Samira and Mounia to situate Mohammad and Djamel within the French school system and in relation to themselves, their classmates, and other "Arabs."

"It's Rare That You Would See an Arab uh—with the Bac, huh?"

1	Samira	*T'as eu ton bac, toi.*	[To Mohammad] You passed your high school exam.
2	Mohammad	*Moi, j'ai tué mon bac.*	I killed my bac. ["I got a really great grade."]
3	Samira	*C'est rare que tu verrais un arabe euh–*	It's rare that you would see an Arab uh–
4	Mohammad	*–avec le bac hein?*	–with the bac, huh?
5	Mounia	*Bah si, pourquoi?*	Yeah you do, why not?
6	Samira	*Ma cousine, elle l'a.*	My cousin, she got it.
7	Djamel	*Non plaisante pas, Mohammad il veut se marier avec elle.*	No, don't joke, Mohammad wants to get married to her.
8	Mounia	*Ils envoient tous les **hala** en BEP.*	They send all the **screw-ups** to trade school.
9	Samira	*Ah no, **balǝk** il la connaît, alors euh–*	Oh no, **watch out** [in case] he knows her, so uh–
10	Djamel	*Mohammad, vas-y maries-toi avec sa cousine! Elle a le bac, vas-y. Vas-y, maries-toi avec elle!*	Mohammad, go ahead, marry her cousin! She has her bac, go ahead. Go ahead, get married to her!
11	Mohammad	*Ah oui c'est la première, je crois. C'est la première rebeu qui a eu le bac. C'est grave.*	Oh yeah it's the first, I think. It's the first Arab who got the bac. That's serious.

12	Samira	*Nan, mais vous êtes pas marrants là.*	Naw, you all aren't funny there.
13	Mohammad	[Laughs]	[Laughs]
14	Samira	***Llah na'l shaytan!***	**God curse the Devil!**

In a pattern similar to the playful, yet confrontational tone of the last example, Samira is using the social label "Arab" and attendant stereotype to voice a commentary both about the immediate interactional context and the larger social context. On the immediate interactional level, Samira seems to be re-voicing a common stereotype—that getting the *bac* is supposedly "rare" for an "Arab"—in order to highlight Mohammad's accomplishment. On another level, Samira is forming a broader assessment about "Arabs," and thus "testing for shared knowledge" (Ziv 1984), about the *bac* and her own and her peers' chances for success in the French educational system.

Here, as in the previous example, the social identity *arabe* is evoked to note and explain a lack—in this case, a lack of educational success—which serves to explain this experience as being contingent upon a particular ethnic positioning in the French context. This time, however, Samira is challenged for her categorical statement that it's rare to see Arabs achieve the *bac* by Mounia's direct counter claim, "Yeah you do, why not?" (turn 5). Further, Djamel mocks Samira's naiveté by teasing that Mohammad would want to marry her cousin because she has her *bac* (turn 7). Samira eventually realizes that Djamel and Mohammad are teasing her and responds defensively, "Naw, you all aren't funny there" (turn 12), and through indirect critique, "God curse the Devil" (turn 14), a traditional Arabic saying that criticizes wrongdoing.

Yet, in striking contrast to the first example, all participants, Mohammad and Djamel, as well as Mounia, reject Samira's stereotypical depiction of Arabs as it apparently mimics dominant French discourse too closely. Also, Mohammad even refuses to use the term *arabe*, preferring instead to use the verlan term *rebeu* (turn 11), which is less pejorative and less racializing because it is attached to a particular French identity: second and third generation of French citizens who are the grandchildren or children of North African immigrants. Here, as in other interactions that I observed with Mohammad, Djamel, and other North African French adults of their generation, the use of the word *rebeu* generally replaced *arabe* or *beur*.

This exchange demonstrates that certain types of joking are particularly "dangerous" (Basso 1979). In the case of revoicing negative assessments about "Arabs," the joking lasts only so long as those involved agree to actively engage in ironically reproducing dominant stereotypes. In the first "white-out" example, Samira's voicing of Arab stereotypes went unchallenged by participants, showing that they were willing to comfortably operate between literal and metaphorical meanings (Gates 1988: 82). However, in this second exchange, Samira's generalizations about "Arabs" fell flat, and she becomes the object of teasing by her mentors.

These examples of racializing joking show the double-edged character of self-referential stereotypes and their use for in-group identity construction. By ironically re-voicing dominant French stereotypes, teens take a risk that their words will be interpreted at face value. While the use of social labels and stereotypes foregrounds the stigmatized status of Arabs and immigrants within French society, their critical power remains ambiguous—they have the power to both critique and naturalize experiences of racism and prejudice. Ethnic in-group humor has the potential to draw attention to and critique the social inequities that are the cause of negative stereotypes. It this way, racializing in-group humor entails potentially different effects than racializing jokes about other groups, which only rarely serve to challenge the status quo. At the same time, ethnic in-group humor may reinstate stereotypes and circulate racist discourse to the detriment of members of the group.

"A Scene of Racism"

Whereas the preceding interaction demonstrates that divergent interpretations of racialization can cause in-group divisions among "Arabs," the following exchange shows that shared perceptions of racism can bring together teens of diverse immigrant backgrounds. Called by participants "a scene of racism," the exchange shows teens co-narrating and circulating their interpretation of a nearby conflict between some Muslim men and a non-Muslim female building caretaker. Their retellings exemplify how stereotypes emerge in everyday conflicts within *les cités*, as well as how stereotypes are produced and circulated in the analysis of such conflicts.

One sunny spring day, a group of adolescent girls and I were sitting in a playground, wedged between two apartment buildings in Chemin de l'Ile. Hamida and Béatrice, both 14, were chatting after school with Naima, only 12. I knew Hamida and Béatrice from *Cerise*, but had just met Naima. The playground was one of the few public spaces unofficially designated for women and girls. A small enclosure provided young children with climbing toys; older girls and mothers used the benches and a concrete wall to sit and socialize. The area was also desirable because it was less visible from the street than the parking lot where men and adolescent boys would often congregate.

As we sat there chatting, the girls and I became aware of an angry dispute occurring 25 feet away, in front of the tall apartment building facing us. The building's caretaker (*gardienne*), a woman the girls assumed to be of "French" heritage but who was in fact of Portuguese background, was demanding that a group of four or five young men disperse from in front of the building. These men were observant Muslim men, or what less observant Muslims in the neighborhood call *frères musulmans* (Muslim brothers) or, more familiarly, *les mus*. Such labels designated young men who vowed to follow a strict practice of daily prayer, dietary prescriptions, and abstinence from sexual relations outside of marriage, which locally constituted the way to become a "true" Muslim or "follow the straight path" (*suivre le droit chemin*).[2] (While the expression "Frères Musulmans" or "Muslim Brothers" in some contexts is used to denote a political affiliation with the Muslim Brotherhood, an international Islamist organization, to my knowledge it was not an active organization in Chemin de l'Ile.)

Dressed in traditional North African religious clothing, wearing skullcaps and the long robes called *djellaba* over their street clothing, the group had just come from the local "mosque," a prayer room in an adjacent building. When these young men did not move away from the building's entrance at the caretaker's urging, she pushed a man in the group on the shoulder. Shortly after this incident, the group did leave the front of the building, walking together and grumbling to us as they passed that the caretaker was drunk.[3] Although we were sitting too far away from the conflict for me to pick it up on tape, I was able to record the reactions that it provoked in the girls sitting near me.

In the first excerpt that follows, the girls develop an analysis of the incident as "racism" and establish a basic conflict between "the French" and "Muslims," which is later extended to a conflict between "the French" and national groups, including Algerians, and immigrants more generally. At no point does Hamida, Naima, or Béatrice self-identify as "French"; rather, together, they articulate a shared non-French position by virtue of their distinct "immigrant" backgrounds. As I will revisit in the text that follows, each girl has a particular and indirect relationship to immigration, in that all three were born in France: Naima identifies as "Algerian" because both of her parents were originally from Algeria; Hamida identifies as *métisse* ("mixed") because her father was originally from Morocco and her mother from Algeria; although Béatrice's father originally immigrated to France from Germany and her mother was born in France, Béatrice identifies as "Portuguese" because her grandmother came to France from Portugal. Whereas Naima and Hamida are both Muslims, Béatrice is not.

Drug Addicts vs. Muslims

1	Hamida	*La gardienne elle est en panique, tellement elle est raciste. Elle voit plein de musulmans.*	The caretaker is freaking out, she's so racist. She sees tons of Muslims.
2	Naima	*Ouais c'est vrai. Et en plus les frères musulmans ils respectent. Et quand c'est des voyous, ils s'en foutent. C'est ça que je comprends pas chez les gens.*	Yeah it's true. And also Muslim brothers give respect. And when it's hoodlums, they don't care. That's what I don't understand about people.
3	Chantal	*Mm.*	Mm.
4	Naima	*C'est vrai! attends! Elle croit que c'est des terros. T'as vu? J'vous ai dit quand c'est les- hé HE! Sur le Qur'an-*	It's true! Wait! She thinks they're terrorists. Did you see? I told you when it's the- Hey HEY! On the Qur'an
5	Hamida	*Oh la la!*	Oh my! [Female caretaker yelling in background.]
6	Naima	*T'as vu? Je te dis, que quand c'est des drogués, ils disent rien aux petits français. Les drogués, hein? Ça m'énerve, ça.*	You see? I'm telling you, that when it's drug addicts, they say nothing to the little French kids. Drug addicts, huh? That bugs me.
7	Hamida	*T'as vu?*	Did you see?
8	Naima	*Je- je t'ai dit, hein? On t'a dit, Chantal. Quand c'est les petits drogués, sur le Qur'an, elle les laisse. **Wallah**, elle les laisse! Et là, quand c'est eux, elle leur gueule dessus là.*	I- I told you, huh? We told you, Chantal. When it's little drug addicts, on the Qur'an, she leaves them alone. **By God**, she leaves them alone! And now, when it's them [Muslims], she yells at them.

9	Hamida	*Ahhhhh!*	Ahhhh! [Female caretaker pushes man.]
10	Naima	*En plus les musulmans, ils re–*	And plus Muslims, they re–
11	Hamida	*Hiiiih!*	Hiiiih!
12	Naima	*Elle a dit quoi? Elle a dit quoi?*	She said what? She said what?
13	Hamida	*[[Elle l'a tapé!*	[[She hit him
14	Béatrice	*[[Elle l'a tapé. Elle l'a poussé. Elle lui a fait ça.*	[[She hit him. She pushed him. She did that to him. [Demonstrating with hand]
15	Hamida	*Elle le sait qu'i peut pas frapper, c'est pour ça.*	She knows he can't hit [her], that's why.
16	Naima	*Ouais par'c'que elle sait que, les musulmans, ils tapent pas. Nous, les musulmans, les hommes, ce qu'ils respectent le plus, c'est les vieux, les femmes, et les enfants. Les femmes, tu peux pas les taper.*	Yeah, 'cause she knows that, Muslims, they don't hit. We, Muslims, the men, those they respect the most, it's old men, women, and children. Women, you can't hit them.

The preceding excerpt shows the girls' initial reaction to the dispute between the building caretaker and *les frères musulmans* and their ensuing interpretations. When Hamida observes that the caretaker is *en panique* ("freaking out") in turn 1, she attributes her anger to the group of young Muslim men standing before the building. Naima's comparison of the caretaker's treatment of *voyous* (delinquents or "hoodlums") and *drogués* (drug addicts) as better than that of Muslims serves as a commentary on the degree to which she believes the caretaker is unfairly biased. Regarded by adolescents as one of the most reviled and stigmatized personas in the neighborhood, *le drogué* is evoked to cast the caretaker as particularly unfair to Muslims, whom she purportedly and mistakenly views as *les terros* ("terrorists," turn 4). Naima and the others thus argue for the ignorance of the caretaker's position, since, from their perspective, devout Muslims are "respectful" and non-violent (turns 15 and 16). Furthermore, Hamida and Naima reason, the caretaker obviously understands that Muslims are non-violent and is taking advantage of this fact since she has dared to push one of the men (turns 13 and 14). This valorizing depiction of Muslim men also draws upon the notion of *le respect* ("respect"), a central cultural trope among adolescents in the neighborhood that I will analyze in detail in Chapter 4. In a creative adaptation and reinterpretation, the Arab cultural value of *ḥshuma* ("modesty/honor," cf. Abu-Lughod 1986) is constructed by adolescents in Chemin de l'Ile as *le respect*, and functions for teens as a major axis of cultural difference between Muslims and "the French," a theme that returns in the excerpts analyzed in the text that follows.

At stake here, in both the original conflict between the caretaker and the Muslim men as well as in the girls' subsequent interpretation, is who can rightfully occupy space, both literally and metaphorically, in front of the building and within French national borders. In the next excerpt, our discussion turns to interpreting the right of Muslims to occupy both space in the *cité* and in France generally. The exchange thereby illustrates the tight connection between racialized stereotypes and (imagined) spaces in France (Anderson 1991). In particular, it shows the centrality of representations of *les cités* to the reproduction of racialized stereotypes in the imagined national community.

Racism and the Cité

17	Hamida	*Hé, elle a dit qu'elle va voter pour Le Pen pour nous dégager.*	Hey, she said she's going to vote for Le Pen to get rid of us. [Whispered talk]
18	Naima	*Bah, va se faire foutre ce qu'elle va voter. Et même qu'elle vote pour Le Pen, qu'est ce que ça va faire? Ils pourraient jamais nous renvoyer. On est plus que eux. Ils pourront jamais. Elle est dingue, hadi[4] là-celle, là.*	Well, [she can] go fuck herself what she she'll vote. [mimes spitting] And even if she votes for Le Pen, what is that going to do? They could never send us back. There's more of us than them. They could never [do that]. She is crazy, **that one**, that one there.

19	Chantal	*Pourquoi elle est aussi fâchée?*	Why is she so angry?
20	Naima	*Parce que, elle est raciste. Elle n'aime pas les musulmans.*	Because she's racist. She doesn't like Muslims.
21	Béatrice	*[[Bah qu'est ce qu'elle fait- qu'est ce qu'elle fait dans une cité alors?*	[[Well what is she doing- what is she doing in a *cité* then?
22	Chantal	*[[Bah elle est mal barrée dans le quartier là.*	[[Well she's bad off in this neighborhood.

In this excerpt, Hamida reintroduces the conflict to the conversation by claiming she has overheard the caretaker say she would vote "Le Pen" to get rid of "us" (*nous dégager*) in turn 17. Hamida carefully whispers the overheard comment to Naima, seemingly to highlight both the inherent violence of the caretaker's statement as well as its potential for creating violence if circulated. Additionally, by repeating the caretaker's words to Naima and subsequently other adolescents, Hamida appeals to the socially powerful act of circulating another's words through reported speech (Shuman 1986). Hamida not only lays claim to authoritative knowledge about the building caretaker's words, she also begins to circulate this knowledge among her peers, who give circulating reported speech a central importance for making and breaking social alliances (cf. Goodwin 1990). Within the neighborhood's physically and socially close space, circulating reported speech purportedly spoken by community members can serve as a powerful mechanism of social control. Many of the 11,000 inhabitants are connected through family networks and local institutions such as associations, subsidized housing complexes, and schools; in this context, possessing first-hand knowledge of the words of community members provides individuals a valuable form of social capital.

The caretaker's supposed wish that she had voted for Jean-Marie Le Pen, former leader of the National Front, the pro-nationalist, anti-immigrant political party, unleashes a powerful symbol among these adolescents; they were painfully aware that the politician had called for the deportation of all "foreigners" (*étrangers*), a category that is often problematically used to refer not only to immigrants but also their French-born children. Despite the implausibility of Le Pen's proposition, his inflammatory rhetoric lives on both through its strategic reproduction by the caretaker and in the girls' subsequent revoicing of this threat to each other. Much as the caretaker frames the Muslim men's supposed misuse of the street as an offense punishable by deportation, our own conversation begins to make connections between local and national space.

Specifically, Naima's response, "They could never send us back. There's more of us than them," in turn 18, reproduces and contextualizes the local struggle over space at a national level. Naima further solidifies the social dichotomy of "us" versus "them" by claiming that Muslims (*on* or "we") are more numerous than Le Pen supporters (*eux* or "them"). The girls' collaborative interpretation of the conflict evolves from one concerning "Muslim brothers" and "racists" to an inclusive discussion of "us" (Muslims) versus "them" (racists, Le Pen supporters), which is extended in the next excerpt to "the French" generally.

In the exchange, all of us mobilize the powerful trope of racism to claim a higher moral ground in this conflict, a move that might also serve to oversimplify the ethnic, cultural, and religious diversity of the neighborhood and to reinvigorate a racist discourse that posits "French" and "Muslim" as nonoverlapping. For example, Naima reinforces the ideology inherent to much anti-immigrant discourse by implying that Muslims are indeed "taking over" France: "There are more of us (than them)." In a similarly derisive tone in which we reproduce racializing talk at the same time that we take a critical stance to it, Béatrice and I simultaneously co-construct the stereotype that the neighborhood and *cités* in general are "full" of Muslims: "What is she doing in a *cité* then?" and "Well, she's bad off in this neighborhood" in turns 21 and 22. Béatrice and I, both non-Muslims, are clearly re-voicing common stereotypes, and yet, in doing so, we are declaring our solidarity with the Muslims in the present interaction by echoing Naima's claim.

As mentioned in Chapter 1, there is a demographic component to the racialized depiction of *cités* in that these spaces are the product of a confluence of poverty, immigration, labor recruitment, social exclusion, and inequitable housing laws. And yet, such spaces are quite diverse in terms of ethnicity, religion, national provenance, citizenship, and even, to a degree, socioeconomic levels, since middle-class civil servants and state workers are readily granted access to subsidized housing. By recycling the stereotype that *les cités* are "full" of Muslims, we align ourselves with Hamida and Naima. That is, Béatrice and I (both non-Muslims) appeal to the stereotypical image of the *cité* as a religiously and racially homogenous space in order to claim the supposed predominance of Muslim–Arab residents as proof of their right to occupy this space.

In addition, Béatrice and I collaboratively use this stereotype to index a prevalent joking genre among adolescents in the neighborhood, who take the opportunity to acknowledge and reify ethnic, religious, and national differences among their peers in order to tease them. Identifying social labels and related, often playful, insults are often used as a means to engage in a joking style popularly called *traiter*, literally "to treat" (someone), often by marking a peer as a racialized other. Adolescents thus employ an extensive vocabulary for describing racialized, cultural, and religious difference and to symbolically position themselves and others in the context of a multicultural and socially contested France. Here, girls of various backgrounds discursively construct themselves in alignment with a generic "non-French" identity in order to collectively position against the "racist" caretaker.

"And Then They Wonder Why … People Don't Like the French"

23	Béatrice	*Mais c'est pas bien. Regarde, après ils se demandent pourquoi on aime pas les fr- pourquoi les gens ils aiment pas les français. Regarde comment ils parlent.*	But it's not good. Look, after they wonder why we don't like the Fr- why people don't like the French. Look how they talk.
24	Chantal	*Mm hm.*	Mm hm.
25	Naima	*[[T'as vu, parce qu'ils nous aiment pas. C'est eux ils aiment.*	[[You see, because they don't like us. They like themselves.
26	Hamida	*[[Oh la la, et là ils sont en train de nous traiter. Ils sont en train de nous traiter.*	[[Oh my, and there they are now dissing us. They are dissing us now.
27	Naima	*Eux, ils aiment personne, les français. Parce que ça y est, on est dans leur pays. Regarde, attends, je vais t'expliquer. Mon père il m'a dit. Il m'a tout raconté ce qui s'est passé dans la guerre mondiale et tout. C'est eux ils sont venus nous chercher pour eux- eux sont venus nous chercher dans le pays pour le pétrole. Après maintenant ils parlent.*	Them, they don't like anyone, the French. Because that's it, we're in their country. Look, wait [to Chantal], I'm going to explain to you. My father he told me. He told me everything that happened during the World War and all that. It's them who came to get us for themselves- them who came to get us in our country for oil. And now they talk.

28	Béatrice	*Ouais, mais il y en a- hé, hé, Naima j'avoue y a des français qui sont bien.*	Yeah, but there are some- hey, hey, Naima, I swear, there's some French who are good.
29	Chantal	*Ouais, bien sûr.*	Yeah, of course.
30	Naima	*La vérité, moi, il y a des français, comment je les aime bien! T'sais ils respectent et tout.*	The truth, for me, there are some French people I like so much! You know they respect and everything.
31	Béatrice	*Ouais, mais c'est pas tous les mêmes. Je veux dire c'est pas tous les mêmes.*	Yeah, but they aren't all the same. I mean they aren't all the same.
32	Naima	*Y a même des français, ils se convertissent à l'Islam.*	There are even some French people, they convert to Islam.

In this portion of our discussion, Béatrice describes her own and others' dislike of "the French" as justified by the way "the French" supposedly talk about others: "But it's not good. Look, after they wonder why we don't like the Fr- why people don't like the French. Look how they talk" (turn 23). In the excerpt, Béatrice initially claims personally disliking the French herself by using the inclusive pronoun *on* ("… they wonder why *we* don't like the Fr-"), but then corrects herself to claim that the more generic category "people" do not like the French. Béatrice's shift in discursive responsibility may be attributed to her own and her peers' complicated identity positioning. All of the participants were born in France, and thus technically would be considered "French" in terms of their citizenship. And yet, as mentioned previously, Béatrice self-identifies as "Portuguese," perhaps as a way to craft a stigmatized immigrant-origin identity that is somewhat equivalent to that of her friends, the vast majority of whom are of Algerian heritage.

Alternatively, Béatrice's self-correction may be related to my presence as an adult and outsider. In any case, her negative assessment of "the French" is quickly corroborated by Naima (turns 25 and 27). Meanwhile, Hamida takes the fact that the building caretaker is talking to bystanders about the incident as evidence that "they" (by implication, "the French") are verbally attacking her and her friends, as well as the Muslim men who have left the scene: "Oh my! And there they are now, dissing (*traiter*) us. They are dissing us now" (turn 25). As mentioned earlier, "traiter" involves a form of insult that usually involves singling out characteristics of that person's identity for ridicule, including racial or religious characteristics, among others. Here, Hamida aligns herself with the insulted young men by claiming insult for herself and her peers.

Naima continues, "They don't like anyone, the French, because that's it, we are in their country" (turn 27). Naima thus designates France as "their country" and not her own, even though in the previous excerpt she points out her own and other Muslims' right to remain in France: "They could never send us back, we are more (numerous) than them." Furthermore, Naima describes the French as responsible for bringing Algerian immigrants into France and then not accepting Muslims: "It's them who came to get us ... and now they talk" (turn 27). Naima bases her claim upon a description of the history of French labor recruitment from Algeria, which the French government actively pursued from the period after World War II until the economic crisis in 1972. Also, Naima mentions that, in addition to labor, the French government was interested in exploiting Algeria for oil. (When the first Algerian petroleum corporation, Sonatrach, was founded in 1963, the Algerian state held only 4.5% of the company's assets while French holdings were as high as 67.5% [Blin 1990].) By attributing agency to "*them* (who) came to get us for *themselves*," Naima locates responsibility with the French for why Algerians are currently in France.

This discussion thus shows the girls co-constructing the category "the French" and their own oppositional non-French (and "anti-French") stance, despite their backgrounds as native-born French citizens of varied religious, ethnic, and national heritage: Muslim and non-Muslim as well as Algerian, Portuguese–German, and Algerian–Moroccan. While the reasons for the girls' identification as non-French are complex—alternately tied to identifying as Muslim, as being of immigrant parentage, and as "Algerian"—the justification for their criticisms of "the French" are based upon the girls' numerous accounts of experiences of exclusion and prejudice that they collaboratively develop over the course of the discussion: "She's racist. She doesn't like Muslims," "The French don't like us," "And then they wonder why ... people don't like the French—look how they talk," "They don't like anyone, the French." In the discursive logic of the girls' discussion, identifying as non-French is tied to claims that the French are fundamentally against the non-French, an identity that the girls collaboratively construct as a shared, albeit shifting, identity, either by virtue of being Muslim, "Algerian," or as having immigrant parents or grandparents. The girls thus essentialize "Frenchness" as an identity that precludes the subject positions they claim to occupy, namely, "Muslim," "Algerian," "Portuguese," and *d'origine immigrée* (having immigrant parents or grandparents).

In the girls' construction, Frenchness is cast as an identity category that excludes non-members due to religious affiliation and immigrant origins, rather than based on citizenship or nationality. Moreover, as it is configured in their talk, nationality functions as a quasi-ethnic or racializing identity, in that the girls present are only "Algerian" or "Portuguese" based on heritage. In this way, the group's constructions of Frenchness and otherness are similar to the anti-immigrant rhetoric that appeals to "culture" as a supposedly insurmountable difference to justify racism and prejudice. It is also striking that prejudice is named and interpreted as "racism" in the girls' interpretations of the conflict between the caretaker and the Muslim men, although the girls initially framed the conflict as concerning religious intolerance. It seems that both culture and religion are being interpreted by the teens as racialized difference, a pattern also seen in dominant, anti-immigrant French discourses.

And yet, in addition to essentializing "the French" and themselves, the preceding example also shows the girls re-evaluating their negative depictions of all French people as racists, even as the girls continue to distinguish themselves entirely from a French social identity. Béatrice contradicts her initial assessment of the French by appealing to Naima with the words, "I swear, there's some French who are good" (turn 28). Of central importance in this positive construction of "the French" is the reintroduction of the trope of "respect," which is used here as the standard to separate the "good" French from the others: "The truth, for me, there are some French people I like so much! You know they respect and everything" (turn 30). This point is further developed in Naima's subsequent claim that some French people even convert to Islam, which by inference is depicted as the utmost form of "respect" (turn 32).

The following excerpt from the same exchange shows how the girls re-narrate an account of the dispute to Omar, a 13-year-old boy of Algerian parentage who has just arrived. (For the sake of brevity, I have omitted some of the earlier, similar retellings of the conflict to Omar.) The following example demonstrates the girls urging Omar to "take sides" relative to the caretaker, the social groups involved, and the imputed insults, which the girls establish as the conflict's cause.

"She Insulted You as Much as Him"

33	Hamida	*Regarde, elle est en panique.*	Look, she is freaking out.
34	Naima	*Elle est hami.[5] Ça y est, il t'a fait quoi? L'autre t'a fait quoi?*	She is agitated. It's over, what did he do to you? What did the guy do to you?

35	Omar	*Oh, c'est bon aussi.*	Oh, that's enough now.
36	Naima	*Moi, je serais elle–*	Me, [if] I were her–
37	Hamida	*"C'est bon?" Ecoute, elle t'a insulté. Elle t'a insulté autant que lui, hein? Elle a dit, "j'aurais su, j'aurais voté Le Pen vous auraient **ka 'b**"[6]*	"That's enough?" Listen, she insulted you. She insulted you as much as him, huh? She said, "if I'd known, I'd have voted for Le Pen [so that] you'd **get out of here.**"
38	Omar	*Elle a voté Le Pen, quoi, pas que–*	So, she voted Le Pen, not that–
39	Hamida	*Nan, elle a dit, "si j'aurais su, j'aurais voté Le Pen."*	No, she said "if I'd known, I would've voted for Le Pen."
40	Naima	*Elle est ḥami, elle est ḥami. Moi, j'serai à sa place, j'aurais honte!*	She's **agitated**, she's **agitated.** Me, in her place, I'd be ashamed!
41	Hamida	*Bon, Chantal, tu viens d'assister à une scène de racisme.*	Well, Chantal, you've just experienced a scene of racism.
42	Naima	*A sa place j'aurais honte. Elle a même tapé le mec.*	In her place, I'd be ashamed. She even hit the guy.
43	Omar	*T'as enregistré, Chantal?*	Did ya record it, Chantal?

In this exchange, Omar seemed to question the girls' continued criticism of the caretaker: "Oh, that's enough now" (turn 35) and "So, she voted Le Pen, not that–" (turn 38). However, Omar is criticized by Hamida for not taking an oppositional stance toward the caretaker: "Listen, she insulted you. She insulted you as much as him, huh?" (turn 37). Again, the motif of "respect" resurfaces in this interaction, since Hamida is constructing the conflict as requiring a response from Omar, implying that any self-respecting person would respond to such an insult. Hamida's position is in synch with the local interactional aesthetic of these adolescents, who express the cultural motif of "respect" by expecting their peers to meet insult with insult, or lose face. The notion of "respect" is also intrinsic to Naima's response in this excerpt, since she repeatedly proclaims that the caretaker's behavior is "shameful."

In addition to the moral authority that criticizing "racist" behavior confers to Hamida, this example shows how speakers gain narrative authority through naming events, for example, "a scene of racism" (turn 41), and through reproducing them as narratives using reported speech for others (Briggs and Bauman 1992; Hanks 1989). In the act of naming, revoicing, retelling, and analyzing the conflict, Hamida employs the power of "entextualization," or the process whereby an event becomes a "text" that is easily reproduced and circulated in other contexts (Briggs and Bauman 1992: 148). Similarly, Omar's question to me, "Did ya record it Chantal?" (turn 43), shows that the technological representation of an event is another way it becomes transferable to other contexts, thus potentially serving to damage the reputation of the caretaker to wider audiences. In this case, re-voicing, retelling, and recording the event are ways these adolescents can label and critique the "racism" they have observed, to denounce it publicly before multiple audiences, and to thereby gain a measure of personal and group "respect" in the face of insult.

This example shows adolescents using widely circulating and stereotypical identity categories (e.g., "the French" and "Muslims") to interpret everyday spatial conflicts in les cités. In a fashion similar to the examples in previous sections, adolescents here filter everyday experience through nationally circulating anti-immigrant discourse that allows them, through reported speech and narration, to achieve a moral higher ground (e.g., "you've just experienced a scene of racism"), but also positions them as marginalized and non-"French" within the imagined French community.

Le Bled: Racializing Spaces and Spacializing "Race" through Pan-Southern Immigrant Heritage

As discussed in the preceding text, the teens analyzed localized conflicts within their cité in the context of the imagined national community and in terms of supposedly non-overlapping, racialized groups such as "the French" and "Muslims." This section continues to analyze connections between racializing discourse and representations of space with a look at how adolescents share stories and performances dealing with another spatial and racialized concept, le bled. Le bled is a term that teens use to refer to their parents' "home country" or "home village," including places such Algeria and Portugal.

In Chemin de l'Ile, French teenagers of pan-immigrant, peripheral, and southern descent express solidarity by evoking le bled to created shared racialized identities. Prominent in teens' discourse, *le bled* is a French word of Arabic origin that was coined during the colonial period in Algeria. In Classical Arabic, *bld* means "country," but in colloquial Arabic dialect the term often means "village." In colonial French and currently in some contexts, *le bled* and the expression *le bled perdu* or *paumé* (the "lost" *bled*) is used to mean a very rural or extremely remote area. For example, in *Tristes Tropiques*, Lévi-Strauss compares *le bled* to the concept of sertão (roughly, "the bush") in Brazil. He claims, "Sertao [sic] … refers to a subjective aspect: bush in relation to man, and in opposition to inhabited and cultivated areas; there are no permanent settlements in the sertao. French colonial slang has perhaps an exact equivalent in the term *bled*" (2012/1955: 162). Although the term is used differently here than in teen discourse in Chemin de l'Ile, Lévi-Strauss' observation that *le bled* is used to create and describe oppositions between modern civilization and rural backwater is relevant, in that teens also use the concept to set up similar distinctions.

Specifically, in Chemin de l'Ile as in other *cités* across France, *le bled* is used to mean "homeland" or "home country" and is usually used by my consultants to refer to Algeria or to an immigrant parent's specific home-town in Algeria, but can be expanded to other "home" countries including Morocco and Portugal. Furthermore, within the context of diasporic (sub-) urban France, *le bled* is a concept that provides ideologically rich fodder to create shared oppositional stances to the dominant Frenchness. These shared oppositional stances bring together teens of various backgrounds, including Algerian, Moroccan, Portuguese, and Cambodian, and revolve around racialized identities, in addition to multivalent discourses regarding moder-nity, gender, and generation.

Rather than merely a place or static spatial signifier, *le bled* is a shifting referent that helps French teens of immigrant descent to express a constel-lation of oppositions and associations with regard to their shifting, often racialized identities (Silverstein 1976). Despite the multiplicity of tropes that *le bled* potentially evokes—race, tradition, generation, and gender, to name a few—the most consistent way that French teens of immigrant descent employ *le bled* is to discursively configure racialized "otherness," whether on the part of themselves, their peers, or their parents. For example, one rele-vant practice relating to *le bled* involves forms of address that collapse a peer's identity with that of their *bled*, that is, the town or country from which one or more of their parents emigrated. These practices include calling peers directly by the *bled* their parents are from, such as the nickname "Tolga" used for a boy whose parents came from this desert town in Algeria (cf. Geertz 1983, regarding similar naming practices in Morocco).

By ironically calling each other by their "hometown" such as Tolga, teens collapse person and place as a way to display intimate knowledge about a peer and to thereby exert interpersonal power, whether this takes the shape of social control or rapport, or a mixture of both. These and other playful performances can involve highly public rejections of their own or their peer's "personal" *bled* as stigmatized, backward, underdeveloped, and racialized. Such exchanges are all the more performative because these kids are explicitly NOT from *le bled*. All of the consultants involved in this project were born and raised in France. Of course, the "real *bled*" (that is, one's parents' overseas hometown) is a resource for kids from *les cités* to reconfigure and deepen social relationships during summer vacations. In addition to its value as a conceptual framework for diasporic identities, they experience *le bled* as an actual place in which to forge intimate relationships.

In France, however, *le bled* constitutes a central resource for teens to construct shared notions of ethnic and racialized belonging, in that the concept invokes a shared but ever-shifting southern-ness and peripheral-ness, configured alternately as one's village, as Algeria, or the "underdeveloped" edges of Europe, including Portugal. In this way, *le bled* exists for adolescents not only as a destination for summer travel or homeland, but, at least in discursive terms, as the idea of a place that is embodied by adolescents through naming, kinship, and discursive practices.

On the day that the following excerpt was recorded, five girls ranging from 12 to 15 sat with me in the small playground near their house. With the exception of Béatrice, all girls present were French of Algerian descent, with family mostly originating from the western Algerian town Maghnia, situated between Tlemcen and Oujda. As mentioned earlier, Béatrice's grandmother was originally from Portugal. Béatrice's identification as "une portos" (derogatory slang that she used to describe herself as Portuguese) granted her claims on a peripheral, southern *bled*, useful since most of her friends were of Algerian descent.

Discussion had turned to politics and Naima the youngest girl of 12 was making an argument about her preference for Jacques Chirac over other past French leaders, despite the older girls' insistence that Mitterrand and Jospin were preferable. In her argument, Naima claims to prefer former President Chirac due to his supposed commitment to the welfare of "blacks" and "Africa." In voicing her opinion, Naima distinguishes between sub-Saharan "countries where there's not a lot" of material wealth and the girls' "own countries," that is, "Arab countries" and "Portuguese countries," where "there are not a lot of problems." Hamida, an older girl who is also present, accordingly gives a plug for her own *bled* with the claims that there are especially not a lot of problems in Maghnia, the town where her mother is from originally.

Naima's inclusion of "Portuguese countries" involves a clear reference to Béatrice's background. In response, as soon as Naima completes her statement about Chirac, Béatrice launches into a humorous narrative in highly stylized voicing about her experiences in Portugal. Her description serves as a counter-narrative to Naima's claim that, in "their countries," there are not a lot of problems, in that it focused on the supposed preponderance of gypsy caravans and her own (non-gypsy) Portuguese cousin's supposed habit of dressing like a gypsy.

Arab and Portuguese Countries

1	Naima	*Parce que t'sais toujours il va sauver les noirs et tout. La vérité, t'sais bon, nous, dans nos pays, les pays arabes, portuguais et tout, y a pas ce- beaucoup de problèmes.*	Because ya know he [Chirac] always goes to save blacks and everything. The truth, ya know, us, in our countries, the Arab countries, Portuguese and everything, there are not th- a lot of problems.
2	Hamida	*Surtout pour euh surtout pour Maghnia.*	Especially for uh especially for Maghnia. [Hamida's mother is from Maghnia.]
3	Naima	*Mais toujours euh le président il va dans les p- en Afrique, chez les noirs parce que dans les pays où y a pas beaucoup et tout, il va leur rendre visite. Ils nous montrent à la télé.*	But always uh the president [Chirac] goes in the c- in Africa, where blacks live because in the countries where there isn't a lot [of material wealth] and everything, he goes to visit them. They show us on TV.
4	Chantal	*Ah, c'est bien.*	Oh, that's good.
5	Béatrice	*Au Portugal comment c'est blindé en gitans. Partout t'vois de l'herbe, tu vois qu'il y a des caravanes, des sales caravanes rouges en plus.*	In Portugal, it is so chock full of gypsies. Everywhere ya see grass, ya see there are caravans, those dirty red caravans even.
6	Chantal		[Laughter]

| 7 | Béatrice | *Hé, j'étais en sang. J'arrive là bas, j'vois ma cousine. Elle a un tablier jaune, avec une robe violette et des chausettes rouges. Faut le faire!* | Hey, I flipped out. I get down there, I see my cousin. She's wearing a yellow apron, with a purple dress, and red socks. Gotta do it! [Ironic tone] |
| 8 | Chantal and Naima | | [Laughter] |

The preceding excerpt demonstrates the complexity of the ways that competing notions of *le bled* intersect with discourses surrounding modernity, development, and racialization. This complexity is demonstrated by the contrast between younger Naima's pro-*bled* argument (indicating her belief that "their countries" are not underdeveloped like countries of sub-Saharan Africa) and older Béatrice's humorous performance indicating a contrary perspective, with outrageous claims that all the grass in Portugal is covered with gypsy caravans.

Inasmuch as the two girls' descriptions of *le bled* differ, so also do their own stances toward themselves and to the racialized identities they construct through their talk. In Naima's scenario, Arabs and Portuguese are unlike "blacks" from Africa, and are similar to the extent that they (she and her French-born peers) are "from" countries without many problems. In this way, Naima positions herself and her peers as more modern and as racially distinct from Africans who need "saving." In Béatrice's formulation, she and other Portuguese are racially marked by affiliation with "gypsies" (Romani)—perhaps the most uniformly reviled group in Europe—and to their "dirty" red caravans as well as "gypsy"-like behavior such as her cousin's loud, coarse style of clothing.

In such exchanges involving narratives and performative teasing, adolescents articulate a shifting but polarizing set of relationships regarding race/ethnicity, nation, and modernity through the discursive nexus of *le bled*. By invoking *le bled*, French teenagers of immigrant descent simultaneously express their identifications with "home" countries as well as ironic distancing from these places through humor. In addition to geographic space, teenaged discourses regarding *le bled* map onto experiences of immigration, generation, race/ethnicity, gender, and modernity.

Although positive and negative associations with *le bled* compete in these exchanges, the construction of this symbolic space and attendant behaviors exist in contradistinction to France and the North. For example, Naima constructs *le bled* as an entity composed of "Arab" and "Portuguese" countries that is distinct from France, in the position of extending aid, and black or sub-Saharan Africa, in the position of receiving it. Countering Naima's depiction of their *"bled"* as more modern, Béatrice renders a performance of her non-modern-*bled* Portugal, by humorously depicting it as "full" of "gypsies," thereby achieving a non-modern, stigmatized, and racialized representation of her *bled*, a move that serves to locate her in solidarity with "non-modern" "non-French" sub-Saharan-African countries as well as to both critique Naima and to locate herself as racialized. Whether exhibiting or lacking "development," both Naima and Béatrice formulate *le bled* as a pan-southern, peripheral homeland that is available as a resource for solidarity by French teenagers in ethnically mixed and racially stigmatized *cités*. Adolescents are thus actively engaging with and transforming dominant French stereotypes about *le bled* as racialized and non-modern in ways that are central to their personal identities and to social interactions among peers.

Cultural Puns and Racializing Play

In addition to the ways that teens use racializing talk to confront and criticize dominant French society's politicized challenges to their social identities and their occupation of space in *les cités*, teens use racializing talk among themselves for discursive play. Teens ironically reproduce and reconfigure stereotypes in peer-based interaction for fun and to create intimate solidarity with peers and mentors through racialized teasing. In comparison to the use of stereotypes for interactional goals described in the previous examples, this section deals with a case in which full-blown stereotypes are reduced to iconic references for the purpose of verbal and social play. In such instances, teens created fantastical insults that transformed racialized stereotypes to an absurd degree, creating fun and solidarity in the process. These practices are akin to teens co-constructing a transcultural, symbolic mirror to "reflect back" the larger society's dominant racializing images, thereby distorting these images in a carnivalesque or purposefully "grotesque" way (Bakhtin 1984).

In the following example of verbal play dealing with stereotypes, Samira and Mounia collaboratively construct a flow of insults that follows the absurdly exaggerated and reactionary "logic" of dominant French anti-immigrant discourses. Moving from "unemployed" to "illegal immigrant" and finally to "refugee from Kosovo," Samira's and Mounia's absurdly anti-immigrant rhetoric is made all the more humorously ridiculous due to her target: their college-educated tutors, Mohammad and Djamel, who are

French born, albeit of North African descent. In juxtaposing these playful but insulting labels for them, the teens demonstrate their competence in dominant French anti-immigrant rhetoric that posits immigrants as a drain on French social services.

This exchange also introduces the racializing image of *le clandé*, short for *clandestin* or "illegal immigrant." Teens of North African descent often use *clandé* to insult their peers, usually in connection with behavior that they deem backward or styles of dress that they find unfashionable. *Clandé* was also a term that the teens used in conjunction with the male, often Arab or black immigrants living in two high-rise dormitories (*foyers*) in the middle of the neighborhood, who, ironically, as migrant workers living in subsidized housing, were anything but "illegal." In these ways, the teens' uses of *clandé* indicate value judgments and a negative moral stance toward newly arrived immigrants that is less about their legal status than other projected and assumed things about their identity. These assumed qualities include being single or unattached male migrant workers living without their families, a lack of competence in French, non-urban styles of clothing, supposed "backward" or non-cosmopolitan behaviors, a lack of education, and lack of social networks and strong kinship ties that their own families enjoyed in the neighborhood.

The excerpt that follows shows a collaborative interaction in which Samira and Mounia construct discursive connections between stigmatized social labels, that is, *chômeur* (unemployed person), *clandé* (illegal immigrant), and *réfugié* (refugee), and link them with their adult, college-educated tutors, Mohammad and Djamel, to indicate their supposed laziness. The exchange begins with Samira asking Mohammad if he misses working at the association *Cerise*.

A Refugee from Kosovo

1	Samira	*Ça vous a manqué Cerise?*	Did you miss *Cerise*?
2	Mohammad	*Ouais, bah–*	Yeah, well–
3	Mounia	*Non en fait ils sont contents d'esquiver parce qu'on les tue.*	No, in fact they're happy they split because we kill★ them. [★"use them up," "abuse them"]

4	Mohammad	*Regarde, on arrive et tout de suite "les maths! les maths!" Hoh!*	Look, we get here and right away "math! math!" Whoa!
5	Samira	*Hé tu fais quoi maintenant?*	Hey, what are you doing now?
6	Mohammad	*J'fais rien.*	I'm doing nothing. [Laughs]
7	Samira	*Au chômage!*	Unemployed! [Mohammad laughs.]
8	Mounia	*Clandé!* [Slang form, *clandestin* is the complete form]	Illegal immigrant! [Djamel and Mounia laugh.]
9	Djamel	*Non, il a les papiers quand même.*	No, he has papers at least.
10	Samira	*Et là tu fais quoi Djamel? Ha!*	And what are you doing now, Djamel? Ha!
11	Djamel	*Moi? J'fais un stage.*	Me? I'm doing an internship.
12	Mounia	*[[De quoi?*	[[In what?
13	Samira	*[[Où?*	[[Where?
14	Djamel	*En informatique.*	In computer science.
15	Samira	*Ta' les chômeurs!* [*ta'* is a possessive form in Arabic]	**Of** the unemployed!
16	Djamel	*Ta' les chômeurs.* [Group laughter] *Un stage ANPE.*	**Of** the unemployed. [Group laughter] An internship from the welfare office.
17	Samira	*Ta' un réfugié du Kosovo!*	**Of** a refugee from Kosovo!

In the preceding exchange, Samira and Mounia tease their former tutors Mohammad and Djamel about their current (chosen) joblessness by initiating a series of insults regarding unemployment and immigration. Although both of the young, mid-twenties men had been tutors to help put themselves through university, they had since graduated and no longer worked at *Cerise*. They had decided to pay a social visit to the association that night, but are quickly asked to help with math homework.

In the excerpt, the girls and their former tutors collaboratively make symbolic and semantic connections through a chain of emergent derogatory social labels and identities. The exchange begins with Samira's seemingly neutral question to Mohammad, "Did you miss *Cerise?*," but the interaction quickly takes on a contentious tone, as Mounia accuses Mohammad and Djamel of not having missed them: "No, in fact they're happy they split because we kill them," in reference to the girls' demands for math help. Rather than deny Mounia's claim, Mohammad counters, "Look, we get here and right away, 'math! math!' Whoa!," laying the blame of his purported lack of enthusiasm for *Cerise* with the girls and their mistreatment of Djamel and himself. This playful but oppositional tone continues throughout the rest of the exchange as the girls tease Mohammad and Djamel about their current unemployed state.

Samira takes the opportunity of Mohammad's admission that he's "doing nothing" to reframe his current status as "unemployed." The teasing is humorous because Mohammad does not fit the stereotypical French image of the "unemployed"; at the time of the recording, he had just finished a very prestigious master's (*maîtrise*) degree in math that made him eminently employable in the growing high-tech industry in France. While he was indeed without a job at the moment of the exchange, Mohammad was taking time off before beginning his search, and subsequently found a high-paying job at a start-up Internet company.

However, the calculated misnomer "unemployed" sparks a humorous chain of increasingly absurd insults that operate much like dominant stereotypes directed at immigrants and Arabs generally in France. A single feature or signifier of Mohammad's identity is singled out and constructed as essential to his person. For example, Samira reframes Mohammad's admission that he is temporarily out of work as proof that he ranks among the "unemployed." Mounia takes the opportunity to improvise on Samira's theme by labeling Mohammad a *clandé*, implying that if he is out of work, he must be an illegal immigrant. The term *clandé* is complex in that it combines racial stereotypes and immigration status with assumptions of ignorance, provincialism, and laziness. Another aspect of the term's complexity is pragmatic—it is largely used by adolescents of Algerian descent to refer without irony to recent immigrants from North Africa who are generally single men, and who have come, either legally or illegally, to labor in France, much like Abdel, whose pun started this chapter. However, the term is also ironically used among adolescents to refer to each other, although they were born in France and have never immigrated.

The initial encouragement that Samira receives from Mohammad's laughter is echoed by Djamel's laughter in response to Mounia's comment. Yet, Djamel's laughter and response seem to make him vulnerable to the same type of teasing that Mohammad has just experienced. Djamel's corrective intervention on Mohammad's behalf ("no, he has papers at least") turns the group's attention toward him, opening him to questioning and criticism by the two girls. For example, when Samira asks Djamel what he is doing now, she punctuates her question with a challenging "ha!" as if to note that he has become the new object of teasing. Similarly, Djamel's "legitimate" response that he is doing an internship (a very common activity after university graduation in France) is met with challenging by Mounia and Samira, who simultaneously ask "where?" and "in what?" When Djamel tries to further legitimize his current status by responding "computer science," Samira counters that he is doing an internship "of the unemployed," meaning state-sponsored and designed to be a handout rather than a legitimate vehicle to future employment. Finally, Samira uses the expression ta' *les chômeurs* ("of the unemployed") as a further means to imply that his internship is just a cover for his being merely unemployed. Unfortunately, for many young people in France, cycling through unpaid or badly paid internships is indeed their only protection from complete unemployment, but this was not the case for Djamel and Mohammad, who were more generally educated and highly qualified in technical fields that suffered less unemployment at that time.

Throughout the exchange, the insults become increasingly absurd, in that they are being applied to college-educated French citizens (Mohammad and Djamel), who both later went on to get well-paid jobs in computer science. For example, the progression from "unemployed" → "illegal immigrant" → "Kosovo refugee" seems to convey increasing levels of social stigma in terms of the purported "drain" on the French state. Not only does each successive identity seem increasingly socially "pitiful," but also more and more fanciful in relation to the two well-educated and hardworking French citizens standing before Samira and Mounia. Moreover, the intensification of Samira's and Mounia's insults seems to grow with the encouragement she receives from Mohammad, Djamel, and me in the form of laughter, co-construction, and recycling of terms.

Adolescents' transcultural verbal performances are permeated with the fragments and semiotic traces of ideological French categories dealing with "race," immigration, culture, and belonging. Seemingly disparate speech genres and linguistic events demonstrate the prevalence of racialized stereotypes and social labels in adolescents' performances of social and interpersonal identity. As children of predominantly Algerian immigrants who live in a *cité*, these adolescents occupy a particularly stigmatized position with respect to dominant national discourses and cultural ideologies. Hence, it seems logical that these adolescents position their social selves "in relation to" widely-circulating dominant representations of a monolithic "French" identity.

However, a totalizing depiction of these cultural and linguistic practices as merely hegemonic would be too narrow, and would invest dominant French discourse with too much power to determine the ways that these adolescents perform social identity in interpersonal interactions. Rather, I will appeal to Cantwell's (1993) discussion of stereotypes in order to contextualize these adolescents' verbal and cultural practices as intrinsic to cultural expression itself, and not only as the exclusive behavior of marginalized groups. In his ethnography of the Smithsonian Folklife Festival, Cantwell writes that stereotypes are "a way of sorting information … a kind of shorthand," and that, rather than static, their use can indicate "less an urge to fix something than a need to set something in motion" (ibid.: 154–155).

Teens' transcultural uses of stereotypes that I explore here seem to indicate that adolescents are making sense of the ways that they are both integral and marginal to notions of "the French." Thus, the adolescents described here are not only exploring the gap between dominant representations of themselves and their own experience, but are also redirecting, subverting, and appropriating these stereotypes and categories to their own ends, including the performance of emergent transcultural identities. Adolescents' critical appropriation of French stereotypes regarding *les arabes*, Muslims, and *le bled* show them negotiating their community's standing in relation to widely circulating stigmatizing discourses. In this regard, identity performances for peers and adult mentors that appropriate and challenge dominant French stereotypes provide a means for adolescents to attempt to reconfigure symbolic relationships between the diametrically opposed figures in discourse, *le français* and *l'arabe*. In the process of voicing their own social identity in opposition to and through stereotypes, teens reproduce, elaborate, and challenge these essentializing categories.

Notes

1   As such, the aim of this chapter is akin to Bourdieu and Wacquant's "reflexive soci-ology," which looks to everyday practices as a means to understand large-scale processes (1992). For example, in *Weight of the World* [Bourdieu et al. 1999: ix], Bourdieu argues for analytically obtaining "the emblematic from the idiosyncratic" and achieves this "transformation" by juxtaposing interviews and narratives from the everyday experience of people who occupy polarized subject positions in France—for instance, white union factory workers and unskilled immigrant laborers, who are often depicted as vying for the same employment opportunities. Bourdieu's intended goal for creating such a conversation is, "through simple juxtaposition, to bring out everything that results when different or incompatible points of view confront each other, where no concession or compromise is pos-sible because each one of them is equally founded in social reason" [Bourdieu et al. 1999: 3].

2   For women, the practice of covering one's hair or wearing *hijab* holds a similar symbolic function. However, I have never heard women referred to as *les mus* or *soeurs musulmanes* (Muslim sisters). This may be because relatively few local women wore a headscarf in Chemin de l'Ile while I conducted my fieldwork. Furthermore, Muslim women are generally more likely to pray at home than at a mosque, and so it is possible that "the devout Muslim woman" has not congealed into a social persona in the neighborhood.

3   This type of open conflict is reminiscent of Bourdieu's description of other low-income housing projects in *Weight of the World* as "places which bring together people who have nothing in common and force them to live together, either in mutual ignorance and incomprehension or else in latent or open conflict" [Bourdieu et al. 1999: 3].

4   Normally, this Arabic term would take the feminine form **hadia**, but adoles-cents did not always follow conventional rules for gender agreement in Arabic, especially when using loan words.

5   *Ḥami* (Arabic) was often translated in French by adolescents as *excité*, but is better translated in English as "agitated" than "excited" due to the term's nega-tive connotation.

6   **Ka'b** may originate from the Arabic term for "heel," as it is used as an insulting way for someone to leave, as in the expression "ka'b chez toi" ("go home"). However, the term was alternately used in the expression "je t'ai **ka'b**," meaning "I got one over on you." Both the term and its usage are particular to speakers in France; the same term in Standard Arabic means "heel" (of a shoe) or "cube."

CHAPTER 4

LA RACAILLE AND *LE RESPECT*

Chapter 3 demonstrated the ways in which teenagers in Chemin de l'Ile critically appropriate French stereotypes regarding *les arabes* and Muslims in order to negotiate their community's standing in relation to widely circulating stigmatizing discourses. The relationships among racialization, space, and stigma that adolescents articulate when they re-voice such dominant stereotypes are distilled and magnified in teens' talk about *la racaille*, a volatile representation of male drug-dealing street toughs. Broadly circulating French political discourses have established *la racaille* at the center of a national moral panic (Hall et al. 1978) that attributes violence and criminality in *les cités* to this social group, rather than to such issues as discrimination, economic exclusion, and police brutality.

The 2005 violent events in French *cités* and their interpretation by public figures placed *la racaille* front and center in French media and political rhetoric. On October 27, 2005, the fatal electrocution of teenagers Zyed Benna and Bouna Traoré while they were evading police in Clichy-sous-Bois sparked civil unrest in suburban housing projects across France. On October 30, on national television, French President (then Interior Minister) Nicolas Sarkozy proclaimed "zero tolerance" for *la racaille* and threatened to "pressure wash" them from *les cités* (Ridet 2005). Then, at a November 19, 2005, political rally and in an apparent bid for the presidency in 2007, Sarkozy renewed this threat to *la racaille*, adding that "the central cause of

Transcultural Teens: Performing Youth Identities in French Cités, First Edition. Chantal Tetreault.
© 2015 John Wiley & Sons, Inc. Published 2015 by John Wiley & Sons, Inc.

unemployment, of despair, of violence in the suburbs, is not discrimination or the failure of schools … it is drug traffic, the law of bands,[1] the dictatorship of fear and the resignation of the Republic" (Ridet 2005).

Transcultural identities in Chemin de l'Ile are forged at the intersection of broadly circulating discourses and local forms of talk. Similarly, the highly pejorative and stigmatizing national discourses that circulate about *la racaille* inform teens' local moral valuing of this social type as well as the local spaces of *les cités*. The figure of *la racaille* is mobilized in teens' everyday discourse to imagine and socially create specific stigmatized spaces such as *la rue* ("the street"). As in current political rhetoric, inhabitants in Chemin de l'Ile and other *cités* have come to regard *la racaille* as emblematic of the stigmatized urban spaces in which they live. For example, in dominant French discourse as well as in adolescent talk, *la racaille* is constructed as ethnically non-French, and most often Arab or black in a pattern that conflates racialized identities with the stigmatized *cités*. In depicting *la racaille* as intrinsic to and contaminating of *les cités*, dominant French discourses symbolically cast these spaces as masculine, youthful, non-ethnically French, and morally corrupted.[2] Just as these national discourses stigmatize the spaces of *cités*, dominant moralizing discourses in France influence how residents in Chemin de l'Ile imagine and use local space, particularly in relation to gender and generation.

However, whereas in national discourse this conflation is undifferentiated—that is, *la racaille* comes to stand in for *cités* as a whole—in Chemin de l'Ile *la racaille* symbolically stands in only for particular stigmatized spaces, commonly referred to as *la rue* ("the street"). Furthermore, teens' local discourses about *la racaille* are highly ambivalent and reveal both identifications and dis-identifications toward this social type. In this way, broader national discourses that attribute a moral panic to *la racaille* do inform the local valuing of spaces and social types, but only partially in that these stigmatizing discourses are only partially adopted and often critically assessed in teens' talk. Following Goffman, I argue that stigma must be understood as a process interpreted through social relationships rather than measured in terms of static characteristics (1963: 3). The following discussion examines stigmatization of *la racaille* through a series of inter-related social and discursive relationships that are established in national political rhetoric about *cités*, local discourses in a particular *cité*, and in the narratives of two adolescent girls.

Narratives and talk about *la racaille* constitute, in essence, discourse about space and racialized identities, but they are also about gender and generation. Consequently, these stories organize the gendered moral landscapes of *les cités* in addition to local perceptions of their physical spaces (cf. de Certeau 1984). In emphasizing the ways that discourses shape the spaces of *les cités* in moral terms, I draw upon Hall et al's (1978) analysis of the "moral panic" relating to urban space, racialized youth, and mugging in London, which has resonance with ways that the current "crisis" regarding *les cités* is articulated in French media and politics. Stories told by adolescent girls provide evidence for how stigmatizing national discourses about *la racaille* come to play a central role in the construction of spatialized gender norms in the *cité* of Chemin de l'Ile. In particular, teenage girls in Chemin de l'Ile mobilize the symbol of *la racaille* to evoke culturally informed prescriptions regarding gendered and generational uses of space in their neighborhood.

Due to their symbolic affiliation with "the street" and assumed ties with *le business* (illicit commerce including the sale of drugs), *la racaille* potentially compromises the transnational Muslim–Arab sensibility that my consultants refer to as *le respect* or "respect." *Le respect* is a concept of central importance to adolescents in Chemin de l'Ile, and refers to a set of behaviors constructed as commensurate with proper cultural and religious practices derivative of North African and Muslim beliefs. At the same time, the set of moral discourses that constitute *le respect* in Chemin de l'Ile and in other *cités* is central to the experience of being Muslim and Arab within the diasporic context of France. That is, *le respect* is not just a reproduction of Arab Muslim values that are imported wholesale from North Africa but a set of moral discourses and practices that emerged in France, and particularly in the stigmatized spaces of French *cités*. Thus, adolescents in Chemin de l'Ile construct "respect" as a major axis of cultural difference between generations (experienced via both age and immigration), but also between Muslim and French values.

More specifically, *la racaille* is seen as morally threatening to culturally respectful spaces, such as Muslim butcher shops and weddings, but also to the "respect" of women and adolescent girls. In Chemin de l'Ile, adolescent girls' contested use of spaces such as *la rue* ("the street"), and more generally *dehors* ("outside"), elicits moral pressure from their older relatives and sometimes their peers to "go inside," "stop loitering like a bum," and "stop acting like *la racaille*." In these ways, although the term generally refers to a group of young men, adolescent girls' moral standing is implicated in talk about *la racaille*. During storytelling and discussions among their peers, adolescent girls evoke the image of *la racaille* to construct and resist "proper" gendered and generational uses of public space in their *cité*. After a general discussion of the linguistic and symbolic meanings of *la racaille*, I will analyze several adolescent girls' stories to show how the figure of *la racaille* takes on particular moral weight precisely because of the ways that this social persona has come to symbolize stigmatized public spaces.

Linguistic and Social Meanings of *La Racaille*

La racaille is a term that is complex grammatically as well as semantically. Grammatically, the word is a non-countable noun and hence is singular, although it generally refers to a social group. Due to its status as a non-countable noun, *la racaille* is more readily used to describe a type of person, or social persona, rather than specific individuals. Also, the feminine gender attached to the term is merely grammatical and does not reflect the gender of the referent. In fact, the term most frequently connotes pathologized masculinity.

La racaille literally means "trash" or "refuse," but has historically referred to those individuals rejected by mainstream society and so might translate more figuratively as "scum" or "riffraff." However, in recent years, the term has come to refer more narrowly to young men living in *cités*, usually of North African or sub-Saharan-African parentage, who are assumed to be violent and affiliated with drug trade or other forms of illicit commerce. As such, *la racaille* evokes a persona that intersects with gendered, generational, racialized, and spatialized social categories. This referential specificity, combined with grammatical vagueness, allows the term to be used in a morally accusatory manner without identifying individual actors. Depicted as dangerous, racialized, masculine, youthful, and outside the law, *la racaille* has served as a rallying point for mobilizing the conservative right-wing electorate in France.

Within *cités*, usage of the term demonstrates a social ambivalence toward *la racaille*. In interviews I conducted in 2006, several consultants mentioned that the term and the social figure it represents elicit both negative and positive associations. Rashida, a 21-year-old woman, noted, "It's a term that the [then] Interior Minister [Sarkozy] used because in these neighborhoods they often refer to themselves like that, *racaille*." She added, "when we use the term it's normal, it's positive," but that Sarkozy's use of the term was taken as the highest insult. Another young woman named Hamida initially defined *la racaille* as "groups of youth, young boys … who are there breaking things [vandalizing]" and then qualified, "but not always [because] … it may be just a group that hangs around together." Although 23, married, and working at the time of the interview, Hamida had passed through a stage in which her own behavior and style of clothing replicated that of *la racaille*: "when my brothers saw me like that they would say 'you're a real little *racaille*'. They also called me 'the little mafia'." In instances such as these, siblings and peers use the term *la racaille* to critique, often in the guise of teasing, individuals who embody personal styles supposedly typical of *la racaille*, including aggression, tough language, and masculine, urban-styled clothing (e.g., men's polyester warm-up suits), but, crucially, who would not otherwise be considered a member of this group. For instance, Hamida's brother's use of the labels *racaille* and *mafia* are mitigated by the qualifier "little," throwing into question the extent to which he considered his sister to be *la racaille*.

Only very rarely is the term used as an earnest descriptor for specific people, although I will be dealing with such a use later in this chapter. Based upon my interview data, this is because many find the term too stigmatizing to use non-ironically, and prefer, as with Hamida's brother, to use it to tease non-*racaille* for supposedly *racaille*-like behavior. Of central importance to this semantic ambiguity is that one interpretation of *la racaille* is "drug dealer." Although several of my interviewees claimed that one is not necessarily a drug dealer when one is considered *la racaille*, these same consultants sometimes conflated the two categories in everyday conversations. Furthermore, young people's use of the term to teasingly mark non-normative behavior in their peers (such as Hamida's tough dress and demeanor) indicates that *la racaille* is strategically evoked to voice moralizing discourses, even though these discourses may be contested and ambivalent. These practices demonstrate a larger moral ambivalence toward *la racaille* in Chemin de l'Ile and other *cités*. Just as behaviors affiliated with *la racaille* (e.g., toughness, aggression) are alternately valorized and stigmatized, *la racaille* is constructed as the anti-hero of French *cités* and represented alternately as a positive and negative social force.

La Racaille within the Parallel Economies of Les Cités

From the perspective of the French state, a significant portion of the economy of *cités* is constituted by illegitimate economic pursuits. Both women and men participated in the parallel economy of Chemin de l'Ile, but in different sectors. Women's informal economy centered on childcare, catering (especially baking bread and sweets), sewing, and beauty services such as applying henna for weddings. Many skilled male laborers worked illegally as carpenters, masons, plumbers, and other craftspeople because they were unable to obtain work in legitimate businesses due to the lack of immigration papers. As an Algerian woman remodeling her apartment bragged to me, "you can get any kind of work you wanted *au noir* ('under the table') and at half the market price."

Other entrepreneurial activity in Chemin de l'Ile skirted illegality more narrowly. In particular, *le recel*—the resale of stolen or contraband clothing and electronic goods—was widespread in the neighborhood as it is in other *cités*.[3] This type of parallel economic activity, called *le business* or *le biz*, made it possible to buy all manner of luxury items in *cités*, such as cell phones, perfume, jeans, and tennis shoes, for about half the market price and tax-free. Adolescent girls and young women were generally excluded from this type of trade; it is often passed down from so-called "big brothers" (*grands frères* or simply *les grands*) to "little brothers" (*petits frères*) in Chemin de l'Ile as elsewhere in French *cités* (Duret 1996). Within this parallel economy, generation, in addition to gender, shapes access to work as well as attitudes toward work. For male adolescents and young men, establishing a foothold in *le biz* presents a way to gain social status and economic independence.

However, tacit acceptance of the parallel economy in Chemin de l'Ile breaks down with regard to drug dealing, which was strongly stigmatized by older generations and often younger generations, who made a moral distinction between the sale of drugs and the sale of stolen goods and contraband. The degree to which drug dealing was stigmatized in the neighborhood was demonstrated in the ways that money from drug trade was considered to be morally tainted, even when it was invested in other economic endeavors. Discourses regarding which local butcher shop was reputed to be *ḥalal* (ritually pure) illustrates this point.

In Chemin de l'Ile, the two main *ḥalal* meat shops in the neighborhood were owned and operated by local Muslim butchers of North African origin. Both butcher shops sold *ḥalal* meat, that is, from animals slaughtered in the traditional Islamic way and bearing the official inspection stamp indicating that it was blessed by an imam.[4] Yet, some residents disparaged the meat from one butcher shop as inauthentic or not truly *ḥalal*. This distinction was based upon the knowledge that this particular shop had been "built by drug money," and the fact that the owners were previously known as *la racaille*. Meat from the other butcher shop was twice as expensive, yet many families—including the Hamdani family that I lived with—preferred to go without meat (as we frequently did) rather than buy meat that was potentially morally tainted by its association to drug trade and *la racaille*.

The way that the seemingly banal question of where to buy one's *ḥalal* meat was framed by older, "respectable" residents of Chemin de l'Ile as a moral dilemma illustrates how *la racaille* was viewed as morally contaminating of spaces central to Muslim cultural practice. In this case, the butcher shop affiliated with former *racaille* came to be symbolically marked as a morally compromised space, such that its putatively ḥalal meat was considered tainted or less authentic. In this diasporic Muslim community, the moral legitimacy of ḥalal meat is of utmost importance since its consumption is central to everyday "respectful" ritual practice in a potentially morally contaminating non-Muslim French cultural context.

At the same time, it is specifically their illicit economic pursuits that grant la racaille a reputation as resisters of the exclusionary French state, an entity that is perceived as economically and socially marginalizing to a majority of cité inhabitants. Young inhabitants of French cités, including female teens, are particularly sympathetic to la racaille as participants in the parallel economy of French cités. In valorizing the illicit behaviors of la racaille, teenagers growing up in cités position themselves in opposition not only to the authority of the French state, but also to their parents' expectations for their own "respectful" behavior. These generational discourses map onto experiences of immigration, with French adolescents of non-French and particularly Arab Muslim descent positioning themselves in relation to and, at times, in resistance to their parents' "immigrant" values, articulated in adolescent discourse as la mentalité du bled or "the mentality of the home country."[5] Central to adolescents' construction of their parents' values is le respect, which is constructed as being in conflict with illicit activities such as drug dealing and gratuitous violence, two hallmark activities associated with la racaille.

As with attitudes more generally toward la racaille, the moral distinction between legitimate and illegitimate ḥalal meat is shaped by generation; adolescents seemed largely unconcerned about whether to buy a merguez-frites (beef sausage and fries) from the less expensive, and putatively less ḥalal butcher shop. In rejecting the putatively morally tainted ḥalal meat, adult female and male heads of families consolidated their "respectful" personal identity in the eyes of their neighbors. This "respectful" persona is constructed in contradistinction to the potentially "disrespectful" behavior and attitudes of the young, and, in particular, of la racaille. In these ways, le respect, similar to Goffman's notion of stigma, is relationally defined (1963: 137–138). In Chemin de l'Ile, older residents and heads of households construct their own respectful behaviors and personas in relation to disrespectful behaviors and personas of younger generations. Moreover, individuals shift into new roles as they get older; during follow-up research in 2006, young people whom I had begun talking to when they were teenagers complained to me that new generations of teens "lacked respect."

The moral quality of distinct spaces in Chemin de l'Ile is also established relationally. The correlation between drug dealing and morally tainted meat illustrates how local, potentially "respectful" spaces, here a *halal* butcher shop, may be considered morally compromised by their affiliation with *la racaille*. This process of (de-)valuing local spaces occurs by circulating moral discourses that seem superficially similar to moralizing dominant French discourses that circulate nationally about *la cité*. A closer look, however, reveals distinctions between these sets of moralizing discourses that merit further exploration. For example, President Sarkozy's repeated threat to "pressure wash" *cités* constructs *la racaille* as a corrupting force that threatens the morality of the entire collective space of these neighborhoods. In local discourses in Chemin de l'Ile, however, it is those spaces related to respectful moral Muslim practice (such as the *halal* butcher shop) that are considered threatened by illicit activities such as drug dealing. Whereas Sarkozy's depiction of the moral corruption of *cités* is absolute—these spaces are depicted as entirely contaminated by the "scum" of *la racaille*—local renderings of moral corruption regarding *la racaille* are specific and partial (non-totalizing). Within the Muslim community of Chemin de l'Ile, respectful practices and spaces are of particular concern since they may be potentially corrupted by the illicit behaviors of *la racaille*, such as drug dealing. Indeed, there is little impetus to protect outdoor public space from the corrupting nature of *la racaille* because these spaces, namely *la rue* ("the street"), are already considered to be morally corrupting of respectful behavior. Similar to "the street," *la racaille* is often constructed as incompatible with morally respectable spaces, such as the *halal* butcher shop and Muslim weddings, a topic of the stories analyzed later in this chapter.

Le Respect, Cultural Change, and Gender

As noted in the preceding text, *le respect* refers to a set of behaviors constructed as commensurate with proper cultural and religious practices derivative of North African and Muslim beliefs. However, *le respect* is a set of moral discourses and practices that emerge in France, and particularly in the stigmatized spaces of French *cités*. As such, adolescents in Chemin de l'Ile constructed "respect" as a major axis of cultural difference between generations (experienced via both age and immigration), but also between Muslim and French values. For example, on an outing with adolescent girls to Paris, our group passed by a street famous for prostitution. One of the girls present, Rashida, exclaimed in disgust, "There is no respect here!" ("*Il n'y a pas de respect ici!*"). In framing her aversion to prostitution through the cultural code of "respect," Rashida articulated her own moral standing as differential not only to the selling of sexual acts but also to a French society that legally allows such acts. In this way, Muslim adolescents such as Rashida who are growing up in highly stigmatized working-class neighborhoods create codes of morality for themselves and their communities in contradistinction to "French" values and cultural practices.

Adolescents in Chemin de l'Ile interpret *le respect* as a social code that prescribes showing deference for one's elders. Its local practice is loosely based upon an age-and-gender hierarchy typical of North African and Arab culture more generally (Abu-Lughod 1986; Goodman 2005).[6] *Le respect* involves the expectation that supposedly less powerful groups will be protected by those potentially stronger or more powerful. As noted in Chapter 3, Naima, a 12-year-old girl, constructed *le respect* as both relational and hierarchical: "… Muslims, they don't hit. We Muslims, the men, those they respect the most, it's the old men, women, and children. Women, you can't hit them." Rather than depending upon others to receive *le respect*, adult men here hold the power to confer it; they are expected to give respect to those who are more socially vulnerable than they, namely, elderly men, women, and children. The power to give respect to others (thereby marking them as socially vulnerable or weak) is a power that is unevenly distributed; men hold more power to give or withhold respect than women, just as middle-aged adults of both genders can give or withhold respect from the young or the elderly.

Le respect represents a code of behavior that applies to both adolescent girls and boys, but in concert with local gender ideologies. Maintaining *le respect* dictates refraining from publicly exhibiting illicit behaviors such as dating, smoking cigarettes, drinking alcohol, and drug use in general, but particularly within view of older relatives and adults of one's parents' or grandparents' generation. In Chemin de l'Ile, *le respect* involves a higher level of social constraint for girls, since they are expected by their parents and peers to attain "respect" through projecting a public image that they are sexually unavailable and inactive. For many adolescent girls in the neighborhood, maintaining a respectful image involves avoiding "too much" time spent *dehors* ("outdoors") in the neighborhood, since doing so might be interpreted as sexual availability.

While there is some overlap between the concepts *la rue* ("the street") and *dehors* ("outside"), the former is semantically more restrictive than the latter. Whereas *la rue* specifically refers to the area in and alongside roads, *dehors* refers to all outdoor spaces, including the open-air market and those more secluded areas such as playgrounds. Loitering and conducting *le business* ("illicit trade or sale of goods") in *la rue* were activities conducted mostly by men and teenaged boys; however, some spaces located "outside" (*dehors*), such as playgrounds, were largely the domain of adult women and children. In Chemin de l'Ile, by way of semantic slippage, *la rue* was often euphemistically used to refer to illicit behaviors such as the sale of drugs or *le recel*, the sale of stolen merchandise. *Dehors*, on the other hand, was often used euphemistically among women to refer to an inappropriate use or over-use of public space, as in the expression *traîner dehors* ("loiter outside"). Whereas young men were expected to "loiter outside," it was highly stigmatized behavior for young women, and even those adolescent girls occupying normally gender-appropriate spaces, such as their front stoop or the playground, might be admonished by older relatives or neighbors for spending "too much" time *dehors*.

And yet, some adolescent girls in Chemin de l'Ile choose to strategically occupy public outdoor spaces and adopt styles of dress and speech affiliated with *la racaille* in order to craft an alternate type of "respect." These girls in Chemin de l'Ile dress in baggy men's warm-up suits and instigate rounds of ritualized insults and bragging that are considered emblematic of a tough local identity, and, by symbolic extension, the masculine image of *la racaille*. Girls frame their use of these styles as a way to build a youthful, personalized form of *le respect* that is non-traditional, or, in the words of one teen, unlike "those girls that stay home and do the dishes." Strategies for crafting this alternative form of "respect" include displaying toughness, verbal and sometimes physical aggression, and an intimate knowledge of illicit spaces and activities such as drug dealing within their own and other *cités*. Likewise, adolescent girls construct discursive stances toward *la racaille* that reflect their personal and moral stances toward local public spaces within their neighborhood. Adolescent girls' shifting and often contradictory discursive valuing of *la racaille* provides insight into their own ambivalent positioning toward stigmatized public space in their *cité*.

Language is constitutive of gender only indirectly: language practices such as voice quality and styles of speech index (or point to) stances and social acts that constitute gendered meanings, such as "toughness" (Ochs 1992: 341). Stance—the expression of attitudes and evaluations—is central to adolescent girls' narratives about *la racaille* because it provides a means to voice moral positions not only toward this stigmatized group, but also toward "respectful" cultural representations of femininity. In the following section, two adolescent girls construct distinct gendered personas for

themselves by aligning with and differentiating themselves from the stigmatized and hyper-masculine figure of *la racaille*. These girls construct their
(female but not necessarily feminine) gendered personas through discourses
about the hyper-masculine *racaille*. That they do so illustrates how teens
actively reconfigure understandings of "masculine" and "feminine" at different social levels and for different contexts, including peer interactions in the
local context of *les cités*, but also in response to their parents' generation and
to gender norms within the French society at large (Barrett 1999; Bucholtz
1999; Butler 1990; Hall 1997; McElhinny 1995). In the case of girls adopting
discourses and emulating behaviors purportedly associated with *la racaille*,
such transgressive gender performances are alternately valued and stigmatized among peers because they allow teens to carve out a separate identity
from their parents' generation, but may also be interpreted as undermining
community values.

Adolescent Girls' Discursive and Moral Positioning toward *La Racaille*

While conducting research in Chemin de l'Ile, I had to learn how
to interpret the gendered and moral import of local spaces in order to
conduct daily fieldwork and to eventually live with a family in the neighborhood. Initially, I routinely crossed through the parking lot in front of
the high rise where I would later live, to the amusement of the young
men gathered to conduct *le business*. I had not realized that although
doing so was the quickest route, most women and young girls in the
neighborhood walked around the parking lot (especially during the evening) to avoid this overtly masculine space. This is a small example of the
way that, as an American outsider, I had to learn the moral spatial
landscape of the *cité* in which I researched and lived. Through my own
exposure to circulating discourses similar to those that I discuss in this
chapter, I learned to navigate morally demarcated spaces in a manner
commensurate with *le respect*. Whereas adolescent boys and sometimes
adult men may spend time outdoors *traîner* ("loitering") in the street,
parking lots, and entrances to buildings, women and adolescent girls are
mostly on the move, walking through the neighborhood on their way to
somewhere, unless they are tending to small children in local playgrounds.
This gendering of space is such that many outdoor, public areas are occupied by men, whereas oftentimes for women, in the words of de Certeau,
"to walk is to lack a place" (1984: 103).

In contrast to the highly gendered use of outdoor public space in Chemin de l'Ile, many indoor, state-sponsored public spaces are gender mixed, including schools and neighborhood associations such as *Cerise*. Adolescent boys and girls used the association as a means to talk and socialize, even though they would tend to avoid each other in public outdoor space to uphold an image of *le respect*. Interspersed between tutoring sessions at *Cerise*, teens would tease, flirt, joke, gossip, and brag with one another, using competitive verbal genres combining linguistic repertoires from French, North African, and global hip-hop cultures.

I recorded the conversation analyzed in the following text while several adolescents socialized informally in a small game room within *Cerise*. Present was Mina, a 15-year-old girl of Algerian background who typified what residents locally referred to as a "girl from the *cité*" (*une fille de la cité*), in that she crafted a tough personal identity through emulating the verbal and dress styles often associated with masculinity and local spaces. Girls such as Mina craft this type of transgressive persona for themselves, in part, by openly valorizing *la racaille* and behaviors attributed to them. Although Mina's peers appreciated her tough personal style and "masculine" clothing, they also often criticized her for these very same qualities.

On this particular afternoon, Mina sat with Pierre, a 15-year-old boy of Antillean origin, and Cécile, a girl of 14 whose father was Moroccan and mother was French. Cécile, as with Mina, often wore masculine dresses such as baggy sweatpants and used competitive verbal genres associated with the *cité*. However, unlike Mina, Cécile's relationship to her own *cité* was mitigated by her desire to one day leave it and her distaste for its physically decrepit and economically depressed status. For example, Cécile once asked me if I liked the supermarket chain called "Ed," short for "Europa Discount," that constituted the only choice for food shopping inside the neighborhood. When I said that I thought it was useful for some things, Cécile responded by expressing her strong distaste for the store, claiming that it represented everything that was wrong with the neighborhood, being reputed for cheap goods of low quality.

Unlike Cécile, Mina gained a certain amount of prestige by associating herself with the tough ways of Chemin de l'Ile and other nearby *cités*. While I sat with them and recorded their casual conversation, Mina talked about a new boy at school, Dumont, who was a "céfran," *verlan* (inverted slang) for *français* and a common way to label individuals who are ethnically French.[7] At the end of her narrative, Mina claimed, "you know the wild guys are the little French [kids]. They all think they're *racaille*."

1	Mina	*Un mec des Quatre Chemins est venu dans notre collège, il a atterri dans notre classe, et quand il était pas dans la classe, la classe elle était calme, mais laisse tomber quoi!* [Smiling gleefully]	A guy from Quatre Chemins came to our school, he landed in our class, and when he wasn't in class the class was calm, but [now] forget it!
2	Cécile	*Après elle est partie en couille.*	Afterward, it [the class] went to hell.
3	Mina	*En fait elle était pas calme, il y avait du bordel, mais bon, il y avait pas comme la fin de l'année.* [Suppressing laughter]	In fact, it wasn't calm [before], people raised hell, but not like at the end of the year.
4	Pierre	*Ouais.*	Yeah.
5	Mina	[Laughing throughout] *Et les profs ils disent, "oui c'est l'arrivée de Dumont—il nous entraîne." Et toute la classe a commencé à dégénérer. Même les premiers de la classe ils répondaient aux profs et tout.*	And the teachers, they say, "yes, it's because Dumont [the 'guy'] came—he drags us into it." And the whole class started to fall apart. Even the best students talked back to the teachers and everything.
6	Pierre	[Laughter]	[Laughter]
7	Mina	[Continuing to laugh] *Il répondait, il se battait en cours, il disait "oh foutez-moi la paix" et tout, mais tu sais les mecs chelous c'est les petits céfrans. Ils se prennent pour de la racaille.*	He [Dumont] talked back to the teacher, he fought in class, he said "oh leave me the hell alone" and everything, but you know the wild guys are the little French [kids]. They think they're *racaille*.

In this narrative, Mina gleefully describes the way that their class had "gone to hell" since Dumont had joined them from Quatre Chemins, a nearby *cité* reputed to be much tougher than their own neighborhood. Similar to other narratives that Mina often told, this story dramatizes and exaggerates disruptive behavior at the same time that it also valorizes this behavior. Mina's narrative serves the double function of reporting her contempt for school authority and of portraying her classmate Dumont, and by association herself, as disruptive in school, presumably to gain the respect and approbation of Pierre. At the time, Pierre had a reputation for being tough because he had assaulted a teacher and had been expelled from school for it. In this sense, he is a well-chosen audience for Mina's narrative, in that he is associated with the kind of tough reputation that Mina is attempting to craft for herself. Although the bulk of this story is built around her classmate Dumont's aggressive behavior, Mina provides the face-saving caveat that "In fact, it [the class] wasn't calm [before]" to illustrate her own and other classmates' disruptive behavior.

A main way that Mina establishes Dumont's and, by association, her own reputation for toughness at school is by comparing her "little French" class-mate's behavior to that of *la racaille*. In doing so, Mina creates a complex discursive hierarchy of toughness that intersects with ideologies of space, ethnicity, and gender. Mina's evaluation of Dumont as a *céfran*, or ethnically French, establishes by comparison *la racaille* as ethnically non-French. Mina's contrast also serves to highlight the irony of the "little French" guy, Dumont, who mistakenly thinks he is *la racaille* even though he is (in her estimation) just an uncooperative student.

In distinguishing *la racaille* from "little French" troublemakers, Mina creates a hierarchy of toughness, at the top of which she locates the ethnically non-French *racaille*. Her use of the dismissive term "little" to refer to her "French" classmate further diminishes the gravity of his disruptive acts in school. In this way, at the same time that she valorizes the disruptive behavior of her ethni-cally French classmate, Dumont, Mina depicts him as less tough and less mature than "true" *racaille*. By contrasting *la racaille* with this image of Frenchness, Mina evokes essentializing and authenticating discourses (Bucholtz 2003) that establish *la racaille* as both inherently tough and ethni-cally non-French, thus strategically co-opting the dominant stereotype that *la racaille* are exclusively Arab or black. Mina's comparison also rests on the impli-cation that, although Dumont is from a very tough *cité*, Quatre Chemins, he is not as tough as what she infers to be the true or authentic inhabitants of her own and other *cités*, namely *la racaille*. Such a distinction relies not only upon contrastive comparisons of ethnic groups but also on a contrastive anal-ysis of space; Dumont cannot be *la racaille* and go to school since the realm of the "real" *racaille* is outside of the domesticating context of formal education.

Mina's contrastive categories thereby distinguish between the "little French" boy in a school setting with the Arab or black *racaille* in the street.

This example demonstrates the ways that certain adolescent girls valorize *la racaille* as part of crafting a tough, transgressive identity for themselves. Similar to *la racaille*, Mina crafts her own tough persona by evoking a strong affiliation with her local *cité* and *cités* generally. Her stance depends upon adopting negative, dominant French images of *cités* and *racaille* as tough and dangerous, and yet she also simultaneously valorizes these characteristics. In these ways, adolescents who are racially and spatially marginalized in the broader French society construct counter-discourses of social power by positively revaluing the pathologized figure of *la racaille* and the stigmatized space of their *cité*. In Mina's case, her valorization of *la racaille* and her use of affiliated styles of dress and speech, in her words, "make her respected" (*se faire respecter*) in the neighborhood. In so doing, Mina resists a normative construction of femininity that relies on being socially absent from public outdoor space, and instead adopts a tough, masculine style to achieve an alternative form of *le respect*.

La Racaille *at a Wedding*

Not all girls in Chemin de l'Ile engage in self-valorization through an affiliation with *la racaille* as Mina does. For example, in a discussion about Muslim weddings, Mina and Cécile describe contrasting images of *la racaille*. Drawn from the same recording of casual spontaneous conversation as the preceding excerpt, *la racaille* re-emerges in this portion of the discussion when Mina asks Cécile if she attended a recent wedding. Cécile responds decisively that, although her older sister had invited her, she had declined the offer, remarking that, "When I go to a wedding, frankly I don't want to see all the *racaille* that you always see in the *cité*." In the ensuing discussion, both Mina and Cécile co-construct a moral discourse that separates *la racaille* from the respectful context of a Muslim family wedding. However, whereas Cécile's discourse constructs *la racaille* as generally stigmatized, Mina constructs only the mixing of *la racaille* with respectable female guests as disrespectful and continues to valorize *la racaille*.

"I Don't Want to See All the Racaille That You Always See in the Cité*"*

1	Mina	*T'es partie à son mariage?*	Did you go to her wedding?
2	Cécile	*Ma soeur, elle m'avait invitée, après j'ai fait "Non, j'y vais pas."*	My sister, she had invited me, but I said "no, I'm not going."

| 3 | Chantal | *Pourquoi tu voulais pas?* | Why didn't you want to? |

| 4 | Cécile | *Parce que quand tu vas dans un mariage, franchement, j'ai pas envie de voir toute <u>la racaille</u> que tu vois toujours dans <u>la cité</u> et tout ça. C'est bon, j'ai fait "non, j'y vais pas."* | Because when you go to a wedding, frankly, I don't want to see all <u>the racaille</u> that you always see in <u>the cité</u> and all that. It's ok, I said "no, I'm not going." |

| 5 | Pierre | *Mais non mais là c'est un mariage, tu crois quoi? C'est-c'est pas <u>la rue</u>.* | But no, but, this is a wedding, what do you think? It's- it's not <u>the street</u>. |

| 6 | Mina | *Non mais même, attends, hé franchement quand ma cousine elle s'est mariée, mes cousins pendant qu'ils y étaient ils avaient que ramené ah, <u>les mecs des Canibous, les mecs des Pâquerettes, les mecs des Côtes D'Auty</u> mais ils ont fait, "Non, c'est un mariage pour entre la famille. C'est que leur famille qui va, pas <u>les bicots</u>."* | No but still, look, hey, frankly when my [female] cousin got married, my [male] cousins, as long as they were there, could have brought, um, <u>the guys from Canibous, the guys from Pâquerettes, the guys from Côtes D'Auty</u>, but they [the male cousins] said, "No, it's a wedding for between family." It's only their family that goes, not the <u>Arabs</u>.★ [★*bicots*, a highly pejorative word for Arabs] |

| 7 | Pierre | *Bah ouais.* | Well, yeah. |

| 8 | Mina | *Bah normalement je n'sais pas pour le moindre <u>respect</u> c'est un mariage à sa soeur ou à sa tante ou j'sais pas à qui que ce soit, la moindre des choses, il ramène personne, pas de leurs copains ou pas qui que ce soit.* | Well normally, I don't know, for the least amount of <u>respect</u> [whether] it's a wedding to one's sister or aunt or I don't know to whomever, the least thing [is that] they bring no one, not their buddies, or anybody. |

| 9 | Chantal | *Mais le marié euh Azim c'est pas de <u>la racaille</u>, lui? Non.* | But the groom, uh, Azim, he's not <u>racaille</u> is he? No. |

10	Mina	*Bah il vend du <u>it</u>.* [Short for "le shit" or hashish]	Well, he sells <u>hashish</u>.
12	Cécile	[Clicks tongue against teeth to express her displeasure with Mina's comment about groom]	[Tongue click—"tsk"]
13	Silence	[5 seconds of silence]	[5 seconds of silence]

In this excerpt, Cécile's discursive formulations of public space, *la racaille*, and the *cité* rely upon many of the associations found in Mina's discourse in the previous example. Similar to Mina's connection between public space in the *cité* and *la racaille*, Cécile stipulates that she does not want to see *la racaille* "that you always see uh in the *cité*," implying that you would not find *racaille* elsewhere, for instance, in central Paris. However, despite similarities, Cécile articulates a very different moral position toward *la racaille* than Mina. In particular, Cécile articulates the desire to avoid *la racaille*, and implies that their presence is inappropriate at a wedding. The concern that Cécile articulates about "seeing" *la racaille* may, in fact, have more to do with being "seen" by and among *la racaille*. Here, Cécile is apparently hoping to maintain her own respect by remaining separate from *la racaille*, whom she casts as potentially morally contaminating, seemingly not only because they are non-male relatives, but because they represent stigmatized public space in her neighborhood: "I don't want to see all the racaille that you always see in the *cité*."

Cécile's hope to remain separate from the contaminating presence of *la racaille* falls in line with her general attitude toward the space of the *cité*. It is a place that she hopes to escape one day, and her wish to escape *la racaille* is representative of that desire. Although Cécile also uses styles of dress and speech affiliated with the *cité*, she is very clear about her eventual intent to leave it, remarking that she finds the neighborhood profoundly depressing. Cécile hopes to get a job as a flight attendant to achieve her dream of traveling far away from the *cité* that encloses her. Privately too, Cécile is critical of Mina, whom she claims acts too often like *une fille de la cité* ("a girl from the *cité*"), meaning that Mina's identity is too enmeshed with the dense social networks of the *cité* itself, supposedly causing her to gossip about other girls and keep tabs on who is dating whom within the neighborhood. Cécile seems to have adopted aspects of the dominant French discourse regarding her own *cité*, which she casts as more than just a place, but as a set of interactional practices that negatively shape the social identities of those affiliated with it.

Cécile's negative valuing of her own *cité* is mirrored by her unambiguous critique of *la racaille*. In contrast, Mina simultaneously adopts two distinct stances with respect to *la racaille*. She positively values the transgressive behaviors of *la racaille* while criticizing their infringement upon the respectful feminine space of a family wedding. Mina implies that her male cousins are quite familiar with *la racaille* by claiming that they could have invited the "guys" from several tougher nearby *cités* to a past family wedding. By laying claim to her cousins' and by extension her own familiarity of *la racaille*, Mina lays claim also to an intimate knowledge of the workings of *le business* (including drug dealing) in her own and nearby *cités*. In short, she is laying claim, for herself and her cousins, to a tough and symbolically masculine social identity commensurate with *la racaille*.

For example, although Mina self-identifies as Arab, she uses the word *bicots,* a derogatory term for Arabs to describe *la racaille*. In so doing, she demonstrates how pejorative dominant national discourses are appropriated and subverted among *cité* teens for their own transgressive identity performances. By using this racial slur, Mina verbally performs the tough identity akin to that attributed to *la racaille*. Similarly, in response to my question at the end of the discussion, "But the groom, uh, Azim, he's not *racaille* is he?," Mina implies that the groom can be considered *racaille* because he deals hashish. Mina's open claim to knowledge of this fact serves to strengthen her tough reputation as someone who knows about drug dealing. In contrast, Cécile's more discreet demeanor is reiterated when she admonishes Mina ("tsk") for divulging this inappropriate information, after which we all fall silent for several seconds.

Mina further displays the link between spatializing practices and narratives when she invokes the names of nearby infamous *cités*: Canibous, Pâquerettes, and Côtes D'Auty. Mina's iteration of these nearby *cités* allows her, as an adolescent girl with relative immobility in the space of her own *cité*, to embrace the illicit freedom of her cousins and *la racaille*, who circulate among *cités* in order to conduct *le business*. Through listing infamous nearby *cités*, Mina's narrative serves to "traverse and organize places" and thus to make "itineraries out of them" (de Certeau 1984: 115). Mina casts herself, similar to *la racaille*, as a transgressive agent who, through her narratives about specific *cités* with tough reputations, creates spatial trajectories that exist in resistance to the authority of schools, parents' expectations for respectful behavior, and the French police or "forces of order."

Yet, Mina simultaneously adopts a second, traditionalist discourse when she acknowledges that the "respect" of female relatives must be preserved by excluding *la racaille* from the feminized, semi-private space of a wedding [turn 8]. In so doing, Mina embraces the cultural requirements of *le respect* by discursively secluding adult female guests and a few close male relatives in the respectful space of a wedding. Thus, Mina simultaneously voices two seemingly contradictory discourses, one that valorizes the disruptively violent, masculine *racaille*, and another that valorizes the moral virtue of older female relatives in the context of a Muslim wedding.

Central to this second discourse is a moral imperative to protect older, married female relatives—"sisters" and "aunts"—who represent a generation with different ways of achieving respect than the adolescent Mina. By casting herself as distinct from this feminine group needing protection from *la racaille*, Mina positions herself outside of the restraints and requirements of respectful femininity, even as she extols it as a virtue in other women. In this way, Mina appears to strategically craft a youthful and masculine style of respect for herself; she identifies herself as familiar and comfortable with *la racaille*, but also forwards a desire to engage in the moral protection of the older female generation, which is normally a stance that adult males adopt. Mina's ability to position herself in this protective masculine stance, however, depends upon depicting *la racaille* as a contaminating social element. In this way, both Cécile and Mina cast *la racaille* as morally contaminating to the space of a respectful Muslim family wedding and the respect of female guests.[8]

Narratives dealing with *la racaille* are central to how these adolescents evoke moralizing discourses regarding gender, generation, and space. At one point in this group discussion, Pierre attempts to assert a different stance, that the *racaille*, taken out of *la rue* are not morally corrupting to the respect of a family wedding, arguing, "but it's a wedding, *it's not the street.*" Yet, both Cécile and Mina clearly disagree, for they, like President Sarkozy, construct *la racaille* as discursively and morally metonymic—that is, as symbolic for the whole—of stigmatized public space in the *cité* and the illicit activity, namely drug dealing, that takes place there. At the same time, Cécile and Mina represent two distinct moral positions toward *la racaille*— Cécile's overtly stigmatizing and Mina's implicitly valorizing. Mina refrains from casting *la racaille* as immoral in their own right, but rather depicts their presence in the context of a respectful wedding as morally corrupting.

The divergent moral stances that Cécile and Mina articulate in relation to *la racaille* demonstrate the social ambivalence that adolescent girls experience in relation to their use of public, stigmatized spaces in Chemin de l'Ile. Although these and other adolescent girls in Chemin de l'Ile strategically use stigmatized public spaces in their *cité*, they are also morally implicated in gendered discourses that advocate their avoidance, and by extension, avoidance of *la racaille*. And yet, by articulating divergent moral positions toward *la racaille*, Cécile and Mina display their individually divergent spatializing practices and negotiate competing local definitions of *le respect*. For Cécile, this exchange constitutes the opportunity to craft a respectful persona for herself that involves avoiding the morally contaminating influence of *la racaille* just as she would like to avoid the contaminating influence of the *cité* by becoming a flight attendant. Mina constructs a very different persona for herself, while simultaneously constructing *la racaille* as threatening to the moral integrity of adult female guests at a family wedding. Rather than construct her own moral standing as commensurate with that of adult sisters and aunts, Mina crafts an alternate youthful and masculine form of respect for herself by implicitly valorizing the transgressive behaviors of *la racaille*.

In discourses that circulate at both national and local levels, *la racaille* are constructed as spatially and morally metonymic of stigmatized spaces in *cités*. In turn, narratives about *la racaille* come to invoke specific stigmatized spaces such as *la rue* ("the street"). In these ways, stories about *la racaille* contribute to the moral ordering of spaces. In mainstream French discourse, *la racaille* is a social group that is identified as morally corrupting of *cités* generally and constructed as needing to be removed (or "cleansed" as per Sarkozy's rhetoric) if a moral order is to be restored to these spaces. In Chemin de l'Ile, *la racaille* do not semiotically represent *cités* in a totalizing way, and yet neither is their supposedly corrupting moral influence confined only to "the street." In circulating stories about a Muslim wedding and *ḥalal* butcher shop, *la racaille* bring the stigma of the street with them when they move into these culturally sanctified spaces. Narratives about *la racaille* in Chemin de l'Ile thereby regulate "changes in space (or moves from one place to another)" (de Certeau 1984: 115).

Moreover, narratives about *la racaille* organize gender and generation in spatializing terms. In the casual talk analyzed here, adolescent girls position themselves in relation to *la racaille* in ways commensurate to their own use of (or desire to use) public space in their *cité*, but, in so doing, discursively construct an image of "the street" as masculine and stigmatized. Cécile and Mina collaboratively define and delimit this stigmatized masculine public space through their discursive construction of the respectful feminine space of a Muslim wedding and the supposedly endangered respect of its female participants. However, the gendered and generational discourses defining space here are quite complex; Mina discursively establishes public spaces in nearby stigmatized *cités*, Canibous, Pâquerettes, and Côtes D'Auty, as tough and masculine at the same time that she grants herself symbolic (if not physical) entry into them. Mina uses narrative to discursively navigate her own symbolic movement into these reputedly tough *cités* even though her actual physical access is impeded. Mina thereby establishes simultaneously a youthful, masculine style of respect for herself and "the guys" from these *cités* by displaying knowledge of these stigmatized spaces.

Dominant discourses such as those circulated in French politics and media about *la racaille* and *les cités* are formative for how individuals living in proximity to these social actors and spaces construct moral stances toward them. And yet, rarely are dominant discourses adopted wholesale. Here, dominant discourses are re-valued and transformed to suit political and social realities situated outside the French bourgeois mainstream. In the case of Mina and Cécile, adopting divergent stances toward the masculine and stigmatized social category *la racaille* becomes a way to construct divergent stances toward a normative "respectful" Muslim femininity and toward public space in their *cité*. Mina adopts many attributes of the dominant discourses about *la racaille*—in her narratives, they are stigmatized males, ethnically non-white, and socially contaminating drug dealers. And yet, she valorizes *la racaille* for their resistant stance toward authority and attempts to emulate their supposedly disruptive social behaviors and their reputation for a tough masculinity. Cécile's strategy is to distance herself from *la racaille* and *la cité* in order to craft an upwardly mobile and "modern" femininity in the guise of the flight attendant, equally unlike a "girl from the *cité*" and the supposedly demure "traditional" femininity of aunts and older sisters. The next chapter develops these issues by looking at a variety of communicative and stylistic strategies that teenaged girls use to broker a middle ground between conflicting models for femininity.

Locally circulating narratives about *la racaille* constitute one way for adolescents, and in particular female adolescents, to voice struggles over traditionalist and modern representations of femininity and to elaborate their own transcultural identities in relation to shifting notions of "respect" in their immigrant community. The French dominant discourses that have established *la racaille* at the center of a national moral panic about *cités* do influence how their inhabitants experience and perceive their neighborhoods, but in unexpected and contradictory ways. Mina and Cécile both employ but move beyond mainstream discourses in order to innovate forms of social recognition within their *cité* as well as to elaborate emergent norms regarding gender, space, and generation.

Notes

1   In my translation of Sarkozy's words, I use the term "bands" (*les bandes*) in order to preserve a crucial distinction between it and the American term "gangs." "Bands" (*les bandes*) is used in France to refer to groups of (usually) young men

who may or may not be involved in drug trade; they are not organized into nameable entities, and membership is informal.

2   A robust scholarly tradition has charted the political effects of similar criminalizing and racializing discourses in Europe, the United States, and elsewhere (Balibar 1991; Fairclough 2001; Hall et al. 1978; Gilroy 1991; Silverstein 2004; Smitherman-Donaldson and van Dijk 1988; van Dijk 1987, 1993). Far less scholarship has addressed how these discourses shape inhabitants' experience and use of space in the local communities that they purport to describe. Notable exceptions include Bourdieu et al. 1999; Essed 1991; Ghannam 2002; Modan 2007; Silverstein 2004; Urciuoli 1996; and Williams 1991.

3   For the some of the adolescents with whom I worked, stealing occupied a moral gray zone, with stealing goods from warehouses or work sites considered to be less morally offensive than stealing from individuals. Also, stealing within the neighborhood was considered by most to be completely immoral, whereas stealing outside of it was considered by some to be morally ambiguous.

4   *Halal* meat comes from an animal that is killed by having its throat slit so as to drain the body of blood and impurities. During the process, the animal must be blessed by an imam (Muslim religious leader).

5   Although in the discourse of these adolescents, this *mentalité* ("mentality") is located within the *bled* (usually Algeria), Jane Goodman (2005: 165–169) notes that anti-traditionalist and pro-modernist discourse against "old mentalities" also exists in Algeria, and is currently a major source of inspiration and conflict among younger generations of Algerians. She notes too that these conflicts over differing visions of society are often centered upon gender, much like the conflicts around "respect" that I discuss here.

6   In past literature on the Middle East and Mediterranean, scholars have referred to a similar moral code as *honor* and *shame*, thus compartmentalizing masculine and feminine behaviors (Peristiany 1976). In preserving adolescents' use of the term *le respect* for both genders, I avoid mapping a simple dichotomy onto a complex model of moral behavior. In this effort, I follow pathbreaking feminist scholarship, and in particular, Abu-Lughod (1986), who argues that both men and women experience both honor and modesty (rather than "shame"), but that they are differently conceived when applied to each gender. Also, my discussion of *le respect* resonates with Goodman's (2005: 166) discussion of "relationships of respect" in Algeria, in terms of the age-graded and gendered nature of deferential treatment of elders and/or "social superiors," but also in terms of the ways that younger generations are challenging the ideological basis of this system as an old-fashioned "mentality."

7   Similarly, *chelou* in this example is *verlan* (inverted slang) for *louche*, which means shifty or suspicious.

8   In addition to a social commentary on *la racaille*, this discussion provides insight into shifting cultural attitudes toward weddings as public social gatherings in the context of stigmatized French *cités*. Goodman documents that, although

weddings in 1960s Algeria were semi-private events held at home and attended by "members of each subpatrilineage," they have currently shifted to being public events that all villagers are expected to attend (2005: 89–90). As such, Algerian weddings currently provide a context where non-family members are able to socialize with the opposite sex in a public setting. In contrast, adolescents in Chemin de l'Ile express discomfort with the overly public nature of weddings in their *cité*, because they potentially conflict with the cultural value of *le respect*, which prescribes deference toward female relatives through seclusion from potentially contaminating social elements, such as *la racaille*.

CHAPTER 5

"YOU CALL THAT A GIRL?": GENDER CROSSING AND BORDERWORK

Further developing the relationships I have articulated thus far between gender and space, this chapter examines girls' use of purportedly masculine styles and social behaviors associated with the *cité*, as a way to identify with the local neighborhood and an alternative way to gain *le respect* among their peers. Such gendered style crossing constituted a main way that adolescent girls of Algerian descent in Chemin de l'Ile performed their transcultural identities as French teenagers living in a *cité* and as Arab Muslims attempting to fulfill culturally informed expectations of "respect" in their community. Nevertheless, girls were sometimes criticized by their peers for "trying to be men," demonstrating the contradiction and ambivalence central to many girls' experiences of adolescent identities and gendered norms within *cités*.[1]

In one exchange that involved both gender crossing and policing, I observed Hatice, a more typically feminine girl who tended to dress in jeans and tunics, say the following to Mina in reference to her baggy, brand-named sweat suits: "I like your style, it's funny (*marrant*)—half man and half woman." In the guise of a compliment, Hatice indicated that Mina had crossed appropriate gender boundaries by dressing "half man." Tellingly, rather than capitulate to Hatice's depiction of her, Mina provocatively corrected Hatice, "I'm half dyke and half fag" (*Je suis moitié gouine et moitié pédé*), showing that she was beyond such conventional gender identities as "woman" and "man." Mina's claim to be "half dyke and half fag" positioned

Transcultural Teens: Performing Youth Identities in French Cités, First Edition. Chantal Tetreault.
© 2015 John Wiley & Sons, Inc. Published 2015 by John Wiley & Sons, Inc.

her not only between genders, but also between transgressive homosexual identities. Her choice to evoke and blend the pejorative categories of "dyke" (*gouine*) and "fag" (*pédé*) was all the more transgressive due to the widely and openly espoused ideology of heteronormativity in the neighborhood.

Although Mina's claims might be interpreted as a literal expression of her sexual orientation, the comment seemed rather to reflect her choice to enact a transgressive gender identity. Mina was always openly interested in boys, and when I saw her several years later, she had a steady boyfriend. Nineteen at that time, she had started dying her hair blonde, wearing jewelry, and very feminine styles of clothing that displayed cleavage. When I commented on her new feminine look, she explained to me, "I have to, Chantal. Otherwise I look like a boy" (*C'est obligé, Chantal. Autrement je ressemble à un garçon*). Being rather slight and small, Mina decided to play up her shape as a way to be clearly feminine once she became an older adolescent. While seemingly incongruent, Mina's switch from an overtly masculine look to hyper-feminine style indicated her non-conformist attitudes toward gender norms in the neighborhood.

A similar, non-conformist pattern emerges in the examples explored in this chapter, in which adolescent girls sometimes resist local gender norms by adopting locally "masculine" styles and speech genres; in turn, their peers sometimes attempt to police girls' identities by constraining access to these gendered stylistic practices. In Chemin de l'Ile, girls confronted conflicting expectations for their behavior and communicative styles, including speech and dress. Girls were often pressured by their parents and peers to conform to a standard of feminine behavior commensurate with *le respect* ("respect"), which advocates avoiding most outdoor spaces and certain public places, as well as adopting modest dressing styles. And yet, teenaged girls in Chemin de l'Ile sometimes chose to occupy outdoor spaces in the neighborhood, and were often expected by their peers to adopt a tough demeanor as well as verbal and dress styles typical of the (sub-)urban spaces where they lived. In an effort to satisfy both potentially conflicting sets of expectations, many girls adopted spatial practices and styles affiliated with *cités*, but also locally with masculinity, in order to eschew an inappropriately sexualized femininity while exhibiting a high-profile personal identity.

As discussed previously, *le respect* is a transcultural prescriptive code of social etiquette that applies to teenaged boys and girls as well as to adults, but in ways that are gender and age specific as well as context specific. During ethnographic fieldwork and in my data, I observed evidence that adolescent girls were enacting both female-oriented "respect" as well as male-oriented "respect," depending upon the context and individual choices regarding self-presentation (Goffman 1959). In longitudinal interviews conducted in

2006, I asked Mina why she chose to adopt purportedly masculine clothing and language styles as a teenager, even when she was criticized for it. She answered, *"pour me faire respecter"* ("to make myself respected"). Here, Mina uses the reflexive verb *"se faire respecter"* to evoke a masculine-styled "respect" that is contingent upon exhibiting the tough, street-smart speech and dress that are typical of masculine etiquette in Chemin de l'Ile.

At the same time, another teen, Latifah, explained to me that she had "fought very hard" in the neighborhood to "make herself respected": *"Comment j'ai lutté pour me faire respecter!"* ("How (hard) I have fought to make myself respected!"). In this instance, although using identical language to Mina, Latifah was referring to her choices to remove herself socially and physically from the neighborhood by attending a high school in another *cité* and not dating (or even befriending) anyone from Chemin de l'Ile. In contrast to Mina, who embodied a masculine-styled *respect* by achieving a high-profile personal identity contingent upon her use of public space and masculine-styled dress and speech, Latifah sought to achieve personal freedom by embodying a feminine-styled *respect* through avoiding an overt, public presence in the neighborhood.

Le respect thus cannot be understood as a code that applies uniformly to all women and girls, but is rather a contextually based concept that is changing and variable, depending upon the individual and the presentation of self that she is attempting to craft. Similarly, in her work with Bedouin women, Lila Abu-Lughod notes that, rather than "honor" and "modesty" belonging to men and women exclusively, both men and women have honor but it is differently configured over the life course and in relation to gender identity. However, a difference between Abu-Lughod's observations and the patterns here is that, in addition to *le respect* being configured differently for women and men, it appears that teenaged girls in Chemin de l'Ile are working to achieve both feminine-styled and masculine-styled "respect," depending on individual and contextual sets of opportunities and constraints.

In some ways, this shifting between masculine-styled and feminine-styled "respect" is reminiscent of Abrahams' (1975) distinction between "reputation" and "respectability." Abrahams' work is based on his observations of working-class African-American women in the early 1970s caught between the social bind of attending to masculine-styled "reputation" through competitive verbal performance and to feminine-styled "respectability" through their own effacement from public space. Although helpful for my analysis of the conflicting gender expectations for girls in Chemin de l'Ile, Abrahams' distinction falls prey to essentializing women and men into uniform groups, as well as to prescribing two polarized social codes that are supposedly also non-overlapping, complementary, and mutually exclusive.

That said, some of the conflicting standards that Abrahams' observed for American working-class black women are relevant to teenaged girls in Chemin de l'Ile, such as his claim that working-class black women were socially expected to conform to a standard of both "respectable" behavior and to a code of tough, reputational verbal style. While conducting fieldwork, I observed that girls in the neighborhood were pressured by parents and peers to adhere to a standard of *le respect* that involved self-effacement from outdoor spaces and maintaining their virginity until marriage. While virginity is obviously not an outwardly perceptible quality, avoiding outdoor spaces and adopting modest dress styles were considered a way to secure a respectable image in the neighborhood.[2]

At the same time, other girls chose to adhere to local codes for masculine-styled "respect" among their peers, and many female teens were interested in demonstrating their prowess in competitive verbal practices and speech genres that I refer to here and in Chapter 2 as "*cité* styles." Such choices are not without risk; Mina was often criticized by peers for being too masculine. At the same time, Latifah was able to keep her personal identity separate from the neighborhood only for so long; several years down the road, after she got her own apartment and lived, unmarried, with her boyfriend, one of her brothers still refuses to speak to her out of anger that she did not conform to locally normative gender and sexual expectations for young women to remain virgins until marriage in their early to mid-twenties.[3]

In this chapter, I deal with the ways that girls are pressured to conform to a standard of *le respect* that delimits their access to outdoor spaces and local styles in Chemin de l'Ile. The tough reputation that adolescent boys often aspire to in *les cités* is constituted by linguistic and symbolic resources that are less available to adolescent girls. I examine how the boundaries of gender are enforced through a variety of practices, including teasing and evaluative comments by peers. Integral to these processes are the ways that spaces and uses of space come to be gendered within the neighborhood; spatial configurations and ideologies about space are tied to gender ideologies and embodied stylistic practices, including language and dress.

All the same, girls attempt to access speech genres and dress styles that are central to a tough, local aesthetic of adolescent interaction, even though they are symbolically considered masculine. Adolescent girls thereby make a bid for a tough reputation among their peers and thereby challenge normative gender roles. Nevertheless, teenaged girls' choices in representing themselves are achieved in dialogue with their peers' critical evaluations of their behavior.

Barrie Thorne's (1993) pair of metaphors to describe gendered symbolic work, *borderwork* and *crossing*, are particularly useful for describing the pattern of episodic enforcement and infraction of symbolic divisions between genders that I describe here. In Thorne's terms, girls' strategic use of styles and attributes associated with masculinity constitute forays across gender boundaries, or "crossing," which are countered by their peers' social and verbal patrolling of the borders of gender identity, or "borderwork."[4] Tracking the push and pull of transgression and constraint present in adolescent girls' performances of *cité* styles reveals the mutually informing yet often conflicting relationship between emergent gender identities and extant ideologies of gender.

Le Respect, Gender, and Space

As Gal (2002: 3) notes, the metaphors "[P]ublic and private do not simply describe the social world in any direct way; they are rather tools for arguments about and in that world." Discursive constructions of space are thus ideological and must be considered in the context of cultural and political landscapes. In Chemin de l'Ile, a central organizing spatial metaphor that is ideological is *dehors* ("outside"). Much like "public" and "private" in Western discourse (Gal 2002; 2005), *dehors* seems, at first blush, to be merely referential; however, in local discourse, this term indexes a cascade of associated behaviors, persons, and moral judgments. Within this associative system of indexes, *la rue* ("the street") is locally constructed as the most potentially dangerous and stigmatizing space that is semiotically situated under the rubric of *dehors*.

Gal (2005: 26) notes that public/private distinctions come to stand in ideologically for other sets of relations in a three-part process that involves "differentiation," "fractal recursivity," and "erasure." A similar process is at work in the set of distinctions made with respect to ideologically motivated spatial metaphors *dehors* and *la rue* in Chemin de l'Ile. A contrastive, ideological difference is posited by the spatial metaphor *dehors*, in that it is implicitly compared in local discourse with *chez soi* or "home." For example, a critique of adolescent girls by adult relatives or neighbors that was so formulaic that I overheard it many times (either in jest or in earnest) was, "*Tu es tout le temps dehors. Rentre chez toi!*" ("You're outside all the time. Go home!"). Whereas in an English-speaking context this critique loses its bite, in Chemin de l'Ile, among French-speaking North African descendants, *dehors* was often used to index the inappropriate use or overuse of outdoor space. Much like the ideological distinction "private" and "public" that Gal analyzes, *dehors* was used metaphorically in local discourse to describe a host of activities and persons, as in the commonly used expression *se traîner dehors*, roughly meaning, "to loiter outside," or literally, "to drag (oneself) along outside."

Although young or adolescent men were often expected by their parents and older relatives to spend time *traîner dehors* (whether their caretakers fully approved or not), such behavior was considered highly stigmatized for young women. In addition to certain persons, *traîner dehors* was ideologically associated with certain activities such as *le business* ("illicit trade or sale of goods"). Furthermore, through three often linked processes of differentiation, fractal recursivity, and erasure that Gal and Irvine identify (2000), *dehors* or "outside" was further divided into spaces considered more and less exposed and/or stigmatized. For example, inhabitants in Chemin de l'Ile drew a sharp distinction between the most stigmatized, most exposed "outdoor" space, *la rue*, which was routinely associated with youthful masculinity, illicit economic exchange, as well as *la racaille*, and more protected, less public outdoor spaces such as *le terrain de jeu* or "playground," which were often occupied by adolescent girls, young children, and women. Thus, through fractal recursivity, distinct spaces "outside" (*dehors*) were improbably (in that all of these spaces were literally "outdoors") but ideologically divided and contrasted into spaces considered "more" or "less" exposed/protected, masculine/feminine, and public/private.

And yet through erasure, such differences could also be elided or temporarily suppressed, as in the case when I observed an adolescent girl sitting on a bench hanging out with friends in the playground and watching younger children play. She was told (laughingly, but pointedly) by an adult female relative and neighbor, "*arrête de traîner sur cette banquette comme un clochard*" ("stop loitering on that bench like a 'bum'" [homeless man]). In an instant, the more enclosed, feminine, and less stigmatized outdoor space of the playground was metaphorically transformed through erasure into a public park bench upon which was no longer a female adolescent watching children play, but a decrepit man who had no home at all. Similar to Gal's discussion of the ideologically motivated set of metaphors, public and private, here erasure occurs through the conflation of differing scales in which a delimited amount of time outdoors in physically protected and feminized space is re-cast as the ultimate, permanent "outdoor" experience—having nowhere inside to go due to homelessness. In this case, the process of differentiation, fractal recursivity, and erasure is used as an ideologically laden, if humorous, warning to the young woman not to venture "too far" physically and morally.

In these ways, ideological discourses concerning *dehors*, *traîner*, and *la rue* informed gender norms in Chemin de l'Ile. Young men are also implicated in these discourses, but on different terms. Whereas adolescent boys and young men are expected to spend more time *dehors*, stigmatizing discourses around *la rue* and *traîner* could also be used to mark them as troublemakers or *la racaille*, who come to stand in for *la rue*, discussed in Chapter 4. Young women are not expected to spend much time outdoors or to loiter. When younger, girls are told that they are "acting like men or boys" when they are *dehors* and *traîner*; when older, they are presumed to be acting in inappropriately sexualized ways, looking for sexual encounters. Although adolescent boys and young unmarried men are expected to *traîner dehors* more than girls, when they exceed the expected amounts or limits of this behavior, they are presumed to be involved in illegal economic pursuits or criminality.

For example, Aïcha, a 40-year-old mother whom I met while conducting literacy training at the neighborhood association *Les Acacias*, spent hours standing by the window each night to watch her 16-year-old son, Amir, in the parking lot below her building, due to fears that his time *dehors* with friends might mean that he was involved in *le business*. At the same time, whereas she would not allow her daughter Latifah, the 18-year-old teen mentioned earlier, to spend time *dehors* that was unaccounted for, Aïcha acknowledged that, because her son was 16, "*je n'y suis pour rien—il est grand maintenant*" ("I can do nothing—he is big (adult) now"). Instead, she worried and spent time surreptitiously monitoring his activities outdoors, hoping that the extended time he spent with neighborhood friends in the parking lot below was not an indication of illegal activity. Amir never got involved in drug dealing, but he was open about his intention at that time of wanting to be involved in certain kinds of *business* such as the local sale of either smuggled or fenced cellphones, perfume, and clothing.

On one evening when I was visiting Aïcha, the "street" and "home" collided when Amir brought home a cell phone that he tried to sell to his father, who initially expressed interest, at which point his mother, Aïcha, said "*jamais chez moi!*" ("never in my home!"). Hence, even though there was an overt understanding that young men's movements in outdoor space could not and should not be controlled or curtailed to the degree that girls' were, there were limits, and, in many families, conflicts revolved around establishing such limits for boys as well as girls.

In addition to different expectations for the amount of time spent *dehors*, *le respect* posits a preference for men and women to occupy separate outdoor, public spaces in Chemin de l'Ile. Further, because most outside and many public spaces in the neighborhood (parking lots, building entryways, areas around housing for single male workers, the Sports Center, the Municipal Youth Center, the train station, the local café) were occupied by men and boys, there was a general preference among parents of adolescent girls that they limit their time outside (*dehors*) as much as possible. Thus, prescriptive discourses about how girls and boys should use outdoor, public space are central to the construction of gender norms in Chemin de l'Ile.

This discrepancy also derives, in part, from the widespread and contested ideology in Algeria, and across North Africa generally, that because men occupy most outdoor public spaces, these spaces are potentially dangerous to an unmarried woman's virtue (i.e., virginity), and generally for her own and her family's "respect."[5] However, this assumption is also prevalent in local discourses that associate outdoor spaces in the *cité* (referred disparagingly to as *dehors* or *la rue*, "the street") with immoral or dangerous behavior considered especially inappropriate for women and girls, such as prostitution and selling illegal drugs. Among the few spaces in Chemin de l'Ile that are unofficially designated for women and girls are several small playgrounds with children's climbing toys; these areas are located in between tall apartment buildings and are often less visible from the street than parking lots and the local café, where adolescent boys and unmarried men tend to congregate. In contrast, as a place designated for small children, these playgrounds were regarded as appropriate spaces for mothers and adolescent girls to use to sit outside and visit, weather permitting. One such playground consisted of a small cement structure enclosing a play space with slides and ladders for older children and a fenced space with toys for toddlers. Benches and a low cement wall surrounded the space, making it a pleasant place to sit on sunny days. Adolescent girls who lived nearby, and once in a while a boy or two, used this playground to hang out and talk after school.

In addition to the informal segregation of women and men into separate if contiguous outdoor spaces, girls and women generally carefully limited their time outdoors. While some married women sat in the small playground described earlier to chat in the afternoons, others avoided outdoor socializing for fear that doing so would foster gossip about them. I remember one afternoon walking to the market with Madame Hamdani, an adult, married woman from Algeria whose family I eventually lived with. She was worried about seeing her father-in-law on the street, claiming it was not good that he see her, because it made it look like she was "outside" (*dehors*) all the time.[6] Although she did not routinely wear a headscarf, she used the hood of her sweater to quickly cover her hair and walked on. When it came time to cross his path, she greeted him as briefly as possible with a few words and a warm smile and we scurried on our way, no time for chitchat.

Personally, I was particularly aware of the code of *le respect* because, as a single woman, I was initially not always accorded respectful treatment when alone. Once I moved into Chemin de l'Ile, any local trip involved crossing the public parking lot in front of my building—a regular hangout for many young men in the *cité*. (I later learned that most teenaged girls and young women avoided crossing the parking lot when possible.) When alone in the parking lot, and particularly before I moved into the neighborhood, I was loudly greeted and flirted with. One man went so far as to publicly ask me out on a date in front of his friends as I walked by. However, whenever I walked by with Madame Hamdani, none of the young men would speak to us unless she initiated the interaction, conceivably out of respect for her. Chatting adolescent boys and young men allowed her to pass by in feigned anonymity unless she initiated the verbal exchange. Madame Hamdani felt completely justified in doing so. A main way that she would initiate a verbal exchange might be in the form of a request for help—lugging something to her front door, for example, if one of her older sons could not be found. Adolescent boys and young men in this case would follow local rules for *le respect* of one's elders by doing what was asked, with no complaints or questions.

The type of cross-gendered and cross-generational respect that Madame Hamdani enjoyed among her teenaged sons' peers was largely due to her status as a married woman and mother who generally complied with gender norms for avoiding outdoor space, except when conducting "official" family duties, such as going to the local open-air market. Such was not automatically the case with young, unmarried women, however. Take, for example, Aïcha's daughter Latifah, the 18-year-old woman whom I introduced earlier. Latifah often described the great effort that she exerted to attain "respect," often by avoiding neighborhood space entirely. Once Latifah explained to me how happy she was on a night during her walk home from the RER (train) station. There was a car full of young men from the neighborhood sitting in a car parked in front, playing the radio very loudly. As she passed by, they lowered the sound, an act that Latifah interpreted as highly respectful. She felt that night that all of her "hard work" (as she put it) had paid off, because she had finally won the respect of young men in the neighborhood. Some of Latifah's ongoing "fight" or "struggle" (*lutte*) for this respect had taken the form of absenting herself from the neighborhood itself, including attending high school in a neighboring suburb.

In addition to attending a more academically challenging school than the one in Nanterre, Latifah was able to avoid all of the hassles of daily interactions with young men from the neighborhood and escape the possibility of surveillance, by her peers and, indirectly, her parents. Her strategy worked quite well throughout high school because she was able to neatly separate her school life, including friends, from her life within the local neighborhood, preserving a level of anonymity in Chemin de l'Ile that seemed to ensure her more access to the "respect" that she desired.

As second- and third-generation adolescents within a predominantly Algerian immigrant community, girls in Chemin de l'Ile are negotiating more than just so-called "traditional" gender norms, a misnomer since many local norms are the product of an intersection of the effects of diaspora and the physical spaces of *cités*. Adolescent girls are negotiating conflicting social expectations inherent to a context where discourses about femininity shift between transcultural rejections of "French (im)morality" and local re-imaginings of "Arab or Muslim traditions." Also at play are emergent *cité* codes of conduct that often conflict with both of these ideological positions, but which still posit public, outdoor space and, more generally, a *cité* identity as the domain of boys and men, adding to the ambivalence about social roles for girls and women in the community. Girls' own interpretations of these performances were more akin to rejecting constraining discourses about femininity and *la mentalité du bled* ("*bled* mentality"), including the tendency to associate femininity and masculinity, respectively, with domestic and outdoor spaces in the neighborhood.

Gender and Generation in Gatherings at Local Associations

Whereas, in an effort to preserve *le respect*, even members of the same family might avoid publicly acknowledging a member of the opposite sex on the street, this kind of respectful distance is often impossible to maintain at gatherings in the public spaces of neighborhood associations. Ritualized avoidance between genders is both challenged and reinforced through the ways that local associations organize gender in such public events.

In a consciously labeled "inter-generational" event, the association SMJ (*Salle Municipale de Jeunesse* or "Municipal Youth Center") sponsored a picnic and cultural event, to promote communication and understanding between generations in the neighborhood. "Generations" in this event, both during the planning meetings that I attended and the event itself, were mainly interpreted as immigrant parents in contrast to "second-" and "third-generation" adolescent children. Events to foster mutual understanding and communication included cultural displays, music performed by an older Italian man (even though the presence of the Italian community was next to none), and performances by young neighborhood kids, and rap and vocalist performances. There was an after-party as well that was deejayed by a local professional. As usual, a good portion of the North African food on sale at the event was prepared by mothers of adolescent association members at no cost to the association except the groceries. Barbecued *ḥalal* sausages were also grilled by a few male adolescents to earn proceeds for an upcoming beach trip, chaperoned by SMJ.

Despite all of the well-intentioned discussion and planning about inter-generational participation, the actual event was fraught with tensions about improprieties regarding generation and gender mixing in a public space. For instance, I spent a large portion of my time during the deejayed dancing urging Madame Hamdani to dance with me, to no avail. I found out later from her daughter that her teenaged son had begged her not to dance for fear of embarrassing him and seemingly in an effort to uphold standards for respectful mixed-gender interaction. His sister interpreted his request as evidence of how a young man's "respect" among his friends is contingent (in part, at least) upon his female relatives' behavior.

As with Madame Hamdani, no other mothers or fathers danced at this party. In fact, almost no fathers actually attended this party, which repre-sented in itself a type of informal gender segregation typically practiced among North African families in the neighborhood. Events associated with school, youth associations, and school-aged children were considered the domain of women and their responsibility, since they are often primarily responsible for raising children. Conceivably, in an effort to foster "inter-generational" exchanges (which the organization seemed to interpret as largely father–son interactions), the Municipal Youth Center had neglected to allow for the fact that mothers in Chemin de l'Ile generally participated more in children's activities.

Even with the general absence of fathers at this particular party, other intergenerational interaction seemed to embarrass the adolescents present, perhaps lending justification for the need of such events. For example, when I tried to dance with a group of teenaged girls, some of whom I knew from *Cerise*, they too expressed embarrassment about my presence by exclaiming "oh no!" and stopped dancing when I approached. Undoubtedly, my status as an adult tutor at the association made it embarrassing for them to dance with me, particularly in front of the adolescent boys watching nearby whom the girls were likely hoping to impress. The inter-generational goal of the event was overshadowed by an overtly youthful, co-ed feeling at the gathering, in which the young were distinctly uncomfortable with dancing in the presence of adults.

Part of the apparent tension at the gathering stemmed from the fact that cross-gendered and "intergenerational" mixing were so at odds with everyday practices in the SMJ and in Chemin de l'Ile. This association spent most of its resources targeting boys and young men, presumably due to the fact that its mission was oriented to crime and gang prevention, activities assumed to involve boys more than girls. Many adolescent girls told me that they never used the resources at SMJ (free Internet, career counseling, etc.) because they just did not feel comfortable in that space—there were "too many guys" (*"trop de mecs"*). However, at this particular event, the tensions surrounding gender mixing seemed specific to the context of the "inter-generational" setting, rather than tensions about gender mixing per se. Had only teenagers been present, the mixed-gender dancing would not have been nearly as problematic, and indeed as adults (myself included) started leaving at around 8 pm, I noticed that a group of boys began to dance across the room from some of the girls whom I had originally pestered. All of this is to say that public gender mixing is not simply considered shameful in relation to girls' virtue, but also inappropriate in terms of an age hierarchy, which dictates that younger people show *le respect* to older folks by maintaining the appearance of gender segregation.

The need for such public propriety between generations is entirely contingent upon whether the event involves gender mixing. For example, a very different setting in which I experienced "intergenerational" dancing was a couscous party at another neighborhood association called *Les Acacias* ("The Acacia Trees"). The director, Pascale, who had started a program of women's literacy classes, decided to sponsor an all-women party to promote "cross-cultural friendship and understanding" among the North African and sub-Saharan-African women belonging to the association.

Having completed extensive preparations of couscous and North African teacakes earlier that day, about 20 women arrived to eat and dance, including some impromptu guests, despite the express desire articulated by Pascale and Rebecca that only *les adhérents* ("paying members") should come. Also, although children were not encouraged to come, several women had brought their children anyway, making it an organically "inter-generational" event. One Algerian woman, Hanan, brought her sister, Leïla. A Moroccan woman, Fatiha, brought her niece. Aïcha brought her oldest daughter Latifah. Madame Hamdani brought her adolescent daughter Yemina, as did Madame Mira with Zeinab. Miriam came with her mother, Madame BenHabib.

Dancing was central to the event, and everyone participated. Leïla told me that she had only agreed to bring her 8-year-old daughter on the condition that she dance. Her daughter was apparently quite shy, and she initially refused. Eventually she warmed up to the idea toward the end of the evening. When I complimented her on her dancing (she really was dancing well), her mom said something like "You see? You can dance when you want to." Aïcha's daughter Latifah danced, but regretted her choice of wearing pants—it was not the same without a skirt, she claimed. Women's dancing across the Maghrib is characterized by vigorous hip movements that are better executed and more visible in a skirt. Additionally, women and girls often tie scarves around their hips when dancing to further accentuate their movements.

Within this single-sex, inter-generational space, participants were open to sexualized dancing and bawdy joking, demonstrating the contextual nature of sexual discourses and practices with respect to gender and space. Madame BenHabib, Miriam's mother, came out with the first batch of tea, shaking her behind and dancing in an exaggerated, raunchy way. I jokingly pinched her butt and then looked around the room nervously to see if people were offended. Far from it—Aïcha started to play drums on Madame BenHabib's backside, offering simply the explanation dərbuka! or "drum" in Arabic. We all laughed. Afterward, Madame BenHabib made everyone laugh all the harder because she said in Arabic: "I only did that because there's no more tea!" That is, she was jokingly shaking her behind as a distraction so that those without tea would not feel slighted.

A generation older than Madame BenHabib, Madame Mira was one of the most respected and politically active women in Chemin de l'Ile. She had grown up in the shantytowns (bidonvilles) that epitomized the early Algerian immigrant experience in Nanterre and had hidden there, alone with her sister, the night of Paris massacre on October 17, 1961. During a pro-independence protest of 30,000 led by the Algerian FLN party, an estimated 200 were murdered by police, often by being drowned in the Seine (Swedenburg 2001: 77). Fortunately, although Madame Mira's parents were there at the demonstration, they were not among those killed. On the present night, however, Madame Mira was quite the image of playful impropriety as she danced with a woman from Cameroon, Agnès, who was closing in on her, hips leading the way. Madame Mira protested in a rough, masculine, and seemingly aroused voice, "You're turning me on! You're turning me on, there!" ("Tu me provoques! Tu me provoques, là!"). As she said this, Madame Mira took the two ends of the scarf tied around her hips and pointed them toward Agnès, in the shape of an erect penis. Predictably, the only shocked woman in the room was the ethnographer.

This party shows the ways that neighborhood associations can create spaces for women and girls to participate in the irreverent, albeit confined, subversion of their public "respectable" personas. During daily operations of local associations, however, sex segregation was often a less conscious mode of operation that served to reinforce negative aspects of this cultural practice. One of the ways that the separation of girls and boys in public space is perpetuated is through neighborhood associations in Chemin de l'Ile that do not mandate co-ed programs. Thanks to Shakira, a feminist social worker from Algeria, the scholastic programs for middle-school adolescents at *Cerise* grew more and more "feminine" over the course of the year and a half that I worked there. However, the association's "prevention" (anti-criminality) programs were almost exclusively used by adolescent boys and young men. Some of this segregation also occurred more "naturally," in that girls and boys would sign up for homework sessions the same night as their friends, resulting in some nights with more girls or boys, respectively. As the association became more popular with middle-school-aged girls, boys stopped attending as much.

Conversely, the "prevention" programs aimed at scholastic failure and criminality by this same association (which took place at another site) were almost exclusively male because adolescent boys constituted their target population for delinquency. However, as several of the boys involved in the program informed me, the "real" delinquents (such as local, small-scale drug dealers) were not usually a part of the various outings and overnight trips that the association planned because they were considered too tough (*dur*) among the association staff. The result of these practices was that non-delinquent adolescent boys with no particular problems with criminal activity tended to go on many more extended outings away from the neighborhood, such as beach and skiing trips, than girls did.

In other municipally funded clubs and centers within the neighborhood, such as the aforementioned SMJ, adolescent girls were also excluded from activities by design. Many of the activities that boys and young men attended at the SMJ were formally organized outings, especially during summer. When I mentioned the lack of services for girls to the director of SMJ, he told me that girls did indeed participate in outings and other services, but that they tended to "organize themselves differently in the neighborhood" (*elle s'organisaient différemment que les garçons dans le quartier*). Girls would apparently approach the Municipal Youth Center with a plan in mind and with many of the all-female participants already secured.

The reasons for this divergently gendered treatment of teens are potentially multiple. On the one hand, as a female association worker of North African descent who had worked in many other neighborhoods outside of Chemin de l'Ile pointed out to me, gender relations among adolescents in a neighborhood largely depended upon the politics of the local structures in place, including associations, and whether they had a policy of creating co-ed environments or not. On the other hand, according to the director of SMJ, the general atmosphere of Nanterre was quite (religiously and culturally) conservative, compared to other, demographically similar suburbs that he had worked in. One aspect of this "conservatism" was expressed in religious practice. Nanterre, which had its own mosque, was a community with supposedly more practicing Muslims than other communities. However, these justifications for what I found to be fairly discriminatory practices with respect to girls and young women ignored the ways that state-funded local associations tended to reinforce or even establish male privilege in the community. Thus, in the name of "respect" for "tradition," federally funded French institutions such as neighborhood "youth" centers often solidified sexism and the exclusion of girls. This pattern of federally funded exclusion is particularly ironic in light of the multiple forms of anti-veiling laws that the French government has passed in a supposed attempt to "protect" Muslim girls and women from discrimination and sexism in their communities (Bowen 2007; Scott 2007; Selby 2012).

In a similar fashion, the local municipally funded Sports Center was often the unofficially designated space of boys and adolescent males. On the few occasions when I visited the Sports Center, girls were only present in organized sports teams and lessons, whereas boys were informally playing sports on indoor and outdoor courts. Only once in a year and a half of fieldwork did a group of girls and I go over to play basketball informally. On this particular outing, I realized that one reason that some girls participated so little at the Sports Center was for fear of "being seen" there or on the way there, either by their parents or by other locals who would tell their parents. Specifically, some girls worried about compromising propriety by crossing in front of the men's residences for single immigrant workers that lay directly in the path between the association *Cerise* and the Sports Center.

Although institutional structures often aligned with conservative gender norms in Chemin de l'Ile, individual actors working within them have the power to challenge the status quo. While I conducted my fieldwork in Chemin de l'Ile, a group of girls formed a soccer team to compete in the annual neighborhood soccer tournament. Sami, a newly hired male mentor at *Cerise*, who came originally from Marseilles and was of Cameroonian heritage, organized an all-girls' soccer team to play in the tournament, which was usually comprised of only male teams. It was the first time in memory that girls had played in the tournament, and they ended up in second place, to the great pleasure of the girls on the team and Sami. Preparations for the tournament, however, were an interesting lesson in how girls and their parents were constantly evaluating and negotiating "appropriate" behavior for girls in public space to a different degree than for boys.

One girl of 13, Kalilah, had originally signed up to play, but dropped out. When I asked her why, she simply claimed that she did not want to. Her continued presence on the sidelines at practice and the way she teased the playing girls, however, seemed indicative of her own (and undoubtedly her parents') ambivalence toward girls playing sports in public. She and other girls on the sidelines would yell, "Oh, look at the guys ("chaps") there" ("*Regarde les bonhommes, là*"), using a phrase that was generally used to criticize girls who dressed "too much like men." Kalilah was not considered one of the girls who dressed "like a guy" in sweats and tennis shoes, but rather dressed in the popular feminine style of button-down tunics over tight black polyester pants with black leather platform shoes. Some of the other girls playing on the team, such as Hamida, appeared to be proud to be called "bonhomme" and referred to themselves that way in their own defense, for example, "yes, I'm a 'guy'—so what?" ("*oui, j'suis un bonhomme— et alors?*"). In these ways, although individual choices and strategies differed, adolescent girls in Chemin de l'Ile generally negotiated difficult choices regarding their gendered self-presentation and how to best manage the pressures of parents and peers.

Intimate Spaces: Dating, Sexuality, and Marriage

In the preceding sections, I describe how women and girls in Chemin de l'Ile negotiate *le respect* through attention to behaviors in the neighborhood space, including *dehors* and the semi-public spaces of neighborhood associations. In this section, I look at how adolescent girls' bodies and related practices such as dating and dress styles constitute an intimate space for contesting and policing the transcultural code of *le respect*. The interconnected and mutually informing frameworks of gender and space are central to social discourses and personal decisions about dating, sexuality, and marriage for teens in Chemin de l'Ile. Similar to the ways that space is operative at multiple levels and scales in my discussion of *le respect* earlier, space is also concerned at multiple levels and scales regarding specific choices and concerns around teens' romantic relationships. Most generally, space is configured and is central to these concerns in two major ways: (1) how *physical space* is configured in the neighborhood and the social effects of that space, and (2) how spatial relations are imagined in terms of *provenance*, that is, where a person is "from" matters at multiple social levels and spatial scales.

Dating among adolescents in Chemin de l'Ile was a complex undertaking that usually involved secrecy regarding the couple's identity and relationship. Physical space in the neighborhood is a factor in this regard; the roughly 11,400 inhabitants in Chemin de l'Ile (according to the 1999 census) live in an area of less than a square mile, of which roughly one-third is occupied by an industrial park. Twelve-story high-rise subsidized apartment buildings located in the center of the neighborhood and one main street meant that most daily activity, including the comings and goings of inhabitants, were easily observed from windows above. Also, close social networks—the majority of inhabitants with Algerian descent had migrated from just two towns—contributed to the focused attention paid to everyday (self- and other-) monitoring of behaviors and reputations.

During early adolescence (13–16 years), the enterprise of "dating" (sortir avec quelqu'un) in Chemin de l'Ile seemed very chaste. Even those adolescents who were purportedly dating someone were generally not sexually active. Thus, the local version of "dating" usually only involved relatively infrequent, illicit meetings during the day, usually inside or, more rarely, outside the neighborhood, and some physical contact such as kissing, but much more interaction through phone calls, texting, and chatting online. Rather than much time spent in intimate contact by "couples," dating habits among teens in Chemin de l'Ile were characterized by intense discussion and interactions among same-sex peers about the romantic relationships. Information about who was dating whom thus became a form of social capital to share or withhold in everyday interactions among peers.

Teens were very protective of information about each other's dating habits; aside from one couple (Sarah and Tarek, both 15) who were openly dating, I had no specific knowledge of other adolescent couples, even though most teens claimed ambiguously to be "seeing someone." Sarah's and Tarek's situation was unlike other teens' in that Sarah was not of Algerian descent; her mother was Cambodian and her father French. Furthermore, Sarah was living in Chemin de l'Ile as a foster child in a North African family along with her brother and sister, adding to the relatively low level of parental constraint upon her. Even so, Sarah and Tarek were never seen holding hands or kissing in outdoor spaces in the neighborhood, presumably to conform to local expectations for le respect, which dictated keeping youthful sexuality separate from spaces and contexts in which older adults were present.

In addition to the general desire on the part of most adolescents to conform, at least outwardly, to local standards of le respect, secrecy about dating among adolescents was strategic, in that it kept such personal information from parents and older siblings. This privacy was considered particularly important for girls, since many told me that they would be made to stay at home or punished if their parents found out they were dating. The importance of maintaining secrecy—for example, never being seen in public with one's boyfriend—was something even women in their twenties claimed to practice in the neighborhood.

One such woman was Dalilah, a volunteer mentor at *Cerise* who had grown up in Chemin de l'Ile, and, at the time of my interview with her, was 23 years old. She explained that she was currently dating a man who had also grown up in the neighborhood, and who continued to live there with his extended family, as did she. She told me that it was "impossible" for her relationship be public knowledge in the neighborhood, and that she avoided being seen with him there. She laughingly complained that, ironically, she and her boyfriend had to take the RER (commuter train) separately to Paris whenever they wanted to see each other. Only when and if Dalilah and her boyfriend decided to marry and got engaged could she feel at ease with their relationship being public information. Such decisions are also made to protect a young woman's reputation with a view to marriage. Dalilah and her boyfriend subsequently broke up, and keeping their relationship out of public view presumably prevented it from negatively influencing Dalilah's future marriage prospects. More serious dating in one's late teens or early twenties may involve sexual intercourse but with serious risks for girls and young women.

In the same informal interview, Dalilah laughingly told me that, when she was in middle school, her older brother would not let his male friends even look at her in his presence, for example, in the schoolyard. Rather than threatening, Dalilah found this behavior funny because her brother never made her aware of it, and because they were both so young at the time. In fact, Dalilah only found out about her brother's protectiveness much later when she attended an academic high school with a number of his friends, whereas her brother attended trade school instead.

This example demonstrates how a potential romantic relationship between a boy's friend and sister may pose problems to the ideology of a male sibling as sexual "protector." However, it also indicates that these issues often arise when the siblings in question are pre-teens or younger teens (middle-schoolers in France), probably due to the high level of anxiety and tension around sexuality that most teens experience prior to becoming sexually active. Furthermore, this is not to say that all adolescent boys and men try to claim this moral authority over their sisters, wives, and mothers. In many families that I was familiar with in Chemin de l'Ile, older and younger brothers had little or no authority over their sisters, as was clearly the case with Dalilah, since she was unaware of her brother's anxiety about her socializing with his friends. At the same time, the fact that there exists a potential for brothers to act as moral "protectors" of their sisters might cause women and girls to censure their own romantic desires in some instances.

Many of the gendered dynamics that I describe here are generalizable to *les cités* and should not be attributed merely to youth of North African descent, since these spaces are culturally, ethnically, and religiously quite diverse. In these ways, diasporic transcultural practices and spatializing practices intersect and transform local moral landscapes. An example from the SMJ intergenerational party gives evidence for how codes of *le respect* are being transformed and adopted by non-North Africans in the neighborhood. Madame Hamdani's daughter Yemina overheard Thomas, a black (non-Arab), middle-school-aged boy say to a boy of North African descent, "Don't stand next to my sister." The other boy answered back "We're just talking," and Thomas said "You're standing next to my sister and you know that isn't done" (*"Tu sais que ça ne se fait pas"*). Seeing that the other boy would not comply with his demand, Thomas told his sister to go home, and she left the party.

In one of the many ways that personal relationships were spatially configured through *provenance*, some teens preferred not to date inside the neighborhood because they considered it "too close" physically and socially. To avoid the potential impropriety of being seen with a boy in the neighborhood, some girls used the strategy of absenting themselves from the local space for dating. I was told by several adolescents that it was "dangerous" to date a boy from the neighborhood because peers and, consequently, relatives could find out and respond by curtailing outings and freedoms for fear of the girl's threatened virtue. Other girls claimed that since "all the guys know each other" among nearby *cités*, it was not safe to date boys from another local neighborhood either. However, in apparent contradiction to the fears attached to openly dating, meeting new boyfriends was sometimes orchestrated by female peers.[7] This practice could lead to conflicts between friends as this next anecdote about Mina and Béatrice illustrates.

At one time, Béatrice was going out with a boy that she really liked, but who had apparently disrespected her in public. (I was not told how.) Mina took objection to this treatment and convinced Béatrice to break up with the boy and to start going out with another boy that she had picked for her. Béatrice did, in fact, begin dating this other boy for a short time, and Mina felt he treated Béatrice better that the first boy. However, Béatrice decided she preferred the first boy, and started going out with him again, to the intense disapproval of Mina. She argued directly with Béatrice about her choice and later criticized Béatrice publicly for her decision to date a boy who would disrespect her. This conflict was so intense that it temporarily interrupted the girls' friendship. An important aspect of this conflict is that it demonstrates that, for younger adolescents, one of the more important components of heterosexual "dating" involves homosocial peer socialization toward sexuality and romance; simply put, for younger adolescents (13–16 years), "dating" is an activity that is played out to a large extent among one's same-sex peers through conversations, gossip, conflicts, and resolutions.[8] Negotiating inter-personal control among same-sex peers was a particularly central activity with respect to "dating" for younger teens in Chemin de l'Ile.

For older teens and young women, negotiations of social and inter-personal control might be more central to the romantic relationship itself. For example, young women might negotiate the level of control that boyfriends would demand over their self-presentation, including dress and hairstyles. Sherazade was a woman of Tunisian descent who did not grow up in a *cité* but rather in non-subsidized housing; she was 22 and a paid tutor at *Cerise* when I knew her. She told me that her four older brothers had never told her who or how to date. Sherazade said that she could talk about everything with them, including guys. However, her latest love interest, a young man who was also French of Tunisian heritage, did not work out because of her perception that he was too controlling of her. Sherazade recounted that she had once gone to meet him in a short (above the knee) skirt and opaque tights, and he complained, "hey, what is that skirt you're wearing?!" (*"hé, c'est quoi cette jupe?!"*). On another occasion, he told her to pull back her hair and not to wear makeup even though she usually wore her hair down and used eyeliner.

When Sherazade decided to break up with him, her mother consoled her, saying, as long as she did not lose her virginity she could do what she wanted. Her mother added that, in the Qur'an, there is nothing that prohibits girls and women from going out on dates, only that they should stay virgins until marriage. However, when Sherazade told this story to me, the American non-Muslim ethnographer, she quipped: "I'm still a virgin, I'm not ashamed to say it" (*"je suis encore vierge j'ai pas honte de le dire"*). The contrast among her ex-boyfriend's behavior, her mother's advice, and her admission to me that she was not "ashamed" to be a virgin highlight the contradiction and ambivalence that young French women of North African descent negotiate when choosing how to date and with whom. On one hand, they might experience potential criticism from peers if they are "too old-fashioned" (*ringard*) and, on the other hand, they might be criticized if they behave in ways that are considered disrespectful of culturally informed but multiple and often conflicting expectations regarding female sexuality.

Whereas Sherazade's family, who did not live in a *cité*, allowed her relative transparency about dating, such was not generally the case for the young people in Chemin de l'Ile. In part, I believe this to be due to the extremely high density of the social networks in the neighborhood; the social gaze of "others," be they extended family, peers, or non-family neighbors, was intense and constant. Among adult parents, however, the prescription on dating was tied to a general recognition among adults and young people of the social value of women's sexual virtue. I once confronted Madame Hamdani's about her strictness regarding Yemina's movements—she was often out of the house but presumably only on school activities and never allowed to go out at night. I claimed (accurately) that Yemina possessed the same sexual mores as her mother in that she intended to remain a virgin until marriage. Madame Hamdani agreed that this was certainly true, but countered by asking what if Yemina were allowed to go out at night and were raped? What would people say about her as a mother then? For Madame Hamdani, protectiveness about her teenaged daughter's movements were aimed not just at controlling her choices, but at controlling the choices of the men that she might come into contact with outside of the supposed safety of home or school.

For teens, however, the connection between preserving virginity and a prohibition on dating was not as obvious. Yemina was desirous of her mother's trust and wanted the freedom that she felt should reward her good grades and (from her view) sound judgment. Yemina, like most other girls whom I met in the neighborhood, shared her mother's high valuing of virginity, calling it her *trésor* or "treasure." She had every intention of remaining a virgin until marriage; yet, she wanted more personal freedom. At the same time that virginity was generally held as a local value, many adolescent girls and young women whom I knew in Chemin de l'Ile were clearly conflicted about its relative merit when weighed against their desires to date and love young men outside of marriage. One 15-year-old teen confided in me that, although she wanted to remain a virgin before marriage, she realized that it would be extremely difficult to do so. Another 15-year-old teen asked for my opinion about whether having a hymenoplasty—an operation to restore the hymen—constituted being a virgin. (Hymenoplasty is elective surgery that is practiced in many places including France and the United States.) When I claimed that I did not believe that hymenoplasty restored virginity because the experience of sexual intercourse would remain even after the operation, the girl in question was clearly disappointed. She perhaps felt that she had a solution to her own and her peers' dilemma—a way to preserve virginity and retain autonomy over one's sexual desires and choices.

Again illustrating the power of spatialized experience as it is shaped by diaspora, these gender and sexual ideologies were seemingly applied more strictly in Chemin de l'Ile than in many parts of current North Africa, particularly in large cities (Goodman 2005; Kapchan 1996; Ossman 1994). For instance, Dalilah, one of the cultural informants discussed earlier, noted ironically to me that when she returned to Algeria to visit her cousins, she was scandalized at how openly they dated men, including men they had "picked up" on the street, as well as by their choice to dress in short skirts.

The relative loosening of cultural constraints toward unmarried women in large cities in North Africa and the apparent "return" to "traditional" values in French *cités* must be understood in the context of immigration. On the one hand, most populations migrating to France have been from more rural areas, often without formal schooling, and so come from backgrounds with potentially different values than a French bourgeois norm that celebrates "modern" sexuality, dating practices, and gender roles. On the other hand, and perhaps more important, the supposed return (and/or invention) of cultural traditionalism in French *cités* seems related to parents' and adolescents' active rejection of the supposedly corrupting influence of French culture and social values.

This "return" to "traditionalism" as well as intense conflict over this trajectory can be seen in wedding celebrations in Chemin de l'Ile. Weddings are social events often fraught with tensions surrounding tradition and sexuality in Chemin de l'Ile, as this next conversation illustrates. One afternoon at *Cerise*, Nora, around 12, described to Hannah, 16, a wedding that she had recently attended. The conversation began with a discussion of make-up and when and how it was appropriate to wear it. An adult mentor, Emmanuelle, who was French of European heritage, took out a lipstick, put a bit on her lower lip, and teasingly offered Nora some. Being only 12, Nora laughingly refused, but then asked Hannah why she never wore lipstick. Hannah claimed that she did not because, having full lips, "it shows up too much on me" (*"ça se voit trop sur moi"*). Nora then recalled a recent local wedding that she had attended and exclaimed, "wow, she [the bride] was beautiful!" noting that the bride did not usually wear make-up, but that she had at the wedding. Nora then opined that wearing makeup everyday could take away from one's beauty because then there is nothing out of the ordinary about special events. Nora also mentioned that her mother would not let her wear makeup, telling her to wait until she got married. Hannah, however, who often wore eye makeup but not lipstick, claimed that 16 (her age) was the "right" age to start wearing makeup.

Nora then mentioned that the wedding she had attended was "traditional," asking Hannah, "Do you like traditional weddings?" (*"Tu aimes les mariages traditionnels?"*) Hannah initially refused to respond, and so Nora offered: "They're stupid, I don't like them" (*"C'est nul, j'aime pas moi"*). I asked Nora what she meant by "traditional," and she replied that the wedding lasted 3 days, and the men and women were separated the whole time, adding, "we didn't even see them [the bride and groom] together. It's stupid" (*"Oui, ça durait trois jours et les hommes et les femmes étaient separés—On les voyait même pas ensemble. C'est nul"*). Hannah asked Nora, "Maybe that's because the girl was 16? That's why isn't it?" (*"C'est peut-être parce qu'elle a seize ans la fille? C'est pour ça, non?"*). Nora confirmed, "Yes, she's 16," and Hannah claimed that "wasn't good" because she was "too young" (*"C'est pas bien, c'est trop jeune"*).

This short interaction reveals a profusion of contestation surrounding girls' embodied practices with respect to make-up and marriage. On the one hand, both girls are clearly interested in make-up and weddings, but are together struggling to determine appropriate limits to each, both in terms of what they perceive to be respectable limits to sexualizing their bodies through make up, and "reasonable" cultural limits in the practice of weddings, including the age of the bride and social tone of the ceremony. Pressure on girls to marry early was especially strong for young women in Chemin de l'Ile. Whereas a young man unmarried at the age of 30 could possibly raise suspicions that he might be gay, such a delay would not usually hamper his ability to get married or find suitable partners, including women much younger. On the other hand, young women were expected to marry early, or potentially risk diminished choice of partners or the chance of getting married at all. For example, Aïcha's sister was unmarried at 40 and had largely given up trying to find a husband; due to her age and the possibility that she would not be able to have children, she felt her only choice was to marry a man much older (60 or more), which she refused to do. Instead, she continued to live with her parents and to work as a legal assistant.

At the same time that women's choices were limited due to age, young women also had fewer choices in terms of a husband's cultural, religious, and regional provenance. For young Muslim men in Chemin de l'Ile, even a non–Muslim wife was considered suitable as long as the woman was willing to convert. In my experience, cross-national (country of origin) and inter-racial marriages were also more accepted among sons than daughters, who were expected to remain not only within the religion, but also nationality, or even village or region. For example, Rashida, a woman of 23 whom I worked with as a teen, seemingly married the perfect match: a young Frenchman who was also of Algerian–Arab heritage and a Muslim. However, Rashida's mother refused to attend the wedding due to the fact that the groom's family was not from the same village (*bled*) as her own, but rather from a village in Algeria 50 kilometers (30 miles) away. Although the mother's perspective was considered *spécial* ("unusual") by many of Rashida's peers, it was still in the realm of possible. While the importance of provenance in marriage choice took on a singular importance for Rashida's mother, provenance was clearly central to most unions.

More usual types of expectations for young women entailed a preference that the boy in question would be "from" the same national group (e.g., "Algerian," whether born in France or having emigrated), preferably from the same ethnic/linguistic origin (e.g., Arab, not Kabyle), or at the least, of similar regional background (e.g., North African). How a husband was found was also of importance, although contested. Pressure for young women to marry early combined with the general prohibition against (overt) dating meant that some women chose to marry a friend of the family from the country of origin (usually Algeria), or to participate in loosely organized matchmaking through being set up by a relative or friend of the family. For some teens, yearly visits to *le bled* or "home country" were opportunities to meet someone, and such a relationship could be continued by chatting online, phone, and email, or even in person in France if the person was also visiting over the summer.

At the same time that some young women chose to marry men from *le bled*, it was also acknowledged that there were obvious risks to this strategy. Hamida, who did eventually get happily married in such a union, expressed to me when she was a teen that some men only married for the immigration papers they needed to come to France; young women such as Hamida worried that they would be divorced later. Other types of hidden motivations were also a concern. In the case of Faida, her marriage was the product of her religiously conservative father pairing her with the son of a friend; sadly, this young man turned out to be gay and the marriage purportedly an attempt for the family to save face in light of his sexual orientation. Faida was divorced within a year, and the consequences were severe; whether she was technically a virgin or not, her chances of marrying a suitable partner in terms of age and level of education were greatly diminished.

Perhaps because of the many risks involved, local criteria for who, when, and how concerning marriage were highly contested and hotly debated. The provenance of the person was an issue (particularly for young women wanting to find a husband), and how one was "supposed" to find a husband was contested as well. Miriam, a young woman with whom I worked closely when she was an adolescent, had, at the age of 23, a locally idealized courtship and marriage, in that her spouse (Rahim) was of a similar age, a college-educated professional (as was Miriam), had grown up in France (so migration as motivation was not at issue), and was introduced to her by a close family friend (Rahim's cousin). Rahim had grown up in a different, more affluent suburb (not in a *cité*), and so each partner was a relatively unknown quantity to each other, beneficial in that they did not grow up together or know "too much" about each other.

Rather than long-term dating, Miriam's and Rahim's courtship consisted of meeting several times to talk, and they were only together alone a handful of times during the day, including once at a fair where they kissed on the Ferris wheel. They married soon after. From one perspective, Miriam and Rahim embodied a cultural ideal; they did not "date" but did know each other (briefly, a few months) before the wedding. Moreover, they were put into contact by trusted friends and relatives with (warranted) assurances about the good qualities of the other person. However, when I attended their wedding, a guest with a daughter of a similar age commented to me, *"Pas pour ma fille, à se jetter dans le vide comme ça"* ("Not for my daughter, to throw herself into the unknown like that").

Here, a supposedly culturally "ideal" marriage from one perspective was considered potentially a terrible mistake from another view. Some of this conflict has undoubtedly to do with generational, educational, and socio-economic differences. Miriam's mother was an uneducated, illiterate woman who came to France as an adult (to marry), and her ideal for Miriam's marriage was different from her friend's mother, who was raised in France, had finished high school, and was working outside the home. (It should be said that Miriam and Rahim are quite happy, and have one of the most successful marriages that I know of in France or elsewhere.) My point here is that, even under the guise of cultural, national, and religious similarity among many of Chemin de l'Ile's inhabitants, there existed intense conflict and ongoing contestation about what was considered "traditional" or culturally normative with regard to marriage choices.

The Politics of Dress and Hair Styles

Dress styles are another domain in which gender propriety is debated among adolescent girls. Our conversation that day with Nora (aged 12) and Hannah (aged 16) in *Cerise* turned to the practice of wearing a Muslim headscarf (*hijab*) and a debate about the reasonable age limits of this practice.[9] The topic was initiated by Emmanuelle, an adult mentor not of North African heritage, who compared Nora to her mother in terms of looks. Emmanuelle asked me if I knew who her mother was and stated that she thought that Nora looked enormously like her, while Nora looked uncomfortably at both of us. Emmanuelle then asked Nora the culturally insensitive question of whether she and her mother both had the same light, honey-colored hair. Because Nora's mother wore *hijab*, this question was delicate and could have been a provocation from Emmanuelle intended to "enlighten" Nora's thinking about Muslim headscarves. Instead of responding, Nora taunted Emmanuelle: "You have no business knowing that" (*"Tu n'as pas à savoir"*). Emmanuelle exasperatedly replied, "Yes, I should have known you wouldn't say" (*"Oui, j'aurais dû savoir que tu ne dirais pas"*).

Nora then commented that she herself did not want to wear a headscarf, at least until she was 50: "Me, I don't want to veil. I don't want to veil before the age of 50" ("*Moi, je veux pas me voiler. Je ne veux pas me voiler avant l'âge de cinquante ans*"). Here, the age of 50 that Nora gives as the "appropriate" age to begin veiling is of interest because headscarves are more typically worn by elderly women in some Muslim communities, including many in North Africa, as well as the local community in Chemin de l'Ile. It is quite possible that, being only 12, Nora believes that being 50 years old makes one elderly. Relatedly, several people, including Madame Hamdani, who at 40 and as a mother of five did not wear a headscarf, commented to me that elderly women should be well covered up and looked better when they wore headscarves.

Nora then added that she liked to swim and that going to the beach wearing a headscarf was not possible: "For me, I like to swim a lot, and when you veil you can't go to the beach" ("*Moi, j'aime bien nager et quand on se voile on ne peut pas aller à la plage*"). She also added that her mother did not like the beach, thereby rationalizing both her refusal of the headscarf and her mother's choice to wear it: "My mother doesn't like the beach so…" ("*Ma mère, elle n'aime pas la plage, alors…*").

Our discussion turned to Habiba—not present at the time—the only girl who wore a *hijab* at the neighborhood association, *Cerise*. Nora claimed that it was Habiba's father who made her wear it and that, although headscarves were prohibited at school due to French law, she was not granted permission to swim: "It's her father who makes her veil. She's not allowed to swim, even at school" ("*C'est son père qui l'oblige à se voiler. Elle n'a pas droit de nager même à l'école*"). Nora's critique of Habiba's father extended to his purported requirement that all his children pray five times a day, including once at dawn (one of five religious edicts for practicing Sunni Muslims). Nora reported, "And even the little ones at the age of five, six have to get up to pray" ("*Et même les petits à l'âge de 5, 6 ans ils sont obligés de se lever pour faire la prière*"). In a similar fashion to our previous discussion about make-up and weddings, our conversation here attempted to delimit a space between respectable and reasonable standards for cultural and religious practice, including headscarves and prayer. However, just as I discussed in the preceding section on dating and marriage, rather than consensus, individuals of North African heritage in Chemin de l'Ile displayed an extremely wide range of views and practices about gendered and religious practices and, as such, they were commonly characterized by conflict and disagreement.

Our discussion illustrates also the ways that a Muslim headscarf did not shield a woman or girl, or, for that matter, father or husband, from critique in the local community. As is commonly the case in many Muslim communities worldwide, wearing a headscarf was generally extolled locally when it was considered a personal choice based upon a heartfelt spiritual decision by the woman in question. Coerced "veiling" among minors (as was supposedly Habiba's case) was extremely rare, and highly criticized locally, as our preceding discussion illustrates. Furthermore, most women and adolescent girls believed that wearing *hijab* was not only a highly personal and weighty spiritual choice, but also a choice that should not to be undertaken lightly. Many times, people in Chemin de l'Ile explained to me that it was "worse" to decide to wear a headscarf and then stop; better not to "veil" in the first place than make a hasty or superficial decision. For the vast majority of women and girls with whom I spoke, to wear a Muslim headscarf was a religious choice that was between a woman and God and thus not a decision to reverse lightly. At the same time, one or two adult women reported to me that their adolescent sons pressured them to wear a headscarf, most likely as a way to control their teenaged peers' view of their mothers. I never encountered a woman who decided to wear *hijab* for this reason, however.

The motives of young local women who chose to don a *hijab* were often discussed with skepticism by peers. For example, the young woman who expressed to me her belief that it would be difficult to remain a virgin before marriage chose to begin wearing a headscarf at around the age of 18. When I noted this fact in informal conversation to one of her peers, she exclaimed, "Yes, but if you knew the state of her reputation at the time!" ("*Oui, mais si tu savais sa réputation et l'état dans lequel elle était à l'époque!*"). On several occasions, it was noted to me that this young woman's choice to wear a headscarf might be a belated attempt to control her personal reputation in the neighborhood and possibly a way to improve her standing vis-à-vis her peers and her marriage prospects generally. That is, the action of veiling was met with criticism from peers because it was interpreted as merely instrumental on her part.

For older women who were not in the throes of managing their sexual reputations in light of future marriage prospects, the choice to wear a *hijab* might be more overtly strategic without such repercussions. Zayna, a divorced mother of two, explained quite frankly to me that she chose to wear a headscarf because she was always "in the street" (*dans la rue*) in order to visit social service offices for her children. Although she had been an engineer in Algeria, due to her divorce and political unrest in Algeria she had decided to immigrate to France and was initially unable to find employment. As a single, unemployed mother, she was responsible for all the administrative responsibilities for her family with regard to school, housing, and social services. In Zayna's view, wearing a headscarf allowed her to gain an increased measure of personal freedom in the neighborhood as a respectable (if divorced) woman who was out getting things done for her children.

A more overtly coercive type of negotiation occurred among teenaged peers in relation to appropriate secular dress styles among adolescent girls. The following example represents a recording of Samira and Mounia (both around 12) discussing 16-year-old Mina's unconventionally "masculine" dress styles with their adult tutors, Djamel and Mohammad, in the kitchen at *Cerise*. Girls such as Mina, who were perceived by their peers as foraying too far into styles and behaviors associated with a tough *cité* identity, were sometimes criticized by male and female peers as "wanting to be men," either overtly or through playful teasing. Girls and boys tended to have different interactional styles for monitoring their peers' behavior and dress styles, however. Whereas boys tended to use confrontational, direct teasing and mimicry in order to monitor girls' access to verbal and dress styles associated with masculinity, girls tended to use subtler forms of critique such as reported speech. For example, in the following exchange, Samira and Mounia voice their disapproval of Mina's "masculine" clothing by attributing their own critique to their adult male mentors, Mohammad and Djamel. The two younger girls were sitting with the two adult mentors in the kitchen when Mina walked in with a greeting and then left to go to another room. When she had left the room, Mounia initiated a discussion about what she was wearing.

"She's Dressed like a Girl for Once"

1	Mounia	*Hé, elle a son jean Mina? Vous avez pas remarqué qu'elle s'est habillée en meuf pour une fois?*	Hey, is Mina wearing her jeans? You didn't notice that she's dressed like a girl for once?
2	Djamel	*Ah ouais, c'est vrai en plus. J'croyais qu'elle était en racaille avec un gros survêt.[10] Tu te rappelles avec sa veste rouge?* [Laughing]	Oh yeah, it's even true. I thought she was in racaille style with a big tracksuit. You remember with her red jacket?
3	Mohammad	[Laughter]	[Laughter]
4	Samira	*Elle l'a encore?*	Does she still have it?
5	Mohammad	*Allez.*	Let's go. [Let's start your homework.]

6	Samira	*Ḥagar*[11] *Mina! Ils parlent de toi! Ils disent ta veste rouge **Ta' bəkri**. Ils ont dit combien de fois tu t'habillais en mec.*	**Bully!** [Directed at Djamel and Mohammad, presumably to avoid starting her homework] Mina! [Yelling to Mina in another room] They're talking about you! They're saying "your red jacket **from before**."They said how many times you dressed like a guy.
7	Mina		[Mina comes into the kitchen and looks accusingly at Mohammad and Djamel.]
8	Mohammad	*Nan, on se permet pas.*	Nah, we don't do that. ["permit ourselves"]
9	Djamel	*Tu sais très bien qu'on se permet pas nous.*	You know very well that we don't do that. ["We don't permit ourselves."]
10	Mina	*Sur le Qur'an, toujours en train de manger. Vous changez pas, vous.*	[To Samira and Mounia] On the Qur'an, [you are] eating all the time. You two don't change.

In this exchange, Mounia initiates a conversation criticizing Mina's dress styles, by mentioning that she had "dressed like a girl for once" that night. Here, the fashion distinction in question was Mina's choice of wearing jeans as opposed to a tracksuit, the former being characterized by Mounia as feminine in comparison. Djamel further adds to Mounia's description of Mina as masculine, claiming that he had thought she was dressed in *racaille* (roughly "hoodlum") style that night. As explained in detail in Chapter 4, *la racaille* constitutes a highly salient social type that embodies the most stereotypical characteristics of the *cité*—being tough, young, violent, territorial, involved in illicit activities, and, in most cases, male.

However, when Mohammad entreats the girls to start their homework ("*allez*" "Let's go"), Samira turns upon both of her adult male mentors by accusing them, "bully!" and then by yelling to Mina in the other room:

"They're talking about you! They're saying 'your red jacket from before'. They said how many times you dressed like a guy!" In response to Mina's stare, who had by then returned to the kitchen, the two men are forced to deny any wrongdoing: "You know very well that we don't do that." Mina accordingly turns her anger toward Samira and Mounia. Creating a strongly moralizing stance for herself by framing her critique with the words "*Sur le Qur'an*" ("On the Qur'an"), Mina accuses the two younger girls (who were snacking on chips) of "eating all the time." For Samira, in particular, this insult was sharp, as she was a bit heavy—I observed several of her peers accuse her of having a "big stomach."

Both the younger girls' criticisms of Mina's dress styles and Mina's response to them are indicative of the ways that girls who violated the norms for femininity were subject to criticism. In Chemin de l'Ile, norms for dress styles for girls revolved around seemingly minor distinctions such as whether one dressed "like a guy" in a tracksuit and tennis shoes, or "like a girl" in jeans. Strategies for dress styles on summer trips to Algeria, however, often included more typically "feminine" choices of self-presentation. For example, after the preceding criticism of Mina's clothing styles occurred, another conversation ensued (shown in the following table) between Samira and Mounia about Mina's dress styles in Algeria. The exchange serves to contrast the two countries as distinct cultural spaces, with distinct rules for appropriate feminine dress. The evaluative contrast that Samira makes in the first versus second description of Mina's dress styles is thus not only an evaluative commentary about Mina's "masculine" and "feminine" sides, but also a cultural contrast about appropriate behavior "here" in France versus "there" in the *bled* ("home country" or Algeria).

"She Was Going to a Wedding"

1	Samira	*Je suis partie au bled chez elle. Tu sais j'ai vu sa maison, et comment son père, il me fait, **dukhl-i, dukhl-i**, avec les cheveux lâchés avec une robe moulante.*	I went to her [Mina's] house in the "home country" [Algeria]. You know I saw her house, and how her father, he goes to me, "**come in, come in**," [she had] her hair down with a form-fitting dress.
2	Chantal	*Ah bon?*	Oh really?
3	Samira	*Elle partait dans un mariage.*	She was going to a wedding.

In this excerpted exchange, Samira expressed in a longing tone her excitement about having spent time at Mina's Algerian home during a summer vacation there. Samira's voiced approval of Mina *au bled* ("in the home country") indicated her approval of her partaking in normative feminine behavior there—attending weddings, and wearing makeup, and form-fitting clothing—behaviors that Mina avoided in her French *cité*, due to her wish to foster a tough, masculine-styled identity and to avoid appearing sexualized before her peers.

In contrast to Samira's previous criticism of Mina as having a masculine style, this narrative initially seems to serve to position Mina as sharing a type of nostalgic traditionalism that is grounded *au bled* ("in the home country"). For example, Samira appreciatively uses quotative speech to reproduce the Arabic words of Mina's father: *dukhl-i* or "come in." She also notes that Mina was dressed up in preparation to attend a wedding, perhaps the most central cultural activity during which North African traditions are practiced and preserved, including *henna*, traditional Arabic songs, blessings, Qur'anic readings, and traditional cuisine.

However, the nostalgic traditionalism that seems to be communicated by Samira's preceding narrative clashes with her description of Mina's sexualized appearance: hair down with a form-fitting dress, a dress that by its description would not be traditional because it was tight. This narrative is typical of others I heard about teenagers from Chemin de l'Ile who, although they avoided "modern" sexualized styles such as tight dresses and loose hair in the *cité*, felt encouraged and justified to do so *au bled*.

In short, Chemin de l'Ile, a neighborhood of 11,000 people, with its high-rise apartments providing bird's-eye views, its single-road entrance, and dense migration patterns from mostly two towns in Algeria, had created an intense village-like spatial environment with cascading effects for notions of gendered propriety. It was, at times, more village-like than *le bled*. In these discourses, it is France, and particularly the harsh urban spaces of the *cité*, that are envisioned as the impediment to a fully realized and modern femininity and not *le bled*, a pattern seen above in Samira's discussion of Mina's dress styles.

Sometimes the pressures that girls experienced around dress styles in Chemin de l'Ile had less to do with aesthetic preferences than pressures to conform to an image of sexual propriety. In an interview that I conducted with a group of about eight adolescent girls, ranging in age from 14 to 16, dressing "like a man" (*comme un bonhomme*) was touted as a strategy to circumvent criticism for appearing too sexualized. As Béatrice told me, "Chantal, when we wear a skirt, they [the boys] call us 'whores'. When we wear pants, they call us 'men'." Hamida also added a personal narrative about wearing an ankle length skirt to school. She claimed that she was criticized for dressing "like a slut" and so she went home to change back into her sweatpants. Such pressures seemed more intense for younger adolescents in *collège* (middle school) rather than older adolescents in high school.

Criticisms from boys about their female peers' overly masculine dress styles sometimes emerged from their perception of girls as competitors for the same clothing, in that some of it circulated in the *cité* as low-cost luxury goods resold by their older peers (sometimes stolen and sometimes illegally smuggled into France). I was told an interesting story about a teenaged girl, Aurore, who had a bunch of BodyGlove T-shirts that she was selling for roughly €10 to other kids. How she got the T-shirts was unclear, but, in any case, they were selling like hotcakes to both the girls and the boys at the association. Apparently, several of the boys at *Cerise* complained that the girls were buying all the T-shirts, which were "men's styles," the implicit complaint being that because the girls were buying them, there remained less for those boys who wanted to buy them.

Hamida, a girl who was present when the boys criticized them for buying all the T-shirts, exclaimed, "*Oui, on est des bonhommes, et alors?*" ("Yes, we are 'men', and so what?"). She thus answered the boys' critique that they were acting like "men" rather than appropriately girl-like by accepting their critique and minimizing it by her acceptance of it as supposedly factual. Some girls thus acknowledged and publicly accepted their behavior as atypical, "freakish," and even "masculine," to minimize the stigmatizing power of the critique. Hamida, in particular, had a highly sophisticated analysis about the strategic reasons for adopting a masculine dress and demeanor that surpassed concerns about her male peers. She claimed that it was in relation to their mothers that she and her friends chose a masculine identity—in order to avoid work at home. Hamida maintained that as long as she did not know how to cook, her mother would leave her alone—as the youngest child, if she was completely ignorant of how to do "womanly" tasks, then her mother would not depend on her to do them. She ironically noted that her mother would be all too happy if she learned *la broderie* ("embroidery") so that she could count on help around the house. In refusing to learn a more "appropriate" gender role, Hamida exempted herself from participation in household work.

It seems that adopting supposedly unfeminine behaviors and styles of dress was a multifunctional strategy. Not only did girls use non-feminine dress as a way to circumvent parental expectations for normative gender roles, but also to avoid appearing inappropriately sexualized to their peers.

Another reason girls adopted and maintained an unfeminine image was to have access to the tough reputation that boys more typically embodied in *les cités*. However, rather than a rejection of normative expectations for femininity, teenaged peers (female and male) sometimes interpreted these behaviors as emulating masculinity or "wanting to be men."

Teasing and Borderwork

Interactions that involve monitoring women's and girls' embodied practices (by other women/girls and by men/boys) constitute collaborative acts that I call "gender policing," which fit into the larger frame of "borderwork" that Thorne (1993) describes. These interactions can take the form of direct teasing of an individual for supposedly inappropriate gender behavior, forms of dress, sexuality, or more indirect commentary about the gender practices in one's culture or country of origin. As I have discussed throughout this book, and as other researchers of gender and language have noted, teasing is an important mechanism of social control (Thorne 1993; Goodwin 1990). Furthermore, patterns of teasing can reveal locally dominant beliefs and ideologies regarding gender. Understanding how gender ideologies are emergent in discursive practices is central to understanding how adolescents elaborate and transform gendered experience and socialize each other into local gender norms and practices. This is not to say that establishing normative gender roles is a consistent or seamless process—adolescents often struggle to make sense of conflicting, ambiguous, or contradictory gendered practices and ideologies.

Sometimes, borderwork was achieved when boys invoked supposed religious or cultural "tradition" to gain the upper hand in interactions with girls. One day in the association *Cerise*, Habiba, a girl of about 12, was teasing two boys about the same age. One of the boys told Habiba that it was *ḥaram* (forbidden for Muslims) for girls to tease boys. Apparently, Habiba believed their claim, at least initially, because she stopped teasing them. As the only girl who wore a Muslim headscarf at the association (although not at public school due to its prohibition there), Habiba was very invested in her image as a "good girl," both as a Muslim and a student. Her responsiveness to the boys' claim of gender privilege in the guise of supposed religious propriety (the Qur'an does not prohibit girls from teasing boys) shows how girls are subjected to judgments of their individual behavior through revoicings of (supposedly) authoritative religious and cultural discourse. For example, the name "Habiba" literally means "beloved" in Arabic, but, thanks to its widespread use in raï music from North African and Egyptian pop, has taken on a sexualized tone for some. During follow-up research in 2006, Habiba told me that she preferred to use the name Nabila, since she feared that the connotations of "beloved" were too suggestive. In this instance, Nabila chose to police her own self-image in relation to connotations of illicit behavior and sexuality.

An older, 16-year-old boy, Bilal, who frequented the association for homework help, was a veritable study in personal authority, cultural "tradition," and interactional style. I frequently observed him creating authority for himself by talking a strict "cultural tradition" line and using it to intimidate other kids. For example, on one occasion, he publicly accused Gonul, a 13-year-old Muslim girl of Turkish origin, of not observing Ramadan by fasting, which she vehemently denied. On another occasion, he teased Mina, the 16-year-old Muslim girl of Kabyle origin (Algerian Berber) who was mentioned earlier, that she was not really Muslim, seeing as how she was Kabyle and not Arab. In both of these interactions, Bilal used supposed tradition and cultural authority to question the propriety of his female peers. While such adversarial teasing is most likely the product of adolescent gender relations typical of post-industrial societies in general and not specific to Chemin de l'Ile, his appeals to "tradition" were a powerful tool when situated in the context of a diasporic community. In short, Bilal used appeals to cultural and religious tradition to exert power among his peers because these appeals struck a nerve among other teens.

In a different type of interaction with two adult mentors at *Cerise*, Mohammad and Djamel, Bilal questioned the cultural propriety of Tunisian women in general, in an effort to goad Djamel, who is French of Tunisian origin and in his early twenties. (Mohammad is French of Moroccan origin and was around 25 at the time.) The context was a tutoring session during which Djamel told Bilal that he could succeed at school, if he wanted to. Bilal was a notoriously poor student, having repeated the equivalent of eighth grade twice. At the time of the interaction, Bilal was 16 and still in middle school. To my own ears, and undoubtedly to those of Bilal, Djamel's "friendly" advice about school sounded patronizing and overly confident: "You see, you can succeed if you want to. You just have to know when to study. [At your age] I went out a lot, I had a lot of fun. I didn't work incredibly hard in school, but I still succeeded" ("*Tu vois, tu peux réussir si tu veux. Il faut simplement savoir quand il faut travailler. Moi, je suis beaucoup sorti, je me suis bien amusé. J'ai pas énormément travaillé à l'école, mais j'ai réussi quand même*").

To this motivational discourse, Bilal replied with a smile, "Yes, but you aren't as close to your [cultural] roots as Mohammad" ("*Oui, mais tu n'es pas aussi proche que Mohammad à tes racines*"). Bilal continued, "I went to a

Tunisian wedding and the women had dresses cut down to there [pointing to the middle of his chest]. We're losing modesty" (*"Je suis allé dans un mariage Tunisien et les femmes étaient décolletées jusqu'à là. On perd la pudeur"*). As a way to vindicate himself in the face of Djamel's patronizing comment, Bilal questioned Djamel's cultural authenticity. In contrast to the model of success that Djamel proposed to Bilal, he countered that cultural authenticity had real symbolic value, and claimed that Djamel's success had come at the expense of closeness to cultural roots.[12] Through such teasing and the verbal contests discussed in the following text, teens create and elaborate interactional contexts in which to compete for ownership over symbolic and linguistic terrains of self-expression.

"My Name Is Cécile": (Re)Voicing Gender Identities

In the exchange that follows, teenagers engage in a locally recognizable competitive verbal genre called *afficher* or "to display" in which a speaker publicly defames the character of an individual who is sometimes present. In the particular example of *afficher* that I examine here, teens use the socially recognizable persona of the bourgeois French TV host to authorize themselves to publicly perform unflattering character portraits of (usually) present audience members through the use of insults, rumors, and illicit speech. I will address interactions of this type in detail in Chapter 7. Here, I analyze the use of this type of interaction to show how gender crossing and policing are both achieved in a performance in which two boys mock a girl for her supposedly inappropriate masculine qualities.

In the following excerpt, Salim and Tarek "display" (*afficher*) audience members using my microphone and specifically target 15-year-old Cécile. Cécile was often teased by Salim for her supposedly masculine personal style. In this case, Salim and Tarek use stylized voicing to mimic Cécile and to create both "slutty" and "mannish" personas for her. Little matter that Salim and Tarek "displayed" Cécile in such wildly different ways, as a "slut" and as a "man"; in effect, each boy was attempting to craft a performance of her character that would ring humorously "true" with the audience of peers that had gathered around them.[13] In the end, however, the latter tactic was successful with the audience, because it was a better-suited, sharper "display" of Cécile, given that she was often depicted by peers as "acting like a man."

1	Salim	*Une question pour un homme. Il y a un homme devant moi. Je ne sais pas comment il s'appelle. Comment tu t'appelles? Comment t'appelles-tu?*	[Speaking to Cécile] A question for a man. There's a man in front of me. I don't know his name. What's your name? What is your name?
2	Ali	*Cécile!*	Cécile! [Answering for Cécile while laughing]
3	Salim	*Comment t'appelles-tu s'il te plaît?*	What is your name please?
4	Cécile	*Ta gueule.*	Shut up.
5	Tarek	*Attends! Je m'appelle Cécile, une **qhaba**!*	Wait! [Taking microphone from Salim] My name is Cécile, a **whore**! [In falsetto voice]
6	Salim	*Nan, mais là, mais **hshem**. Attends!*	[To Tarek] Nah, but there, but have some **shame**. Wait! [Salim and Tarek struggle over the microphone.]
7	Tarek	*Attends! Attends! Attends!*	*Wait! Wait! Wait!*
8	Salim	*Nique Cerise! Je m'appelle Cécile! Alors je m'appelle Cécile, en fait j'suis alcoolique et toxicomane. J'ai des biscs[14] et euh, bon ferme ta gueule un petit peu hein?!*	[In a loud, explosive voice] Fuck Cerise! My name is Cécile! [Group laughter, not including Cécile] [In the deep, creaky voice of a burnout] So, my name is Cécile; in fact, I'm an alcoholic and a drug addict. I have [big] biceps, and uh, well shut up a little huh?! [More laughter]
9	Cécile	*Ta gueule.*	Shut up.

Using my microphone, Salim initiated the preceding performance by imitating the voice of the polite and formal "French" TV host and by supposedly asking "a man" questions. Insulting speech takes the guise of supposedly innocuous interview questions, phrased in formal grammatical structures such as "*Comment t'appelles-tu?*" ("How are you called?"), rather than the more informal and non-standard "*C'est quoi ton nom?*" ("What's your name?") that adolescents used in everyday speech. To target Cécile, Salim paired this seemingly polite and innocuous voice with bald-faced insults, such as addressing her as a "man": "A question for a man. There's a man in front of me."

In addition to performing the TV host, Tarek and Salim crafted a satirical performance of Cécile through the use of stylized voicing. Whereas Tarek, using a falsetto tone and rapid speech, mockingly performed Cécile as the hypersexual and feminine "slut" or *qhaba*, Salim constructed Cécile in overwhelmingly masculine terms.[15] Using an explosively loud voice, then a deep, creaky voice to emulate this "alcoholic" and "drug-addicted" tough guy with big "biceps," Salim performed Cécile as an example of deviant masculinity. In addition to his depiction of Cécile as a drug addict and alcoholic—both social identities that are considered taboo and especially unsuitable for a young woman—Salim embellished his performance by attributing to her "voice" profanity ("Fuck *Cerise!*") and an aggressive verbal style, complete with bragging ("I have [big] biceps") and insults for her audience ("well, shut up a little huh?!").

In response, Cécile voiced her disapproval of their depiction of her by telling the boys twice to "shut up." Despite these attempts on Cécile's part to break the performance frame, Salim and Tarek continued to achieve a successful satirical performance through stylized voicing that was ratified by audience laughter. The success of this performance is dependent upon gender crossing through stylized voicing on the part of both Salim and Tarek. Yet, these strategies were used to enforce gender boundaries rather than transgress them. Whereas Tarek took on a falsetto in order to mock Cécile, Salim spoke as an "unnaturally" masculine woman.

And yet, the performers and audience members collaborated to establish limits to the performance. Tarek's unsuccessful bid to depict Cécile as a "slut" through falsetto voicing and insults was unratified by audience members through the absence of laughter and by Salim's removal of the microphone while scolding Tarek for going too far: ḥshem, or "have some shame." In contrast, Salim's arguably more clever and more wounding performance of Cécile as overly masculine was highly appreciated and prompted loud laughter from the audience as well as resistance from the target: "shut up."

The preceding example illustrates the centrality of verbal play, and particularly teasing, for the construction and policing of adolescent gender roles. Through satirical performance, the two boys subverted the toughness of Cécile's verbal style by representing it as an imitation of the real thing, for their own comedic purposes. By mocklingly performing Cécile as male, Salim and Tarik pointed out that, while she is not a man, she acts like one, and that is laughable. In this way, the personal authority that girls bid for when adopting *cité* styles of talk was subject to a level of ironic ridicule by their male peers, who, in parodying girls' performances, reclaim these styles for themselves.

By symbolically taking Cécile's voice, Tarik and Salim were performing a representation of what they perceive to be the discontinuity between Cécile's biological sex and her behavior and speech, which they took to be the exclusive property of males. Their overt purpose was to perform a humorous sketch to make their audience laugh, but at the same time they reinforced the social ideology, which attributes distinct essential properties, both linguistic and interactional, to boys and girls. Because the performance constructs boys and girls as two antagonistic groups, this interaction constitutes an example of what Thorne calls "borderwork," an "interaction based on, or even strengthening gender boundaries" (Thorne 1993: 137). This example shows that, when girls attempted to cross ideological borders between masculine and feminine, those borders were often policed and reestablished by their peers. In this very public, mixed-gender setting, Salim and Tarik enacted a competitive performance with Cécile that, despite its playfulness, had nuanced and far-reaching implications. In this example of competitive teasing, the boundaries of gender identity were redrawn using locally available styles of speech, including genres typical of *les cités* as well as formal styles of standard French.

In the preceding examples, girls and boys used interactional styles associated with the local space of the *cité* to strategically assign, subvert, and enforce gender categories. In so doing, these adolescents demonstrated their ability to perform hegemonic gender roles and also transgress those roles. However, a discrepancy exists in how boys and girls interpret the boundaries of gender identity in relation to local space, and to interactional styles associated with this space. Girls who attempted to construct a transcultural gender identity for themselves used linguistic and interactional styles associated with the *cité* to negotiate a middle ground between prescriptions for either "traditional Arab" or "modern French" femininity. To craft reputations for themselves as tough and independent, they challenged local discourses that girls should remain socially dependent as well as avoid most outdoor and many public spaces.

Their male peers, on the other hand, often attempted to construct linguistic and interactional styles associated with the local space of the *cité* as their exclusive symbolic domain. By undermining the girls' communicative crossing through teasing and mimicry, both boys and girls sometimes re-established the boundaries of gender and policed access to interactional styles deemed "masculine" by the local community and by dominant French discourses more generally. Thus, girls' use of *cité* interactional styles and outdoor space for their transcultural gender performances created ambivalent consequences. While adopting masculine-styled "respect" did allow girls to construct positive reputations among their peers and to voice critique of dominant gender ideologies, peers also enacted borderwork to re-establish the normative boundaries of gender that were reinforced by local and dominant gender ideologies.

Notes

1 These contradictions are typical of many post-industrial contexts that privilege a male model for gender identity while often stigmatizing female sexuality (Bucholtz 2002).

2 Walters (1999: 207) notes similar practices in Tunisia that dictate "the ways in which female and male bodies were regulated in public spaces," particularly in small towns. Walters particularly notes the preference for keeping non-related men and women separate within public spaces.

3 The pressure for young women to adhere to this schedule (as the majority of my consultants did) can be intense; as Rashida told me during my follow-up research in 2006 as she neared her 23rd birthday, still unmarried, "You don't understand, Chantal! For French–Arab (*rebeu*) girls, it's finished at 23!" ("*Tu ne comprends pas, Chantal! Pour les filles rebeu c'est fini à 23 ans!*"), meaning that her marriage prospects would plummet if she waited "too long."

4 And, of course, the reverse is also true. Boys' gender transgressions are constrained by the borderwork activities of their female and male peers.

5 As Goodman (2005) notes, however, ideologies regarding uses of space and gender are changing in Algeria, much as, or perhaps more quickly than, in North African communities in France.

6 Madame Hamdani's construction of la *rue* as a male space through talk even while she was physically occupying this space as a woman is akin to Sidnell's (2003) discussion of how Guyanese use language to index rum shops as male spaces even though they are routinely also occupied by women for various purposes.

7 Similarly, Eckert (2000) notes the importance of dating and the heterosexual marketplace for teens' efforts to expand their same-sex social networks.

8   This pattern seems typical of peer-group interactions among teens in many post-industrial places (cf. Shuman 1986).

9   As is indicated here, the meanings and uses of the *hijab* (or Muslim headscarf) are multiple and include not only personal religious expression on the part of the wearer, but can also indicate participation in political movements, kinship practices, and patterns of gendered sociability and social hierarchy, among other forms of communication (Abu-Lughod 1986 & 2002; Badran 1995; Fernea and Fernea 1995; Mahmood 2005).

10   "Survêt" is an informal abbreviation for *survêtement* or "tracksuit."

11   *Hagar* is an Arabic word that locally and colloquially was used to mean "bully."

12   Tunisians are often criticized by Algerians for being too culturally or morally loose, even when compared to Moroccans, who are also mocked by Algerians for their supposed weak character. An Algerian joke that I heard many times in Chemin de l'Ile illustrates this point: "Moroccans are kings, Algerians are men, and Tunisians are women." Here, Algerians (and presumably Algerian men) position themselves as superior, "true" men both in relation to Moroccans, who are weak because they follow a king, and also Tunisians, who are even weaker because the men supposedly let women "rule" and are therefore but women themselves. More generally, Tunisia is known for better legal protections for women and a less conservative national outlook on gender equality.

13   Cameron (1997) observes a similar pattern of seemingly incongruous insults being used to characterize someone as gender deviant.

14   *Biscs* is short for the word *biscotos* ("biscuits"), a slang term for biceps.

15   The letter q indicates a "hard" k sound in Arabic or the letter ق and the letter ḥ indicates a "breathy" h in Arabic, or the letter ح.

CHAPTER 6

PARENTAL NAME-CALLING

This chapter explores how transcultural ideologies derived from North African culture are transformed in local expressions of identity among adolescents in Chemin de l'Ile. In everyday talk, teens circulate seemingly static transcultural ideologies pertaining to generation, gender, and sexuality, but also routinely challenge these ideologies in interactions with their peers. To explore these issues, I turn to a particular communicative practice: the innovative interactional genre that I term "parental name-calling." In these exchanges, French teens of mostly North African immigrant parentage irreverently use the first name of a peer's parent in a public setting as a way to tease that peer. Teens consider parental name-calling to be fun, risky, and potentially insulting because it subverts a name taboo—the avoidance of given names in personal address—widespread across North Africa and practiced by their parents. In the process, teens negotiate their own beliefs and practices regarding generation, gender, and sexuality in both accommodation and resistance to their parents' values, and articulate their ambivalent relationship to the North-African-derived cultural value of *le respect* (or "respect") that I introduced in Chapter 3.

One of the most abbreviated forms of parental name-calling that I observed involved female peers ironically calling each other by their mother's names. Usually, however, parental name-calling was more elaborate than the ironic use of parents' given names for peers, and was either embedded

Transcultural Teens: Performing Youth Identities in French Cités, First Edition. Chantal Tetreault.
© 2015 John Wiley & Sons, Inc. Published 2015 by John Wiley & Sons, Inc.

into ongoing interaction or used to create interactional contexts onto themselves. My introduction to parental name-calling occurred one afternoon when I was teaching a voluntary English class at *Cerise*. The usual participants in my class were a group of 14–15-year-old middle school girls who were all close friends. On this particular day, however, a 13-year-old boy named Omar came to class, to the dismay of the girls present. Their relationship with this slightly younger boy was characterized by a kind of adversarial teasing typical between younger adolescent girls and boys in the neighborhood.

To engage my students in a conversation in English, I attempted a session of role-play, using one of their favorite TV re-runs, "Beverly Hills 90210," as a model. I began to list the names of the show's characters, eliciting help from the others: "Brandon, Kelly, Dylan, and—" to which Omar decisively replied "Habib" with a grin. I laughed, thinking that Omar was making a clever statement about the lack of Arabic names on the list and the monochromatic whiteness of the show. Omar looked startled and then asked me, "*Tu piges?*" ("You understand?"). I initially said yes, but when I explained my interpretation of his joke, Omar shook his head and explained to me, "No, Habib is the name of someone's father." I only later understood that the teasing was directed at another student, Rashida, whose father's name was Habib. I had noticed that a significant look had passed between Rashida and Omar without understanding why at the time. Knowing that responding would reveal her and her father as the target of the teasing, Rashida chose to remain silent.

This very brief, very embedded example of parental name-calling illustrates how performances of the genre can function as covert communication for the peer group. With this type of embedded name-calling, covert challenges are destined for a particular person in the ongoing context, and only those individuals with personal knowledge about the addressee will understand the reference. However, parental name-calling not only relies upon context for meaning, but also allows participants to create contexts of meaning in ongoing interactions. To this end, adolescents sometimes crafted highly elaborate verbal exchanges in which to embed the names of their peers' parents.

In one lengthy performance that I recorded, two teenaged girls and one boy used a classic 1980s French rock song by Daniel Balavoine, entitled *Le Chanteur* ("The Singer"), to embed each other's parents' names. Mimicking the song's original verse, "I introduce myself, my name is Henri" ("*Je me présente, je m'appelle Henri*"), adolescents embedded each other's mothers' names into the "Henri" slot, thereby creating utterances that were generally rhymed and which took the form of couplets. In the initial sequence of the lengthy exchange, participants actively made themselves and their parents available as targets. In this way, performances of parental name-calling sometimes allowed adolescent peers to create peer solidarity in generational opposition to parents through ritualized conflict. The following excerpt demonstrates participants collaboratively achieving a performance of parental name-calling, and, in so doing, sharing solidarity among their peer group through the expression of irreverence toward parents.

"My Name Is Fatma"

1	Soraya	*Je me présente!*	I introduce myself!
2	Zeinab	*Shoush!*	Shhhh!
3	Omar	*Je m'ap—pelle*	My name is [syncopated speech]
4	Zeinab	*Fatma!*	Fatma!
5	Soraya and Zeinab	*[[Je m'appelle Fatma.* *[[Je-*	[[My name is Fatma. [[I-
6	Zeinab	*Je voudrais bien avoir un petit chat.*	I would like to have a little cat.
7	Soraya	[Laughs]	[Laughs]
8	Zeinab	*Bonjour Nashia*	Hello Nashia

Here, Soraya and Omar co-initiate a round of parental name-calling without selecting a target, mutually laying themselves open to Zeinab's "attack." Zeinab in turn targets both of their mothers by first inserting Omar's mother's name, Fatma, into the "Henri" slot of Balavoine's song lyrics, and then completes the rhyme by obliquely referring to Soraya's mother by the second part of her her nickname "*Nashia, le chat*" (Nashia, the cat), and then by her given name, Nashia. (Adolescents often created rhymed, irreverent nicknames for peers' parents, such as "*Galeet, elle fume du shit*" or

"Galeet smokes hash.") By inserting each other's parents' names, they transform the song lyrics into a performative vehicle for parental name-calling. The highlighted sections in the following show how participants co-construct revised lyrics from the song in the form of couplets and even triplets over several turns of interaction. For example, *"Je me présente, je m'appelle Fatma"* was collaboratively achieved by all three speakers above.

Such transformative communicative practices among French Arab teens are transcultural for the ways that they combine multiple cultural referents. Performances of parental name-calling constitute a way that adolescents appropriate a North African cultural practice, a name taboo, and transform it into a new expressive form that is central to identity construction within their peer groups. In performing this genre, adolescents take the social rules for respectful address and bend them to create a transgressive type of symbolic expression for their peers.

A current preoccupation of youth language research is to understand how large-scale societal changes, such as modernity, migration, and globalization, affect young people around the world.[1] An examination of the effects of global change upon young peoples' expressive forms reveals contradictory processes. For example, the local identity practices of French teens of North African descent in my study articulate with transnational ideologies of gender and generation, but do so in contradictory rather than wholly consistent ways. Along these lines, tracing the origins of cultural borrowing among youth is increasingly complex, since many of the "traditions" adopted by youth depend upon creative reinterpretations of the past and hence involve "a kind of neotraditionalism in which elements of the heritage culture are selectively appropriated and resignified" (Bucholtz 2002: 542).

With regard to communicative styles and their practiceteen in Chemin de l'Ile, both innovative and traditionalizing patterns of cultural production are occurring simultaneously. Adolescents selectively appropriate and adapt a communicative form of their cultural background (in this case, a name taboo) and transform it into a means to express their social positioning as young, Arab, and French. In addition to such innovation, the practice of parental name-calling involves neotraditionalism in the form of *le respect* ("respect") through the selective borrowing and re-interpretation of North-African-derived cultural norms in a diasporic context.

That said, I should clarify that, in claiming that parental name-calling is a transcultural practice, I am not claiming it to be an exclusively French or uniquely diasporic speech genre. Indeed, the widespread practice of the name taboo in much of North Africa virtually guarantees that young people, when among themselves, would very likely also opportunistically invert this taboo in order to tease and insult their peers. Unfortunately, I do not have first-hand access to such evidence or to data in the context of North Africa due to the general lack of scholarly research on this topic. However, I have discussed this phenomenon with scholars who study North-African-influenced language and cultural practices and who have deep cultural and linguistic connections to the region.

In 2002, I discussed my findings with Dr. Azouz Begag, in the context of his scholarly presentation "*Immigration, humour, écriture*" ("Immigration, humor, writing"), organized by the Department of French and Italian at the University of Texas. Dr. Begag is a celebrated French-born scholar and author of Algerian descent who served as the Minister of Equal Opportunities under Prime Minister Dominique de Villepin until April 2007. Begag is well known for both his academic scholarship in sociology and economics as well as his novels, especially *Le Gone du Chaâba* (roughly, "The Kid from the Shantytown"), published in 1986, which is a semi-autobiographical account of his early years living in *les bidonvilles* outside Lyon, France. When I presented my findings on parental name-calling to Dr. Begag, he laughed, noting that, from his personal experience growing up, "We all did that," implying the ubiquity of the practice among French youth of North African descent. Dr. Begag then added, "But perhaps not the girls—that seems to be something new."

More recently, in 2013, I presented my research on parental name-calling at the Michigan State University to an audience of sociolinguists, including my colleague Dr. Brahim Chakrani. Dr. Chakrani is a sociolinguist who coordinates Michigan State's Arabic Language Program, and is originally from Morocco. He noted that, although teasing genres are widespread among Moroccan youth, to his knowledge parental names were not used for playful teasing due to their continued taboo status. In the Moroccan context, Dr. Chakrani noted that the mention of parents' names functions to insult and usually leads to physical altercation. He believes that parental name-calling as verbal play has emerged in France, and that it draws influence not only from the name taboo practices of North Africa, but also from African-American speech genres as well as French and American speech patterns more generally, a point to which I return in the following.

My discussions with Dr. Begag and Dr. Chakrani have encouraged me to argue that, while parental name-calling does likely have precedent in ritual insults using personal names in North Africa, there seems to have been a shift among French teens toward more non-serious, playful uses of the practice. These discussions also indicated to me that these forms take on potentially transcultural attributes in France, in that (1) they seem to be more widely practiced by adolescent girls in France; (2) these forms are sometimes adopted by teens of non-North-African descent and, in this way, appear to be affiliated more generally with the spaces of *les cités*; (3) they incorporate cultural forms particular to France and to the French language, as well as to American speech genres, in addition to genres and styles emanating from North Africa; and (4) they often incorporate tropes that frame parents as immigrants or as representatives of immigrant culture, and in this way reflect the larger social and political landscapes of France regarding immigration.

Ethnographic Contexts for Parental Name-Calling

French language influences for parental name-calling not only include cultural references, as in the preceding example where teens use lyrics from Balavoine's song "*Le Chanteur*"; these exchanges also draw upon new French speech genres such as *les vannes*, or mother insults similar in form and usage to "the dozens," an African-American speech genre (Mitchell-Kernan 1971). Popularized during the 1990s in a series of books including *Ta Mère!* ("Your Mother!") and *Ta Mère 2! la Réponse* ("Your Mother 2! The Response") by the Moroccan-born, French-raised comedian Arthur, much has been made of these mother insults and their apparent appeal for *cité* youth. For example, Lepoutre (1997) notes the influence of African-American speech genres, American rap, and American-influenced French rap upon *les vannes* in French *cités*. Similarly, adolescents in Chemin de l'Ile engage in genres such as *les vannes* and thus participate in a global, hip-hop-influenced youth subculture.

As well, North African norms for respectful address constitute a central linguistic and cultural influence. By engaging in parental name-calling, adolescents both foreground and subvert a North African cultural value, that is, the avoidance of personal names. Norms of "respect" prescribe avoiding speaking the first name of a non-relative, and sometimes of a relative, particularly if that person is older than the speaker or not of the same gender. Common forms of address that help North African Arabic speakers circumvent given names include kinship terms, such as "*ukhti*" ("my sister"), which are often used for non-kin. Euphemisms may also be used, as in the common expression "How's the house?" ("*Kaifa dar?*"), which a man might use to indirectly ask another non-kin male "How is your wife?", without needing to mention his wife's name or even the word "wife." The implication of the question is that the speaker is asking about "home" and so is indirectly asking about the keeper of the home, the wife. Such practices point to the ways that respectful forms of address are codified in relation to cultural norms regarding gender, age, and sexual propriety.

Following these rules for politeness, speakers avoid indiscreet reference to non-kin that might offend cultural sensibilities. In parental name-calling, however, teens intentionally do the exact opposite, that is, they publicly voice a peer's parent's name in order to playfully tease, incite anger, or exercise social control. In so doing, French adolescents of North African descent construct their peer group both in relation to cultural ideals of *le respect* and in contrast to those ideals. In this regard, parental name-calling constitutes a particularly important discursive genre for adolescents to articulate cultural ties to both their immigrant origins and their emergent adolescent subculture. These performances constitute expressions of in-group knowledge among peers that are contingent upon foregrounding the parent–child relationship. Performances of parental name-calling highlight adolescents' experiences of both cultural continuity and disjuncture in relation to their parents. As verbal routines in which adolescents symbolically evoke and defend parental identities, instances of parental name-calling are a way to both individuate from and connect to their parents, as well as to create a common feeling of belonging as French teens of North African descent. In solidifying adolescent subculture and social identity, these verbal performances are central in two ways: (1) they are public performances of knowledge about one's peers that constitute the group, and (2) they symbolically pose parents and adolescents in oppositional and yet dependent relationships.

Sometimes, this symbolic opposition demonstrates the ways that teens are actively engaging with gender ideologies. In the next example, two girls both reproduce and challenge ideologies regarding behavioral norms for women and mothers in their community, and in so doing actively negotiate understandings of gender and generation. This performance demonstrates how the main instigator, Hamida, reinforces a conservative gender ideology even as she undermines this discourse in practice.

Le Respect and Le Foulard ("Headscarf")

One evening I was sitting in a playground near a group of apartments with several girls, when Miriam, age 15, walked up to chat. Miriam, like the other girls, lived in the small 1960s apartment complex. Among the first state-supported, low-income housing built in the neighborhood, these units stood only four stories tall and sat cozily clustered around the small playground. Upon seeing her approach, Hamida, age 14, immediately reported to Miriam that her mother had burned something in her kitchen and the smoke had traveled all the way to the playground. Hamida then rendered a bodily pantomime of Miriam's mother who had supposedly used a headscarf, or *foulard*, to shake the smoke out of her kitchen. While she leaned forward and waved her arms up and down, Hamida added a verbal caption for the unflattering image she had created for Miriam's mother, whose first name was Zahra: "*Zahra avec son foulard en train de le secouer*" ("Zahra with her headscarf, shaking it out").

Miriam said nothing but was visibly upset by Hamida's account. Hamida apparently interpreted her look as an accusation of wrongdoing, for she responded: "*T'inquiète pas!*" ("No worries!"). Rather than accept Hamida's mitigation of the seriousness of her teasing, Miriam said to the rest of us, "Hamida always does this kind of thing to me, so that I'll worry and everything" ("*Elle me fait toujours ce genre de truc, Hamida, pour que je m'inquiète et tout*"). With no resolution or further commentary, the girls' discussion about the event ended there in cold silence. This performance of parental name-calling highlights the delicate balance that adolescents negotiate between joke and affront in such teasing. In this case, teasing becomes insult through its interpretation by the listener, Miriam, and not specifically by certain generic codes or inherent limits to these speech events.

In spite of the lack of interpretation embedded within the interaction itself, ethnographic knowledge provides some clues as to why Miriam would think Hamida's story was cause for "worry." The verbal and physical imagery incites affront because of the public spectacle that Miriam's mother has supposedly made of herself, which might compromise her "respect." Hamida describes Miriam's mother Zahra as inappropriately crossing from domestic space to *dehors* ("outdoors") in two ways: first, by supposedly burning something whose smell travels all the way to the playground, and second, by hanging out of the window for people in the neighborhood to see. As I discussed in Chapter 5, ideologies about proper uses of outdoor space map onto ideologies regarding gender and age in the neighborhood.

Hamida's performance of Miriam's mother is seemingly a means to depict her as behaving in socially inappropriate ways. In addition to Zahra's supposed unseemly encroachment into public space by hanging out the window and spreading smoke throughout the neighborhood, her puported use of a *foulard* or headscarf is particularly troubling to notions of *le respect*. A *foulard* (*hijab* in Arabic) is a personal item of women's clothing that for many Muslim Arabs is a symbol, among others, of a woman's modesty or *ḥasham* (Abu-Lughod 1986: 108). It is quite surprising, then, that Zahra would take a headscarf and use it to blow away smoke, rather than a kitchen towel (*torchon*). Hamida's choice of wording is particularly notable since Miriam's mother did not, in fact, wear a headscarf, a point that Hamida may have been trying to highlight, since her own mother did. (None of the adolescent girls present wore headscarves; very few young women in the neighborhood did.) In this performance of parental name-calling, Hamida draws upon cultural symbolism in order to depict Miriam's mother as acting in gender-inappropriate ways.

In addition to cultural symbolism, Hamida's performance of Miriam's mother seems to draw upon symbolism common to French anti-immigrant rhetoric. The accusation that Zahra allowed her burned cooking to infiltrate public space recalls the infamous speech by the former president Jacques Chirac that the "French worker" (read "non-immigrant male citizen") living in *cités* found it difficult to cope with "the noise and the smell" of his immigrant neighbors (*Le Monde* 1991). Such highly negative depictions of supposedly typical immigrant behavior circulate in public discourses in Chemin de l'Ile and elsewhere in France.[2] This exchange demonstrates how children of immigrants appropriate these discourses for their own in-group purposes. In so doing, they create unflattering depictions of one another's parents that draw upon ideals of *le respect* from transcultural Algerian cultural models as well as upon bourgeois French notions of "appropriate" public behavior.[3]

Adolescents articulate their complex relationship to *le respect* in performances of parental name-calling. For instance, in the preceding example, Hamida evokes *le respect* as a set of behavioral expectations for Miriam's mother, Zahra. At the same time, through her use of familiar reference for Miriam's mother and in her description of Zahra's supposedly disrespectful behavior, Hamida herself flouts cultural expectations for the respect of her elders. Thus, even as she is prescribing respectful behavior for Miriam's mother, Hamida is subverting these behavioral norms herself. The contradictions inherent in Hamida's performance demonstrate that parental name-calling is a way in which these adolescents may discursively reproduce conservative gender norms at the same time that they challenge these ideas in practice.

In these ways, conflicting cultural and interactional norms of adolescents and their parents are evoked in parental name-calling. In the next example, interactional expectations of teenagers are explicitly compared to the projected expectations of a parent when a parental name-calling performance is observed by a nearby mother.

Giving Voice to Parents, Symbolically Pointing at Peers

As demonstrated throughout this chapter, performances of parental name-calling constitute an opportunity for adolescents to negotiate social identity by symbolically evoking community-based ideals of "respect" and simultaneously flouting these ideals. In these performances, immigrant parents are constructed as simultaneously worthy of respectful demeanor and as a potential embarrassment to their adolescent children. Parental name-calling demonstrates adolescents' creation of interactional structures with which to both challenge and defend their peers and their own parents' "respect." For instance, when parental name-calling escalated to insulting references involving sexual suggestion, adolescent targets, including girls, sometimes resorted to directly insulting the instigator or to physical fighting.

And yet, in instigating parental name-calling exchanges, teens subvert a basic principle of le respect, namely that only the socially powerful may defend the respect of the socially weak. Here, both adolescent girls and boys cast themselves in the powerful role of defending their parents' "respect" even though, according to a traditionalist reading of le respect, such a power would normally be reserved for males, and especially adult males. Furthermore, performances of name-calling construct immigrant parents as threatening to adolescents' "face" (Goffman 1982). Goffman's concept of "face" represents an individual's positive image of self, which the individual tries to maintain during social interactions (1982). In the previous example, by depicting Miriam's mother as clumsy (burning food), immodest (hanging out of her window for all to see), and culturally vulgar (using her headscarf to shake out smoke), Hamida not only challenges Miriam's mother's "respect," but challenges Miriam's own social face.

In the following example, the theme of the socially blundering immigrant parent is repeated. The excerpt also illustrates the complexity of these issues in an event of parental name-calling among peers that was observed by a nearby parent. In the following, Hamida and Béatrice, both 14-year-old girls, initiated a parental name-calling performance directed at a boy of roughly the same age, Mabrouk, as he passed by on a bicycle. At the time of the episode, the girls were sitting chatting in a playground with a girl of 15, Mina. Just after Hamida and Béatrice called out to Mabrouk, Mina criticized Hamida for behaving this way in front of Hamida's own mother, who was sitting with a few other women at the other end of the playground. The example thus contrasts adolescent norms for interactions within their peer group with the projected interactional expectations of parents. As such, this performance demonstrates how adolescents actively negotiate divergent norms of "respect" in relation to themselves and their parents.

In the example, Hamida and Béatrice revoice embarrassing reported speech for Mabrouk's immigrant parents. They are, in fact, representing speech from a previous incident in which Mabrouk's mother, Yassina

Bendjedid, supposedly publicly embarrassed herself by approaching two adolescents involved in a heated argument. Trying to resolve the situation, she purportedly uttered the words, "My name is Yassina Bendjedid. Is there a problem?" Hamida and Béatrice reuse the words purportedly uttered by Mabrouk's mother in order to tease Mabrouk.

"My Name Is Yassina Bendjedid"

1	Hamida	Je m'appelle Yassina Bendjedid! Y a un problème!? Y a un problème!?	My name is Yassina Bendjedid! Is there a problem?! There a problem?!
2	Béatrice	Yassina Bendjedid! Y a un problème!?	Yassina Bendjedid! There a problem?!
3	Mabrouk	[Sabah]	[Inaudible speech that sounds like a woman's first name in Arabic, probably Hamida's mother's name, Sabah.]
4	Hamida	Je m'appelle Hassan Bendjedid! Y a un problème?!	My name is Hassan Bendjedid! There a problem?
5	Mina	Chut! Chut! Ta daronne[4] est en train de te dire, "Mais qu'est-ce qui te prend? Normale toi?"	Shh! Shh! Your mom is telling you, "What's wrong with you? [Are] you normal?"
6	Hamida	C'est vrai?	Is it true?
7	Mina	Bah, elle te regarde.	Well, she's looking at you.
8	Hamida	Ah ouais, je croyais que c'était ta daronne qui était en train de me regarder. Elle est en panique. Ma mère elle me regarde quand je crie.	Oh yeah, I thought that it was your mom who was looking at me. She's freaking out. My mother looks at me when I yell.

In this collaborative performance, Hamida uses Mabrouk's parents' full first and last names and voices them in mocking reported speech: "My name is Yassina Bendjedid! Is there a problem?! There a problem?!" (turn 1). Béatrice joins Hamida's teasing by recycling Hamida's words, making the performance collaborative (turn 2). At this point, Mabrouk responds, but his words are not completely intelligible; however, it sounds like Mabrouk is uttering a female Arabic name, probably that of Hamida's mother, Sabah. In response, Hamida quips back in Mabrouk's father's voice, "My name is Hassan Bendjedid! There a problem?!" (turn 4).

Through reported speech, Hamida and Béatrice refer back to an earlier event involving Mabrouk's mother and tease him for her supposed naïveté, a common trope in teens' characterizations of both parents and immigrants. From an adult perspective, Mrs. Bendjedid's use of her own name when speaking to two adolescents did not break the preference for avoiding personal names in that she was referring to herself, rather than using a name to address another; furthermore, she was conversing with young people, who themselves are less worthy of "respect" due to age. And yet, for the adolescents she purportedly addressed or who were listening nearby, the use of her full given and last name in public presented an opportunity to tease her son, Mabrouk, for her supposed lack of decorum. Again, in an inversion of "respectful" inter-actional norms, Mrs. Bendjedid's words were considered amusing not because, in using her own name to address teenagers, she had actually broken polite rules for address, but because she had flouted *adolescents'* expectations that parents refrain from using personal names and thus maintain social anonymity within the neighborhood. Indeed, these adolescents' liberal interpretation of "respectful" demeanor and its supposed infringement by Mrs. Bendjedid is evidenced in the revoicing of similar hypothetical speech for Mabrouk's father, Mr. Bendjedid, even though he was purportedly not present at the original dispute and so did not name himself in public at all.

In addition to challenging the respect of Mabrouk and his parents, this example demonstrates adolescent concern for *le respect* of parents as well. The loud performance of parental name-calling has drawn the critical gaze of a co-present parent watching the performance: Hamida's mother. While Hamida's mother stares stony-faced from across the playground, Mina chooses to voice her projected wishes, significantly also through the use of reported hypothetical speech: "Your mom is telling you, 'What's wrong with you? [Are] you normal?'" (turn 5). Here, as in the case of Hamida and Béatrice, Mina verbally embodies a parent, but for a different purpose. Rather than teasing a peer based upon a parent's supposed inappropriate behavior, Mina verbally embodies Hamida's mother in order to evoke expectations for *le respect* by prescribing more reserved behavior in front of older relatives.

While this exchange involves a performance that flouts respect for a peer's parents, it also involves an attempt by a peer to enforce normative respectful behaviors. The example thus shows adolescents' active negotiation of *le respect* through parental name routines, evidenced as well by Hamida's dismissive response to Mina's scolding: "My mother looks at me when I yell" (turn 8). This example illustrates that norms for *le respect* are significantly different in the context of peer interaction than within intergenerational settings. In these verbal performances, adolescents demonstrate their ambivalent relationship to both *le respect* and their immigrant parents, a theme I will further develop below. Through parental name-calling performances, they verbally foreground, challenge, and sometimes reinstate normative values regarding *le respect*.

In parental name-calling, the construction of absent mothers and fathers through reported speech creates a complicated web linking the adolescent "self" with a parental "other." Here, through quoted speech that refers back to an earlier event involving Mabrouk's mother, Hamida and Béatrice embody Mabrouk's mother's and father's voices as a way to communicate to and about Mabrouk himself. Béatrice and Hamida have thus created a representation of this initial event that resembles it, but also diverges from it through mockery—speech that Bakhtin (1981) would call "heteroglossic," in that it combines multiple voices—and are thereby able to tease Mabrouk for his mother's apparently humorous and embarrassing public display. Thus, Hamida and Béatrice teasingly target Mabrouk but also articulate the ambivalent relationship between French-born teens and their immigrant parents. In this way, parental name-calling speech events enact adolescent interpersonal relations writ small as well as adolescent and parent social relations writ large.

Knowledge about Parents as Symbolic Capital among Teenaged Peers

In this section, I explore the ways that performances of parental name-calling can be marshaled to elaborate and enforce teen norms of propriety regarding gender and sexuality through both accommodation and opposition to their parents. As discussed in Chapter 5, many adolescents in Chemin de l'Ile were engaged in dating, but they were also very careful to keep this information from their parents, in partial fulfillment of cultural expectations of *le respect*. By covertly dating, adolescents undermined the intention of *le respect*, that is, to prevent premarital romantic relationships. And yet, by refraining from overtly contradicting their parents' wishes, adolescents engaged in an interesting combination of resistance and accommodation to their parents' sexual morality and notions of le respect.

Teens sometimes used performances of parental name-calling to control the circulation of information related to dating. The following example shows how knowledge about a peer's parents serves as a form of symbolic capital to manage these issues, that is, as a type of "currency" that is not money but which holds intrinsic value for the group (Bourdieu 1987). Accordingly, parental name-calling routines serve as a means for adolescents to monitor their own and one another's emergent sexuality. The excerpt shows an exchange between Hamida (seen in the previous example), Naima (a girl of 12), and Omar (a boy of 13), in which they exchange threats to share sensitive information with one another's older relatives. Adolescents thus use information about kin not only to tease but also as collateral to prevent the circulation of information that is damaging to both personal and parental "respect."

In the following, Hamida engages in a modified version of parental name-calling by referring to Omar as "Ahmed number two," after his older brother. Naima then joins in the performance by referring to their peer Omar as "Omar number two" after his father, who shares the same first name. The initially playful exchange between Naima and Omar turns increasingly combative as each threatens to divulge information about the other regarding adoption and dating.

"Omar Number Two"

1	Hamida	*Fais voir tes yeux Omar. Ahmed numéro deux.*	Show us your eyes Omar. Ahmed number two. [Ahmed is Omar's older brother.]
2	Naima	*Putain, il a de ces beaux yeux, le chien!*	Fuck, he has some of those beautiful eyes, the dog!
3	Omar	*Pourquoi tu dis c'est Omar numéro deux? C'est Omar numéro zéro et–*	Why do you say it's Omar number two? It's Omar number zero and–
4	Hamida	*Omar numéro deux!*	Omar number two!

5	Naima	*Ouais, nan, par contre, c'est la vérité que c'est Omar numéro deux, parce que Omar numéro un, c'est ton daron.*[5] [Laughs] *Je t'ai vexé!*	Yeah, naah, on the other hand, it's the truth that it's Omar number two, because Omar number one, it's your dad. [Laughs] I annoyed you!
6	Omar	*Heeh, t'es contente, haaaa! Ah mais toi, t'es pas une Belkaalool!*	Heee, you're happy, haaaa! Oh but you, you're not a Belkaalool! [Here, Omar is implying that Naima is adopted. Belkaalool is her family name.]
7	Naima	*Va dire ça. Va dire ce que t'as dit là.*	Go ahead and say that. Go say what ya said just now.
8	Hamida	*Il va le raconter à tout le monde pendant une semaine là.*	He's going to tell that to everyone during a whole week.
9	Naima	*Ferme ta gueule aussi. Hé, sur le Qur'an, tu balances, sur le Qur'an, Je vais voir ta daronne et **wallah** je lui dis. [Je vais] voir ton père. Je sais où il travaille, ton père.*	Shut your mouth too. Hey, on the Qur'an, you tell, on the Qur'an, I'm going to see your mom and **by God** tell her. [I'll] go see your father. I know where he works, your father.
10	Omar	*Haaaahh!*	Haaaahh!
11	Naima	*Il travaille à la loge ta*[6] *l'école. Hé, ferme ta gueule. Il travaille avec son frère. Et tiens maintenant j'te l'ai mis dans où j'pense-*	He works at the security gate **of the** school. Hey, shut up. He works with his brother. And now that I stuck it to you where I'm thinking about- [Or roughly, "where the sun don't shine"]
12	Omar	*Moi, j'vais voir ta soeur, ouais, j'sais où elle travaille.*	Me, I'm going to see your sister, yeah, I know where she works.
13	Naima	*Bah, va la voir. J't'ai rien fait du tout.*	Well, go see her. I haven't done anything to you at all.

This exchange demonstrates Naima and Omar wielding information about the other's relatives to prevent the circulation of rumors about themselves. As their verbal contest escalates, Omar threatens to circulate information that Naima is adopted, or, in Omar's words, that "you're not a Belkaalool," her family name (turn 6). Naima's fear that Omar will circulate such personal information is evidenced in her counterthreat to reveal which girl he is dating to Omar's mother: "on the Qur'an I'm going to go see your mother and by God tell her" (turn 9). Just prior to this recorded exchange, Omar had furtively called his girlfriend to warn her that a peer had threatened to tell her brother that they were dating. (To reiterate from Chapter 5, "dating" was very chaste among younger adolescents in the neighborhood and did not involve sexual activity.) In this exchange, the delicate nature of such information is evidenced by the way Naima refrains from explicitly referring to what she will "tell." The referent of her threat is understood and need not be named.

In this exchange, knowledge of a peer's parents constitutes symbolic capital for adolescents in several contexts (Bourdieu 1987). In the immediate context, such information provides the means to provoke one's peer and to retaliate in the case of provocation. In the larger context of the peer group and the neighborhood generally, such information provides important collateral for controlling information about oneself. Specifically, details about parents and older siblings are cited by both Naima and Omar as evidence for why the other should refrain from sharing illicit personal information with non-present peers: "I'll go see your father, I know where he works" (turn 9), and "I'm going to see your sister, yeah, I know where she works" (turn 12). As such, parental name-calling is not merely verbal play but rather serves as evidence for the ability (if not the intent) to damage a peer's "respect" by divulging damaging information to parents and kin.

In performances of parental name-calling, adolescents reinterpret and negotiate an emergent code of *le respect*. By using a peer's parent's first name in public and in an irreverent manner, adolescents subvert norms for respectful behavior toward adults based upon a name taboo. Thus, adolescents foreground the cultural code of behavior they call *le respect* even as they transform this code through its reinterpretation in interactional practice. The enactment of these reinterpretations of *le respect* in parental name-calling demonstrates how these French teens of mostly North African descent reinterpret transcultural ideologies of generation, gender, and sexuality in everyday identity practices.

The varied examples addressed in this chapter demonstrate the centrality of constructions of and knowledge about kin to adolescents' performances of personal and group identity. Performances of parental name-calling indicate that French adolescents of North African descent experience and express peer identity as highly relational to their parents' generation. In these transcultural performances, teens position each other as "daughter" and "son," thereby elaborating personal adolescent identities in relation to parents and older kin. Through parental name-calling, personal names and other information about parents and kin are used to evoke these absent persons as foils for the present adolescent self, and these absent adults serve, in turn, as foils for the peer group.

Finally, collaborative performances of parental name-calling exemplify the ambivalent moral positioning of adolescents in relation to the transcultural value of *le respect*. While most teens in the neighborhood were surreptitiously dating and thus flouting the intention of the behavioral code *le respect*, they nonetheless outwardly maintain social norms of "respect" by keeping such information away from parents and older kin. With regard to these youthful reinterpretations of *le respect*, parental name-calling emerges as a means for teens to elaborate their own sexual morality and to monitor and control information regarding their own and their peers' dating practices.

In these multiple ways, the elaboration of adolescent identities and transcultural identities are mutually informing and occur simultaneously in interaction. In these performances, adolescents negotiate their own emergent youthful code of "respectful" behavior that both reinforces and transgresses parents' cultural norms. In these ways, adolescents use parental name-calling not only to reference French cultural symbols, such as Balavoine's classic rock song, but also to enact their positioning as French teens in a transcultural dynamic with their parents' values.

Notes

1   Contemporary research on this issue includes, but is not limited to the following: Alim 2009; Auer and Dirim 2003; Bucholtz 2011; Chun 2009; Eckert 2000; García-Sánchez 2014; Giampapa 2001; Hewitt 1986; McElhinny 2007; Mendoza-Denton 2008; Rampton 1995b; Reyes 2006; Reynolds 2013a & 2013b; Pennycook 2003; Pichler 2005; Shankar 2008; Skapoulli 2004; Vermejj 2004.

2   However, in a demonstration of the power of discourse and its ambivalence, this particular highly negative slogan was subsequently reassigned a pro-immigrant political meaning when the multiethnic music group *Zebda* produced a CD of the same name: *Le bruit et l'odeur* ("The noise and the smell").

3 At the time that this audio recording was made, grade school children across France participated in a national education project to teach student "civility" and the behaviors of "good neighbors," undoubtedly a response to the perception that "new" French citizens were not learning and adopting unwritten codes of *la politesse* ("politeness").

4 *Daronne*, slang for "mother," is purportedly derived from Romani, the Indic language of the Romani people ("Gypsies") (Goudaillier 1997: 79).

5 *Daron*, the masculine counterpart of the term *daronne* used in the previous example, is slang for "father." Both terms are purportedly derived from Romani, the Indic language of the Romani people ("Gypsies"), and, in France, originally emanated from *les cités* (Goudaillier 1997: 79).

6 *Ta'* is a possessive form in Algerian Arabic.

CHAPTER 7

CROSSING REGISTERS: VOICING THE FRENCH TV HOST

The previous chapter looked at how adolescents of primarily Algerian descent transformed verbal genres deriving from a North African name taboo to achieve peer interactions in French, specifically through parental name-calling. This chapter attends to the ways that teens transform French verbal genres, specifically the styles of interaction typical of game shows and talk shows on French television. In these performances, working–class youth of predominantly Algerian descent show their familiarity with and strategic use of a TV host register (i.e., a socially recognizable speech style usually confined to a particular purpose) that is largely based upon standard French, formal grammatical structures, and elite or "bourgeois" pronunciation and prosody.

I analyze these performances as instances of language crossing (Rampton 1995b) because, in their everyday speech, these adolescents used non-standard French grammar and the pronunciation and prosody typical of the working class, or, as Gadet (1996) calls it, "*le français ordinaire*" ("ordinary French"). Language crossing involves a speaker's use of a linguistic code or style that is associated with a group to which the speaker cannot claim membership (Bucholtz 2011; Cutler 1999; Rampton 1995a, 1995b; Rampton and Charalambous 2010; Jaspers 2010; Vermejj 2004). In addition to the growing body of literature on crossing, much of current scholarship on language and culture is generally devoted to how we, as speakers, "convey

Transcultural Teens: Performing Youth Identities in French Cités, First Edition. Chantal Tetreault.
© 2015 John Wiley & Sons, Inc. Published 2015 by John Wiley & Sons, Inc.

words that are not our own" (Goffman 1981: 150), including how we (1) cross into others' languages and registers, (2) invoke others through reported (quoted) speech, and (3) create others through stylized speech.

This chapter addresses data that reside at the confluence of these three types of language crossing. Specifically, I analyze performances in which teenagers in Chemin de l'Ile strategically use my microphone to imitate an elite French television show host. Then, after framing their subsequent utterances by this TV host register, the adolescents create reported speech and stylized voicing for their peers who are present and thereby mock them as show "guests." The adolescents perform the persona of the TV host by mobilizing a set of linguistic and paralinguistic markers, including grammatical structures, lexical items, pronunciation, and prosody (speech rhythm, speed, and intonation), as well as framing devices and contextualization cues, both of which serve to convey information about a speaker's communicative goals. For example, in the interactions that I analyze in the text that follows, teens repeatedly used the first names of nearby peers to contextualize them as "contestants" and thus to enter the frame of the "game show."

Linguistic crossing by working-class Arab teens has been generally overlooked in French sociolinguistic literature. As mentioned in Chapter 2, studies of working-class, ethnically non-French youth tend to focus on new styles of speech emerging from *cités* and often describe these styles as uniform—that is, as a comprehensive "language" onto itself (Pierre-Adolphe et al. 1995; Seguin and Teillard 1996; Goudaillier 1997; Lepoutre 1997). Relatively little, however, has been written about register shifting among French youth of North African descent. Rather, linguistic research on French *cités* tends to reproduce the assumption that teenagers of North African descent lack standard French and to represent these speakers in terms of their supposed "linguistic deviance" (Boyer 1997).

Boyer's (1997) critique that much French sociolinguistic scholarship previously assumed that *cité* youth only use and possess one, uniform linguistic style that was intrinsically tied to *les cités* demonstrates this scholarship's bias toward putatively "authentic" speech, a pattern also seen in the history of sociolinguistics more generally (Bucholtz 2003). As Bucholtz notes, early sociolinguistic research emphasized a one-to-one relationship between social identities and speech varieties and so fostered nostalgia for a form of essentialized (unchanging and supposedly natural) "real language," which posited the possibility for a "language produced in authentic contexts by authentic speakers" (2003: 398).

In contrast, this chapter deals with language that might be provocatively considered "inauthentic" in several ways.[1] By appropriating my microphone and audio recorder and performing overtly self-conscious language, adolescents marshaled a register of standard French that they did not often use in everyday conversation and, in so doing, subverted its usual association with elite French culture. Furthermore, although adolescents' general familiarity with this register would indicate that they sometimes used it outside the research context, the presence of my audio recorder and microphone established conditions that were unusually amenable to its use. In that sense, the data analyzed here are a unique result of the context created by my ongoing ethnographic research. Finally, rather than use this style as a way to "authenticate" themselves as speakers of standard French, I argue that working-class teens were engaging in what Bucholtz calls a process of "denaturalization," that is, "the phenomenon whereby an identity is held up as inauthentic or unreal—as literally incredible" (2003: 409).

One of the most vexing and interesting challenges for analyzing words "not our own" is to describe how these utterances connect the immediate linguistic context with larger social contexts. For example, how do working-class Arab French teenagers in *les cités* manage to transport their peers into an imaginary French TV show, and for what purpose? Particularly helpful to considering these questions is Goffman's (1981) creation of a conceptual paradigm to move beyond "speaker" and "listener," toward "speaker roles"—for example, whether a speaker is the *author* of words or just the "mouthpiece" (*animator*) for them—and toward "participation frameworks," that is, the structure an interaction takes in terms of turn-taking and participation, including speaking and listening (Levinson 1983: 72). The combination of a participant's role and an established discursive frame allows a speaker to achieve what Goffman calls "footing," that is, the stance or attitude of the speaker in relation to other participants and to the emerging talk. In this chapter, by animating the TV host's voice and by framing the current interaction as a game show, speakers achieve an ironic footing akin to "this is irreverent play; this is non-serious; therefore, I cannot be held fully accountable for these words." In turn, this ironic footing is strategically used by speakers to voice unflattering and insulting speech about and for peer audience members.

Another important part of understanding how and why *cité* teens appropriate the voice of the French TV host involves research on how speakers conjure social personas in everyday talk. For example, Eckert (2004) focuses upon linguistic styles as embodying "social personae," and Koven (2001) upon reported speech in narratives as iconic of "locally imaginable personas." Coming at the problem from a related, but slightly different perspective, Agha (2005) focuses upon the "voicing effects" (grammatical, stylistic, and prosodic features) inherent to everyday uses of social registers.

Agha (2007) also notes that registers emerge in everyday interactions such as the ones presented here. Put another way, as Agha (2005: 57) and Irvine (2001: 31) both note, although "registers" are often interpreted as emanating from relatively stable institutional contexts and activities (such as "medical doctor talk"), any register necessarily entails cultural images as well as inter-actional performances of persons and interpersonal roles (e.g., of a "doctor" and "patient"). Thus, the notion of registers overlaps with social dialects and linguistic styles.

Teens' performances of TV host register hinged on a strategic and comedic mismatch between speaking social persons—working-class Arab teenagers—and the voiced social persona evoked in these perfor-mances, namely the culturally elite, ethnically French adult MC (Master of Ceremonies). Specifically, the adolescents' performances of the TV host register constituted an instance in which teens' speaking styles were at odds with the metapragmatic stereotypes associated with the enregis-tered voice of the French TV host. Whereas "pragmatic" generally refers to language *use* or linguistic *practice*, "meta-pragmatic" refers to beliefs or ideologies *about* language use and linguistic practice. Meta-pragmatic stereotypes include those notions that speakers have about what types of speech are (and should be) attached to which speakers. In interaction, meta-pragmatic stereotypes inform our expectations of who should say what and in which context. These expectations draw upon information and ideologies regarding gender, age, ethnicity, class, sexual orientation, and regional provenance, along with other parameters of identity such as profession and education. The teens' performances of the French TV host style provide a fruitful arena to explore how socially "mismatched" types of speech and types of speakers are strategically used to establish participation frameworks that allow the speaker to tease their peers.

Afficher ("to Display"): Interactional Contexts for the TV Host Register

In the data I analyze here, teenagers use the socially recognizable persona of the TV host to authorize themselves to publicly perform unflattering character portraits of (usually) present audience members through the use of insults, rumors, and illicit speech. These unflattering character portraits are instances of a speech event typical of *cités* across France called *afficher* "to display," in which a speaker publicly defames the character of an individual who may be present. Earlier, I briefly discussed an example of *afficher* in Chapter 5. There, and in the examples of *afficher* that I examine here, teen performers strategically created caricatures of audience members' identities, either by divulging personal information or by depicting them as embarrassing social personas, such as a "slut" or "drug addict." Using the TV host register to mitigate the seriousness but increase the force of their words, performers create a public, unflattering caricature of the target's identity that is both hurtful and humorous because it "rings true" (is plausible), although it may not be completely anchored in reality.

Afficher is not always framed in the enregistered voice of the TV host. In the examples addressed here, adolescents use the TV host register to frame episodes of *afficher* as ritualized, non-serious events. In contrast, the majority of instances of *afficher* are considered serious affronts that can lead to verbal and physical altercations. In everyday, non-ritual or serious examples that I observed, an exchange was deemed to be an instance of *afficher* most often by the target—that is, the recipient of a public verbal "outing" in which damaging or sensitive information was purportedly shared. The seriousness of these exchanges was made apparent by the target's issuing an accusation: "*hé, tu m'as affiché*" "hey, you outed/displayed me," to describe either an immediately preceding event or a previously occurring event to which the recipient was not a direct witness. The accused "displayer" would then deny or confirm the target's accusations.[2]

Similar to the ritualized events that I describe here, serious instances of *afficher* most often revolve around disputing reported speech, either that the "displayer" presumably spoke about the target or that the target presumably spoke in private but that was later made public information. In non-playful instances, the exchange becomes deemed an example of *afficher* when the target claims it so, regardless of the intent of the speaker. In this sense, *afficher* is a speech act in which the perlocutionary effect—the recipient's experience of being publically "outed" or "displayed"—is paramount in defining the event. In other words, the effect experienced by the target of the (supposedly occurring) original utterance may be more important than the actual utterance or speaker's actual intent. In contrast, in the performative and ritualized examples of *afficher* that I analyze here, the speaker overtly engages in outing a peer in her or his presence, making very clear the intent to "display." The general expectation among teens is that the target should respond in kind by "outing" his or her opponent or refrain from getting angry in order to save face. The insults, rumors, and mocking involved in these performances are couched in the voice of the TV show host precisely so that they may be framed and later claimed as "just play."

Linguistic Features of the TV Host Register: Game Show and Interview Formats

Below, I describe the TV host register in terms of its general features. Then I list those features specific to the game show format and the interview format, respectively. All performances, whether they entail game show format or interview format, exhibit all of the features in the first list.

TV Host Register in French

(a)   Use of contextualizing lexical items such as television stations (e.g., TF1 and France 2), actual TV hosts' names (e.g., Julien Lepers), and names of television shows, especially *Questions pour un Champion*.

(b)   Indicating the MC role by contextualizing audience members as "guests" through greetings, introductions, and naming.

(c)   Use of relevant props, especially the researcher's microphone.

(d)   Increased use of formal grammar, for example, *nous* "we" and *vous* "you, plural," pronouns and conjugations rather than those corresponding with *on* "one" and *tu* "you singular."

(e)   Increased use of complex grammar when compared to everyday speech—for example, the use of past perfect tense rather than simple past tense and inverted question format rather than declarative form to ask questions.

(f)   Use of politeness, especially the use of "please" and expressions that exhibit shared positive affect—for example, "Goodbye, friends!" and "Let's rally our spirits!"

(g)   High tendency to use repetition as both a stylistic marker and an attention-getting device, especially in relation to audience members' names, key phrases, and questions.

(h)   Crisp enunciation, indicating formality and elevated social status of French elite (bourgeois).

Specific Features of the TV Host Register in Game Show Format

(a)   Pattern of emphatic stress on first syllable as an attention–getting device (as opposed to emphatic stress placed on last syllable in conversational French).

(b)   Lexical items specific to game shows such as *Truth or Consequences* and *Prizes.*

(c)   Loudness or "throwing" the voice to the audience.

Specific Features of the TV Host Register in Interview Show Format

(a)   Extensive use of questions to engage audience members.

(b)   Use of lexical items/topics common to the "public opinion" interview, such as "pollution."

(c)   Archaic, old-fashioned expressions, such as "Let's rally our spirits."

(d)   Pompous tone that sounds fussy or pseudo-intellectual and is achieved with nasality and at times a lowered, discreet voice. Exaggeration and hyperbole can also contribute here, as in the extensive use of intensifiers—for example, "It's very, very nice" (*"c'est très, très bien"*).

Performance of the TV Host Register in Game Show Format

In the extended exchange in the following, adolescents frame a performance of *afficher* with the game show format of the TV host register. In this performance, two 15-year-old girls, Mina and Hannah, appropriated my microphone in order to direct insults and rumors toward a present peer and three of their adult tutors. Mina and Hannah were not close friends, but each girl regularly attended the neighborhood association, *Cerise*, in which the performance took place. The two girls' personal communication styles were generally quite different. Mina was the consummate iconoclast and risk-taker, an unabashed tomboy who delighted in saying shocking things. Hannah, in contrast, was more socially conservative. She tended to keep to herself and focus solely on tutoring while in the association. Hannah projected a more feminine persona and was more soft-spoken than Mina. Both girls were among the older teens at the association and in their final year of the French equivalent of middle school; they had attended *Cerise* for several years.

Initially in the exchange, the teenaged girls target Jacques, who is an adult tutor and not present. Jacques worked many years as a tutor at *Cerise*. An older gentleman of French background, Jacques was dearly beloved by the students, but was unfortunately reputed to have bad breath. While students generally showed Jacques affection and deference to his face, they delighted in complaining and joking about his halitosis behind his back. In fact, the trope of Jacques's "bad breath" returns several times in both the extended performances that I address in this chapter.

Mina	"*Questions pour un Champion" en direct sur TF1! Avec Kader, Hannah, et Cécile! Voilà [laughs] attends. Kader veut dire quelque chose. Il dit que Jacques qu'il pue de la gueule.*	Questions for a Champion live *on* TF1! With Kader, Hannah, and Cécile! There [laughs] wait. Kader wants to say something. He says that Jacques' breath stinks. [Mina and Kader laugh.]

This example shows Mina using my microphone and the performed voice of a game show MC to ironically frame subsequent mocking of a present peer, Kader. Voicing effects here take on several linguistic forms and pragmatic functions. That is, Mina is not merely stylistically approximating the enregistered voice of a TV host. Her rendering of the voice of Julien Lepers relies upon embedded participant roles (Goffman 1981: 149). Also, although Mina is clearly the animator of the words she speaks, her words also clearly indicate an absent animator, the host of *Questions pour un Champion*, Lepers. To achieve this double-voiced utterance, Mina gives contextualization cues (Gumperz 1982a, 1982b), that is, verbal and non-verbal signs that allow her listeners to infer her imagined identity, such as the words "questions for a champion" and "live on TF1."

An icon of French popular culture and host of the show since 1988, Lepers was born in 1949 in Paris and began his entertainment career as a popular singer, famous for his interpretation of *De Retour de Vacances* ("Back from Vacation"). Considered a charismatic and formal presenter, Lepers is not himself particularly educated. And yet, the show, *Questions pour un Champion*, is a popularized performance of contestants vying to display what the French call *la culture générale*, knowledge about a variety of subjects, including literature, art, natural sciences, history, and geography. Champions are often quite educated, and special competitions among university students are not uncommon. In sum, this show demonstrates the French ideal of a well-rounded citizen embodying the cultural knowledge central to a nation constructed as residing, past and present, at the apex of Western civilization.

Mina draws on an array of linguistic and paralinguistic markers to achieve her transformation into the MC persona. In terms of contexualization cues, Mina identifies the name of the show and station, using the term *en direct* ("live"), and names three nearby peers as contestants—Kader, Hannah, and Cécile. Little matter that the actual TV show *Questions pour un Champion* never aired on Channel 1, but rather on Channel 3, or that the show was usually prerecorded and not live; Mina nonetheless successfully uses these typifying, if inaccurate, cues to evoke a game show frame.

Further, Mina's prosodic and phonological patterns mimic that of a game show host. For instance, as indicated by bold type above, we see that Mina places stress on the first syllable of key words and so mimics the emphatic tone of the game show MC, whereas conversational French places stress on the last syllable. Indicated in the transcript with underlined speech is Mina's careful enunciation of sounds in the words *sur* "on" and the two *n*'s in *Hannah* that conjure the formal (or "proper") speech of a television MC.

Yet, rather than a performance of "high culture," Mina instigates a veritable variety show of insults and rumors for the microphone, performed by herself and her peer Hannah. Mina uses quotation to report embarrassing speech for one of her named "guests," Kader, whom she claims has insulted the "bad breath" of their tutor, Jacques. As Jacques is not present, it would seem that the main communicative goal here is to render a caricature of Kader as rude and insolent, even while the "real" (shy and polite) Kader stands by listening and laughing. Thus, the strategic mismatch of social voices that Mina creates in depicting herself as a well-known game show host is reproduced in the clash between Mina's depiction of Kader "on the show" and Kader in real life.

In addition to juxtaposing social voices, Mina's brief performance juxtaposes speech events and participant frameworks. Specifically, Mina transforms a parody of the game show's habitual introduction of contestants into a way to single out and mimic Kader. By these means, Mina capitalizes upon and yet subverts the television host's main discursive power to contextualize "guests" within an interaction that is largely of the host's making. Rather than show her "contestant's" polite deference, as is common to the TV host role, Mina usurps his voice to create inappropriate speech for him. The clashing voicing effects that Mina establishes with her imitation of the TV host serve to create a generalized ironic footing that facilitates the other double-voiced utterances aimed at "outing" Kader.

Next, following Mina's game show introduction, she and Hannah co-construct a performance of rumors and insults, directed at the two tutors present, Djamel and Mohammad. The two targeted male tutors, Djamel and Mohammad, were both in their mid-twenties, of North African background, and very close friends. However, the two men were perceived very differently by students in the association. Whereas Mohammad was well liked and considered *sympa* ("nice"), Djamel was considered to be too tough (*dur*) with students and was said to unfairly deny them help with homework. Adolescents' negative impressions of Djamel would seem to account for how he is targeted by the girls' *afficher* performance. Despite differences in personal style, both tutors enjoyed a casual relationship with their students, as evidenced by students' common practice of calling them by their first names and addressing them with *tu* (informal/singular "you") as opposed to *vous* (formal/ plural "you").

Hannah	*Djamel, Djamel, venez voir s'il vous plaît. Question Vérité. Verité, vérité, vérité.*	Djamel, Djamel, come here, if you please. Truth or Consequences. Truth, truth, truth.
Zahira	[Whispers something to Hannah]	[Whispers something to Hannah)]
Hannah	*Il n'y a pas—non, Zahira, il a cassé et j'ai entendu la conversation. C'est maintenant, euh Sherazade. Sherazade, Sherazade. Il n'y a pas longtemps Mohammad il m'a dit que tu lui avais demandé qu'il t'arrange un coup. C'est vrai.*	There is no—no, Zahira, he goofed and I heard the conversation. It's now, uh Sherazade. Sherazade, Sherazade. Not long ago, Mohammad told me that you had asked him to arrange a hook up for you. It's true.
Mina	*DE BITE!!!*[β]	FOR SEX!!!
Hannah	*Ça c'est vrai, ça. Ça c'est vrai. Et tu sais ce qu'il m'a dit, Mohammad? Il m'a dit- c'est vrai parce qu'il m'a dit, "De toute façon je veux pas lui arranger un coup," parce que ah t'es assez grand, tu vois, t'es assez grand, euh-*	That is true, this. That is true. And do you know what he told me, Mohammad? He told me- it's true because he told me, "In any case I don't want to arrange a hook up for him," because ah you're big enough, you see, you're big enough, uh-
Mina	*Bah oui ça c'est ta' les gamins de demander à quelqu'un d'arranger un coup.*	Well yeah, that a kids' thing to ask someone to arrange a hook up.
Hannah	*Ta gueule, ta gueule, ta ta ta ta gueule!*	Shut up, shut up, shut shut shut shut up! (sing-song voice)
Mina	*Oui, maintenant euh c'est pas grave. Merci, euhhhh [bijoun]*[4] *Adios amigos! Et maintenant nous allons passer au concours de chant. Oui voilà. Vous allez chanter tous les trois en coeur.*	Yes, now uh it's ok. Thank you, uhhh [XX] Adios amigos! And now we will move on to the singing contest. Yes, that's it. You three are going to sing together as a chorus.

As in the previous excerpt with Mina, Hannah emulates the TV host register through a variety of markers. First, Hannah emulates the formal speaking style of a TV host. Although she would normally address her adult male tutor with the more informal *tu* "you," she here chooses *vous*. Hannah also employs a more formal grammatical verb tense, past perfect, *tu lui avais demandé* "you had asked him," whereas in everyday speech she would more likely use the simple past tense, *tu lui as demandé* or "you asked him." Second, as with Mina earlier, Hannah marks her speech with lexical items typical of a game show format, such as *Question Vérité*. Finally, Hannah exhibits stylistic markers of the TV host register both at the level of prosody and discourse. Specifically, she uses emphatic first-syllable stress (indicated by bold type) as an attention-getting device, as well as the stylized repetition of key terms, such as "truth," and of "contestants," Djamel and Sherazade, much as Mina does earlier.

Using explicit language and with the help of Mina, Hannah uses reported speech to narrate how Djamel supposedly asked Mohammad (the other 20-something male tutor) for help in seducing Sherazade, a female tutor of roughly the same age. Hannah also claims that Mohammad confided in her that he preferred not to do so, implicating him in the mocking "display" she creates for Djamel. Both male tutors are present and, unlike Jacques, are within earshot of the performance. Rather than dispute the truth of Hannah's claims, they sit nearby, smiling to show an unaffected, calm stance. Sherazade is not present. In the course of this narration, Zahira, a female adolescent standing nearby, attempts to challenge the veracity of her claims, but Hannah justifies her attack by claiming to be simply reporting overheard speech.

The lamination of speech events and participant roles that Mina establishes earlier is further developed by Hannah, who acts as both "host" and "guest" to implicate her adult tutors, Djamel and Mohammad. Whereas the last caricature was established upon speech that Kader might be expected to say but did not, Hannah constructs narrated personas for her "targets" based on a supposedly truthful account of their past utterances. In the following excerpt, Hannah continues to frame the performance in the game show by inviting her "guest," Djamel, to come forward for *Question Vérité*, similar to a "Truth or Consequences" sequence. This phrase is uttered when a game show host orders a guest to provide an answer to a question, the veracity of which is then challenged by another contestant or audience member.

In the course of her injurious depiction of Djamel, Hannah does not sustain a formal, socially distanced style. Rather, Hannah downgrades the polite address for Djamel from *vous* to *tu* and breaks from the TV host style in an aside to a peer, Zahira, in order to give first-hand evidence for her claims about Djamel and Mohammad. Yet, Mina completes the episode in

TV host style, thereby reestablishing the initial discursive frame of "game show." Specifically, Mina uses the positive politeness that one would expect from a TV host, "Thank you," which she follows up with a friendly saluta-tion to the audience in "mock" Spanish (Hill 1998), "*Adios amigos*," and then calls for a "singing contest" in which she entreats audience members to "sing as a chorus."[5]

In this extended performance by Mina and Hannah, performing the voice of the TV host creates a context for a derisive performance of an audi-ence member by authorizing otherwise illicit or inappropriate speech. It would seem that assuming the role of a TV host establishes one's authority to speak the normally unspeakable and to take social risks that one might not otherwise dare. For instance, earlier, in a sing-song voice, Hannah tells her audience and presumably the target of her performance, Djamel, to "shut up," and Mina liberally utters illicit words throughout the performance, including *bite* "sex" or "cock," and, later in the interaction (not shown here), announces that the winner of the singing contest will get a *capote en or* "golden condom."

Here, mismatched voicing effects facilitate a lamination of identities and participation roles, in the form of "animators"—combining the present speaker and hypothetical TV show host—as well as "authors," combining the utterer of the original words and the reporter of those words (Goffman 1981: 149). Much as performers blend voices of multiple social personas, they mix playful and serious messages. In terms of such "serious" messages, the two adolescent girls Hannah and Mina, almost 10 years younger than Djamel and Mohammad, use the vehicle of the TV host style to chastise their male tutors for their purportedly inappropriate and juvenile sexual practices.

Whereas constructing the voice of the TV host is achieved here through stylized direct voicing, that is, by approximating an enregistered voice, con-structing the voice of the target is achieved through non-stylized, reported speech, as in "He says that Jacques' breath stinks" and "you had asked him to arrange a hook up for you." In this way, an unflattering performance of the target's identity is based on potentially truthful past actions and utterances. The two girls create this embarrassing but plausible caricature of their tutors by claiming to construct a truthful account of their tutors' own words.

This performance illustrates the two girls using the TV host register to establish a generalized ironic footing that authorizes them to publicly make outrageous and face-threatening claims about their adult male tutors. However, the embedded utterances that the girls use to negatively characterize their tutors' sexual behavior rely on quotation in the form of reported speech and on making truth claims for their words (e.g., that they overheard them). The two girls thus achieve this performance by creating non-stylized reported speech for their tutors and thereby engaging in a somewhat milder, less direct form of *afficher*, when compared to the *direct* stylized voicing—speaking *for* rather than reporting about another person—that is used to mock peers in the next performance that follows.

Performance of the TV Host Register in Interview Show Format

In the next performance, two teenaged boys, Salim and Tarek, direct the majority of their mocking speech toward their adolescent peers present. When compared to the first, the performance creates a wider range of voicing effects, participant roles, and participation frameworks. Rather than reported speech, speakers in the second performance rely primarily on stylized direct voicing (i.e., talking *for* the target) to "display" embarrassing caricatures of audience members. In contrast to the first performance, these attacks are not about putatively "true" prior statements or actions, but rather focus on characteristics supposedly embodied by present peers, such as ugly hair.

In the following, the teenagers engage in a more intensely mocking form of *afficher* when compared to the first performance. This intensity is evidenced by the highly dynamic participation frameworks in which participants compete for the microphone, exchange ritual or direct insults, and engage in "side-play" (Goffman 1981: 154)—that is, derisive comments by audience members who are "non-ratified" or previously unrecognized as active participants (Bell 1984). As in the first performance, this exchange illustrates the use of the TV host register to establish a generalized ironic footing to authorize outrageous and rude claims. Here, however, the TV host voice is used to achieve much more than a frame within which to embed a "display." Rather, performers use the voice of the TV interviewer to orchestrate complex voicing effects throughout the performance, to laminate (overlay) multiple participant roles, and to embed several participation frameworks at once.

Tarek and Salim similarly use mismatched voicing effects to achieve innovative participant frameworks that recast present peers as objects for public "display." As in the last example, an enregistered voice—a recognizable style attached to a particular persona—of the TV show host is employed by performers to achieve a generalized ironic footing that facilitates saying face-threatening, insulting things about a present audience member. Similarly, both performances revolve around the discursive power of the television host to contextualize guests within an interactional context largely of his or her making. However, in this performance, Tarek and Salim perform the voice of another type of TV show host, that of the interviewer who searches for "public opinion." Whereas the previous example created a generalized ironic footing through the juxtaposition of the play or "game" frame and serious accusations, this next example juxtaposes the quasi-serious frame of the television interview with outrageous caricatures of present peers.

Accordingly, participation frameworks are differently manipulated in the following performance. Rather than the enregistered voice of the TV host serving to frame more serious, non-stylized utterances, the quasi-serious and pompous voice of the intellectual interviewer leaks into every utterance. Initially, Salim assumes the role of the "objective" reporter to improvise a mock interview with Tarek about "pollution," which both performers collude to interpret as the bad breath of their tutor, Jacques. Much like the previous one, this performance initiates with a ritualized *afficher* of Jacques, well out of his presence. In addition, they ritually "display" an absent adult female tutor, Michèle, whom they imply is gassy by imploring the need for more electric cars.

As with the previous one, this second performance took place in the neighborhood association *Cerise*. Rather than take my microphone while I was not present, Salim politely asked my permission to "interview someone," as the first excerpt shows in the following. The audio recording took place in a small room at the end of the association building where I sat with Salim and Tarek (both 15-year-old boys), a younger boy Ali (13), and several girls, including Cécile (15), Batool (14), Amina (14), and Sarah (15). Salim and Tarek were close friends, and very much act as co-conspirators to keep control of my microphone. Whereas Tarek was well liked by boys and especially girls his own age, Salim was regarded as someone who could tease mercilessly and so was treated with caution by peers. Nonetheless, teens here jockey for the microphone and targets talk back to their "displayers" with some success. However, the two older boys control the microphone more often than anyone else present; for example, although the younger boy mentioned earlier, Ali, tries repeatedly to commandeer the microphone, it is never directly given to him and so he resorts to "side-play," as do several of the girls present.

| Salim | *Ça enregistre? Ça enregistre? Attends, je vais interviewer quelqu'un, s'il te plaît.* | [To Chantal] Is it recording? Is it recording? Wait, I'm going to interview someone, please. |
| Chantal | | [Nods in agreement] |

Salim	*Bonjour, que pensez-vous de la pollution?*	Hello, what do you think about pollution? [Breathy laugh]
Tarek	*Hé, la pollution. Jacques il fait 35 % de pollution en France. Après il y a–*	Hey, pollution. Jacques makes 35% of pollution in France. After there's–
Ali	*Ecoutez! Ecoutez!*	Listen! Listen! [Ali tries to get Tarek to pass microphone]
Tarek	*Attends, j'ai pas fini. Jacques, déjà, il fait 35% et euh, et euh il a invité des recrues qui font déjà les 70 autres pourcents. Et après Michèle-*	[To Ali] Wait, I haven't finished. Jacques, already, he makes 35% and uh, and uh he invited recruits who make already the 70 other percent. And after that Michèle- [Tarek laughs; Ali laughs, pounds table]
Salim	*S'il te plaît!*	If you please! [Acting the role of the moderator, asks for silence from Ali]
Tarek	*Il faudrait plus de voitures électriques.*	We should have more electric cars.

In this example, Salim initiates a mock interview with Tarek using the performed voice of the TV show host register, in particular an interviewer in search of "public opinion." Salim exhibits this voice first with his greeting to Tarek (*bonjour*) and his polite use of *vous* to address his close friend while holding the microphone as a prop. Next, Salim orchestrates the seemingly banal participation framework of the television interview by asking Salim about the ubiquitous social problem of pollution. Salim's breathy laugh at the end of his question, however, prompts Tarek to interpret "pollution" as code for the target of much mocking among these teens: the bad breath of their tutor, Jacques. Here, the target of a "display," Jacques, is laminated with a topic typical of "objective" reporting on public opinion.

Laminated topics are accompanied by the embedded participation frameworks of a highly uncivil "display" situated within the performance of a "civil" exchange of opinion. For example, Tarek colludes with Salim's mock topic of pollution by repeating bogus percentages (35%, 70%), parodying a common method of forwarding an "informed" opinion by using numerical figures. The solution that Tarek proposes to the problem—electric cars—is actually a thinly veiled accusation of Michèle's supposed flatulence. The participants thus frame "social problems"—central to the public opinion interview—as targets for *afficher*, with pollution and overly "gassy" cars standing in for their tutors Jacques and Michèle.

The practice of embedding semantically loaded information into questions as a way to convey information about targets continues in the next excerpt. It features two additional ways that voicing effects facilitate innovative participation frameworks. First, we see interview questions that embed illicit information about a present audience member who is not directly addressed, but is rather a bystander. In this case, Salim poses a seemingly innocuous question to Batool about her opinion of Paul, who is not present. Entering the mock interview frame, Batool declares Paul "a jerk." Batool happens to be seated next to Paul's sister, Sarah. However, rather than her or the absent Paul, it is actually Amina who is the target of this "interview"; the seemingly innocent exchange serves to "display" her romantic interest in him. That Amina is in fact the intended target of this question is made wholly clear when Salim next provides an answer to his own question for her in a falsetto voice, introducing himself as Amina and declaring Paul "very handsome."

Also of interest in this excerpt is the way that the multiple participant frames and personas within the "interview" become "leaky," that is, bleed into each other (Irvine 1996) at certain key moments. For example, after Salim uses a falsetto voice to mock Amina's supposed opinion of Paul as "very handsome," he continues to talk in a falsetto voice as the interviewer to question Amina about her supposedly "big" hair: "*Que penses-tu de ta coupe?*" "What do you think about your hairdo?" ("Big hair," meaning tightly coiled or kinky, was often a source for teasing both boys and girls, probably because it served as a phenotypic marker of Arabness.) Also, the performance frame of the mock interview is broken when Amina responds to Salim's question with a direct insult about his hair ("I think you have big hair"), and he responds with a threat ("I'll break your face"). Finally, Batool's evaluation of Salim's performed TV host voice as a *voix de connard* ("jerky voice") is of interest because she pinpoints the pompous and fake qualities associated with the persona that he communicates through voicing effects.

Salim	*Que pensez-vous de Paul?*	[To Batool, sitting next to Paul's sister Sarah and Amina]
		What do you think about Paul?
Sarah		[Laughs]

Batool	*C'est un connard euh-*	He's a jerk ah-
Salim	*"Je m'appelle Amina. Je trouve Paul très beau." Que penses-tu de ta coupe?*	"My name is Amina. I think Paul is very handsome." [In falsetto voice throughout turn] What do you think about your hair? [To Amina]
Amina	*Je pense que t'as une grosse coupe.*	[To Salim] I think you've got big hair.
Salim	*Je te fous la gueule. Que pensez-vous de la mauvaise haleine?*	[To Amina] I'll break your face. [To Batool in pompous interviewer voice] What do you think about bad breath?
Batool		[Laughs]
Salim	*Que pensez-vous de la mauvaise haleine, s'il vous plaît?*	What do you think about bad breath, please? [Repeats in intensified pompous interviewer voice]
Batool	*Arrête avec ta voix de connard.*	Stop with your jerky voice. [Laughing]

In this intense form of *afficher*, voices of the interviewer and interviewee are blended through direct stylized voicing and used to mock targets, such as Amina. At the same time, this exchange demonstrates increased friction between serious and non-serious interpretations of the ongoing events. For example, when this interaction devolves into direct insults and threats, Salim returns to the ironic footing of the mock interviewer by repeating a safer, less pointed "display" of the absent Jacques to the audience: "What do you think about bad breath?" Specifically, he signals his return to the ironic voice of the TV interviewer by his use of the formal *vous* form and by his use of positive politeness, "please." He also achieves this shift through an increase in voicing effects, as evidenced by Batool's laughing assessment about the pompous quality of his tone: "Stop with your jerky voice."

Not all targets resorted to direct insult as Amina does here. In other parts of the recording, targets crafted semantically "loaded" questions of their own to have the last word with Salim and to resist the discursive power of the "interviewer." For example, Salim later asked Sarah (who is half Cambodian) "What do you think about Thailand" ("*Que pensez-vous de la Thaïlande?*"), probably to publicly mock her ethnicity through misrecognition and by insinuating a sexualized persona for her being related to the image of wide-spread prostitution associated with the country. In her defense, nearby Batool answered, "What do you think about Tolga" ("*Que pensez-vous de Tolga?*") in mocking reference to the relatively poor, provincial Algerian desert town that Salim's family is from. Similarly, later, in an interesting example of self-display, Salim playfully asked Sarah, "What do you think about Tolga?" ("*Que pensez-vous de Tolga?*"). In response, Sarah embedded her opinion in the semantically loaded question, "What do you think of the desert, yeah" ("*Que pensez-vous du désert, ouais*"). In these instances, complex voicing effects and innovative participation frameworks emerge together.

Another milder, subtler example of "display" is explored in the exchange below. In it, I become the target and am mocked in another "public opinion" interview dealing with my perceptions of France and *Cerise*, the tutoring association. The main performer, again Salim, asks seemingly innocuous questions of me, such as "What do you think about France?" However the ironic footing of the event is established by Salim's use of the pseudo-intellectual and pompous-sounding voice of a news interviewer, or, as his peer Batool puts it, his "jerky voice." I also enter the play frame and respond with my own version of this "jerky" voice, using a pompous tone, crisp enunciation, and emphatic stylistic markers to denote refined fussiness such as *très, très bien* "very, very well."

In a fashion similar to but subtler than the semantically "loaded" questions asked of Amina and Cécile earlier, I am politely coerced to participate in my own "display." Salim, as my interviewer, orchestrates my performance of a polite, refined, and pseudo-intellectual television interviewee, and thus a voice that sounds uncomfortably close to the register that I normally approx-imate as a researcher. And yet, the participation framework that Salim co-constructs with the researcher is far less aggressive, allowing me more "room" to speak than his teenaged peers. In particular, no one creates direct stylized voicing for me, such as the falsetto voice used to mock other female targets.

For my part, I attempt to participate in a playful performance while con-structing myself as earnest. For example, I elect to enter the play frame by mimicking the "jerky" intellectual interview voice, but I also give earnest answers to Salim's questions: "France is very very nice" and "the French" are "very wel-coming." Alternately, I engage in a mild form of *afficher* myself when, in response to the question "What do you think about *Cerise*?," I chastise: "Sometimes we chat more than we should. It is necessary to do more homework."

Although they are ironically voiced in the TV interview register, my seem-ingly well-intentioned and polite responses are overridden by bystanders through their active use of "side-play" (Goffman 1981: 154). Rather than a "nice" country, France is depicted as "racist" with not only too much "bad breath," but more seriously, too much "Pen," a reference to the anti-immigrant politician Jean-Marie Le Pen, former head of the National Front political party. Also, my high-minded attempt to create an inclusive depiction of "the French" that includes "especially the French of Chemin de l'Ile" (the local neighborhood) is challenged when Ali, a bystander, cries out that the association *Cerise* is full of "dirty Arabs" (*sales arabes*), a common racist slur. (Ali is Arab.)

Thus, my attempt at a pleasant depiction of France, the neighborhood, and the association is fairly drowned out by side-play claiming the contrary. The phoniness of my depiction is echoed when Salim, acting as the official interviewer, playfully twice pretends to silence vocal bystanders' derisions by claiming, "It's forbidden to say that. This (interview) is for France 2." France 2 is the largest national public television station and, as dominant national medium, would presumably want to suppress negative images of France entailing racism.

However, some side-play serves to validate my perspective, as when Batool teases the interviewer, Salim, with the words "Yes, we love France, Tolga." Here, Batool seems to validate my position even as she playfully challenges Salim's own anti-France stance by addressing him as "Tolga," by the name of his family's hometown in Algeria. Also, Batool smiles and utters *ouais* in a sweet, seemingly sincere tone when I claim to "especially like the French people of Chemin de l'Ile." The overall seriousness of this exchange is furthermore made questionable when the "interview" devolves into a discussion (again) of "bad breath." With a laugh, I acknowledge that this question may well be about me, as the established pattern throughout has been to pose leading questions to "interviewees" as a means to "display" them for an audience. However, this exchange appears again to be about Jacques and constitutes a relatively safe return to mocking him in absentia. As safe a topic as this seems, given the frequency with which it appears in these performances, Ali proclaims his worry that Jacques will listen to my recording. (Jacques was never given access to my audio recordings.) The older boys, Salim and Tarek, override his naïve concern by playfully and proudly "displaying" each other by claiming that "the other one" insulted Jacques, using both reported speech and direct voicing to do so.

Salim	*Que pensez-vous de la France?*	What do you think about France?
	Que pensez-vous de la France?	What do you think about France? [Uses "jerky" voice: pompous tone, nasality, and lowered voice]
Chantal	*C'est très très bien. J'aime la France. Ils sont-*	It's very very nice. I love France. They are- [Mimics "jerky" voice, nasality, lowered tone, crisp enunciation]

Batool	On aime la France, oui, Tolga.	We love France, yes, Tolga. [Laughingly to Salim, addressing him as "Tolga"]
Ali	Y'a des racistes!	There are racists!
Sarah	Y'a trop de racistes!	There are too many racists!
Salim	C'est interdit de dire ça. C'est pour France 2.	It's forbidden to say that. This [interview] is for France 2.
Ali	Y'a trop de coups d'haleine!	There's too much bad breath!
Sarah	Il y a trop de Pen/peine! [6]	There's too much [Le] Pen/pain!
Chantal	Ils sont très acceuillant, les français, sûrtout les français de Chemin de l'Ile.	They are very welcoming, the French, especially the French of Chemin de l'Ile.
Batool	Ouais.	Yes. [Smiling, to Chantal]
Salim	Que pensez-vous de Cerise s'il vous plaît?	What do you think about Cerise, please?
Chantal	De Cerise? [[C'est très très bien euh. Pffff!	About Cerise? [[It's very very nice uh. Pffff! [Exhales air out of tight lips, in response to the "dirty Arabs" comment]
Ali	[[Que des gamins. Que de sales arabes.	[[Just kids. Just dirty Arabs.
Salim	S'il vous plaît, hein? C'est pour France 2, hein?	[To Ali] Please, huh? It's for France 2, huh?
Chantal	Parfois on discute plus qu'on devrait. Il faut faire plus de devoirs.	Sometimes we talk more than we should. It's necessary to do more homework.

Salim	*Que pensez-vous des mauvaises haleines?*	What do you think about bad breath?
Chantal	*Oh j'éspère que j'en ai pas!*	Oh, I hope I don't have it! [Laughs]
Tarek	*En particulier de Jacques.*	Especially *from Jacques.*
Ali	*Il écoute! C'est lui qui va écouter après!*	He listens! He's the one who's going to listen [to the recordings] after!
Tarek	*Hé, c'est pas moi. C'est Salim qui a tout dit!*	Hey, it's not me. It's Salim who said everything! [Laughing]
Salim	*Je m'appelle Tarek Amrouche. Je parle de Jacques! Jacques, il pue de la gueule!*	My name is Tarek Amrouche. I'm talking about Jacques! Jacques' breath stinks! [Laughter from Tarek and others]

In the two extended performances analyzed here, adolescents render two locally performed versions of the TV host register, that of the game show host and the interview show host. Both performed identities establish mismatched voicing effects that, in turn, create a generalized ironic footing for the exchange. However, each performed voice—the game show host and the television interviewer—helps create distinct participation frameworks that are crafted for the particular performance and the target at hand.

In the first performance, the "game show" format allows for the wholesale embedding of a "display" in which targets attribute damaging reported speech. In this way, the non-serious frame of the "game" is used to embed serious accusations about past actions and utterances that are purportedly based on truth. Although targets are not given the chance to speak, the words spoken for them are putatively their own and merely reported by the game show MCs Mina and Hannah.

In the second performance, the "interview" format allows for complex voicing effects to be achieved in every utterance. Ubiquitous interview topics, such as pollution, serve as pointed critiques of specific individuals. Outwardly innocuous interview questions contain personal information and accusations about targets. Interviewers speak not only for interviewees, but as them through direct stylized voicing. And side-play serves to create an altogether negative counter-representation of the "polite" interview. Moreover, in the second performance, the serious and "objective" voice of the television interviewer is revealed as pompous and phony. This phoniness is then marshaled to mock audience members with exaggerated caricatures.

Clashing voicing effects pervade both performances, but performed voices specific to each serve to achieve distinct participation frameworks that mock targets to varying degrees. In each, the authority to speak unspeakable things and to caricature one's peers and mentors is achieved through the performance of an inauthentic persona: the TV host. In these ways, the concepts of mismatched voicing effects and generalized footing lead us to a better understanding of how language crossing acts as a resource in creating nuanced participation frameworks.

More generally, all of the preceding performances demonstrate that, through mismatched voicing effects, adolescents authorize themselves to voice various kinds of dangerous "truths" with which to critique peers. Primarily, the opposition between the elite white French TV persona and working-class teens of North African descent is used to create very local kinds of "displays" about peers and tutors. These take the form of public "truth telling" (afficher) to reveal and mock bad breath, illicit crushes, sexual and gender deviance, and intellectual phoniness.

Yet the gaps in voicing effects achieved here also display a larger social commentary on the inauthentic, "phony" persona of the TV host and the more generalized "phoniness" of French popular media and society at large. Through clashing voicing effects, such truths revolve around the representational gap between positive and seemingly innocuous representations of dominant French society and ugly truths about everyday experiences of racism and inequality.

In these performances, adolescents re-imagine social personas and speech styles in their peer interactions and local interactional goals. By "crossing" into the register of these socially recognizable "Others," adolescents momentarily de-stabilize recognizable identity categories and create transcultural performances that negotiate moral and social orders for their peer group. In contrast to current scholarship's emphasis on non-standard French speech among cité youth, these performances demonstrate teens' knowledge of and competence in multiple styles of French. At the same time, these performances evidence a related but more pervasive body of symbolic knowledge that is possessed by the teen performers: an understanding of the power relations and hierarchical social structures inherent to the social personae attached to these linguistic registers and language styles.

Notes

1 For other exceptions to a focus on naturalistic data, see Chun 2005 and Schilling-Estes 1998.

2 These serious exchanges and the way that they play out as either outright denials or forced admissions, sometimes leading to verbal and physical conflict, bear many similarities to the "he-said-she-said" routines documented by M. H. Goodwin (1990). However, in the data analyzed in this chapter, the ironic frame that is established by the TV host register elevates these performances to a type of play that targets cannot easily resist through direct verbal challenges.

3 The literal French words co-constructed by Hannah and Mina, *un coup de bite*, might literally be translated as "a fuck (i.e., the sexual act) of cock." I have chosen to translate the phrase as "hook up for sex" because I feel this translation better suits the level of profanity of the original French.

4 This may be *bidun* ("nothing" or "without") in Arabic, and acting as a filler or as a fictitious guest's name.

5 Mock Spanish (Hill 1998) comprises uses of loan words and loan phrases from Spanish by non-Spanish speakers in a way that trivializes the language and its native speakers. Hill's (1998: 683) observation that Mock Spanish comprises a fixture in dominant American media is relevant here in that it is a common feature of French TV host register, along with Mock Italian (e.g., *ciao*), used to project a casual and friendly persona. At the same time, it is unlikely that Mock Spanish entails the same social *effects* in France, in that, as Hill argues, within the United States, the practice evidences racialization and neo-imperial power relations toward Mexico and Latin America that seem to be largely absent from the practice within the context of Europe.

6 This could be a play on words, using the homonym, "Pen/peine." or "Le Pen" and "pain," each of which rhyme with *haleine* ("bad breath"). Both utterances work in the immediate context, in that Le Pen is a logical way to follow up on the previous claims of racism in France, and "pain" also follows logically after claims of so much "bad breath."

CONCLUSION

This book has argued that French teens of primarily Algerian descent living in *cités* have a particularly rich and also fraught set of perspectives and practices to share that illuminate aspects of contemporary French society. Racialized and stigmatizing narratives that highlight *la racaille* and criminality have come to dominate public French discourse regarding *les cités*. This book demonstrates both the centrality of these discourses to *cité* teens' own everyday interactions, as well as their clear inadequacy to explain the complexities of social identity and spatial affiliation among teens in Chemin de l'Ile.

Teenagers actively engage with such stigmatizing discourses, for example, by alternatingly affiliating and dis-affiliating with the stigmatized styles associated with *les cités* (Chapter 2), by recycling dominant stereotypes for in-group purposes (Chapter 3), and in girls' gendered and spatializing narratives about *la racaille* (Chapter 4). They also transcend and transform these discourses by creating new communicative forms that connect to and diverge from their North African heritage, for example, in girls' transgressive stylistic practices and in their uses of public space in their *cité* (Chapter 5) as well as through parental name-calling routines (Chapter 6). By breaching the personal name taboo practiced by their parents, teens articulate cultural connections and express how their experiences diverge from those of their parents, a pattern also shown in how girls alternately construct and affirm feminine-styled and masculine-styled "respect" for themselves. Perhaps most central to this book's critique of stigmatizing French discourses about *les cités* are teens' own positioning of themselves as critics of contemporary France, through their transformation of popular cultural symbols and

---

Transcultural Teens: Performing Youth Identities in French Cités, First Edition. Chantal Tetreault.
© 2015 John Wiley & Sons, Inc. Published 2015 by John Wiley & Sons, Inc.

language syles of French in everyday interactions. For example, teens use and transform a variety of standard French in order to humorously mock the French television MC as well as the "phoniness" and racism inherent to French public discourse (Chapter 7).

I have described these practices as *transcultural* for the ways that adolescents of Algerian descent combine cultural and linguistic referents in their communicative styles and identity performances, and for the ways that they connect and take apart the ideological underpinnings of their multiple social identities in everyday peer interactions. I have argued that, through such practices, these teens construct and express their emergent identities as simultaneously Arab and French, identities that are often constructed as mutually exclusive in mainstream discourses.

Through transcultural performances such as the parental name-calling exchange in the following example, adolescents in Chemin de l'Ile articulate their positing between North African heritage and French culture, including symbols of North African kinship, French politics, and popular media. Here, Zeinab taunts her peers, Soraya and Omar, that they do not know her father's first name and so cannot tease her with parental name-calling. Zeinab's father had passed away many years before, and she had tried to do her best to prevent his name circulating in the *cité* in order to avoid being teased by her peers. Zeinab thus challenges her peers: "You dunno the name—the real name of my real father. It's not worth the trouble." In French, however, the expression "it's not worth the trouble" is "*C'est pas la peine*" and *peine* ("trouble" or "pain") is a homonym for "Pen," as in Jean-Marie Le Pen. Zeinab's peers, Omar and Soraya, seize on this opportunity to poke fun that Zeinab's real father is actually the right-wing politician.

Head of a "Pen," Hurts It's So Ugly

Zeinab	*Tu connais pas le nom, le vrai nom de mon vrai père. C'est pas la peine.*	You dunno the name, the real name of my real father. It's not worth the trouble.
Soraya	*Jean-Marie!*	Jean-Marie! [Sing-song voice]
Zeinab	*Non, le vrai.*	No, the real one.
Omar	*Le Pen! WOOOOOO!*	Le Pen! WOOOOOO!

Soraya	*Jean-Marie!*	Jean-Marie! [Singing in an urgent whisper]
Omar	*Tête de Pen, faire d'la peine,* *à Jean-Marie!*	Head of a Pen, it causes pain, ["hurts it's so ugly"], to Jean-Marie!

In the preceding instance, Zeinab, Soraya, and Omar contextualize their unique position at the cultural and linguistic intersection of North African and French social structures. The teens purposefully and humorously conflate the Arab cultural trope of respect for kin (in this case, fathers) with an iconic French figure who built a political career out of denying respect to their community: the founder of the anti-immigrant National Front party, Jean-Marie Le Pen. The example thereby illustrates the creative symbolic juxtaposition of this anti-Arab cultural icon with local Arab kinship networks. The exchange demonstrates both a structured, poetic form as well as a performative, impromptu quality in the way that speakers forge tight connections at the phonological level (*peine* and Pen), and fantastical leaps on the semiotic level (positing the anti-immigration, right-wing Le Pen as Zeinab's "real" father).

The playful claim that Jean-Marie Le Pen is Zeinab's father is effective because of its implausibility, in that the politician has called for the expulsion of all immigrants as well as supposed cultural/religious "foreigners" (*étrangers*) from France, and thus these adolescents' parents and themselves. Not incidentally, the name "Jean-Marie" is also commonly used to refer to the quintessential Frenchman in popular discourse, similar to the American English expression "John Doe." Thus, "Jean-Marie" represents a social persona, like the politician, that clashes with the identity of Zeinab's biological father, who was an Arab Muslim born in North Africa.

Omar next takes up the word *peine* and puns a rhymed insult that targets Zeinab, which is derived from a popular song by the French singer Zazie: *tête de Pen, faire d'la peine* or "head of a Pen, it causes pain." The original lyrics in Zazie's 1998 song, entitled *Tout le Monde* ("Everyone") were "*Tout le monde, il est beau. Quitte à faire de la peine à Jean-Marie*" or "Everyone is beautiful, even if it gives pain to Jean-Marie." Zazie brokers the homonym *peine* and Pen to create a message of racial tolerance that criticizes Jean-Marie Le Pen's public rejection of a multi-cultural France. In contrast to the liberal, inclusive message of harmony and beauty brokered by Zazie, Omar riffs on the song to call Zeinab a *tête de Pen* ("head of a Pen") that "hurts" or gives pain (*faire d'la peine*) because it is so ugly. Omar thereby manages to create a triply valenced insult—insulting Le Pen, Zeinab, and her imaginary father for the supposed ugliness they share. The juxtaposition of these disparate cultural references serves to perform and subvert the boundaries of "Frenchness" and "Arabness." For example, by purposefully melding the iconic French cultural figure of Jean-Marie Le Pen with Zeinab's father, Omar playfully conflates "French" and "Arab" social categories.

In the adolescent interactions explored in this book, the boundaries of contrasting linguistic and symbolic categories are transgressed through transcultural performances that create a cultural crossroads from which to speak. While the "joke" in this language play is about discontinuity, that is, the jarring choice to blend together the identities of Jean-Marie Le Pen and Zeinab's father, this choice nevertheless serves to blur cultural and linguistic boundaries. In this way, adolescents combine cultural symbols to contextualize their unique location at the intersection of French and North African social systems. The practice of inserting high French cultural references and anti-immigrant political figures into the frame of a kinship name taboo furthermore shows that adolescents are improvising verbal genres and cultural practices that mediate among creativity, "tradition," and social critique. By inserting iconic French cultural symbols within an innovative speech genre that is based upon violating their parents' avoidance of personal names, teens simultaneously achieve cultural continuity and disjuncture.

Also negotiated here is adolescents' intimate awareness of the difficult role that they have to play in a post-colonial, multicultural France in which seemingly perpetual "crises" of national identity target and scapegoat immigrants and their descendants for the cultural and economic "demise" of France. Here, the "personal" truly is "political," in that teens are actively processing and creatively expanding upon the broadly circulating discourses of exclusion and racism in their everyday interactions as a way to create a shared sense of community and belonging within their peer group.

Here, fun, humor, and creativity are born out of exclusion and racism, but at a cost. As "products" of French social, racial, spatial, political, and media environments, these teens are learning and teaching each other about the ways that French dominant society too often rejects them as "less than" French. In this sense, tranculturality among these teens is born out of a shared sense that, despite being clearly situated as culturally, linguistically, and historically *French*—both as children born of a (post-)colonial France and a France that touts universal, equal citizenship as available to all born on its soil—they are too often the politicized target and supposed *cause* of ongoing public, hand-wringing "debates" about the viability and future of the French language and, more troubling, of France itself.

The perspectives that these teens show us are vital if we are to understand the lasting and pernicious effects of publicly questioning the value and even "cost" to society of certain French citizens over others. Whereas too many popular and scholarly representations of *les cités* still cast these spaces as "other," in the form of stigmatizing images such as "linguistic deviance" (Boyer 1998), and as non-French for a variety of supposed racialized, religious, or cultural reasons, I have tried to show the ways that teens in Chemin de l'Ile are engaged in the business of elaborating new and creative ways of *being and speaking French*.

As the same time, this book provides a look at *lived* transculturality in the ways that teens use language to situate themselves within the highly contentious atmosphere of low-income housing projects, within contemporary France, and within the North African diaspora. These teens' experiences and forms of expression are of vital importance in a time of both increasing marginalization and globalization. Through verbal creativity teens not only experiment and play with stigmatizing discourses, they also structure their relationships with peers and forge their place in the world.

REFERENCES

Abrahams, Roger D. 1975. "Negotiating Respect: Patterns of Presentation among Black Women." *The Journal of American Folklore* 88 (347): 58–80. doi:10.2307/539186.

Abu-Haidar, Farida. 1995. "Language Loyalty: The Case of Algerian Immigrants' Children in France." In *Arabic Sociolinguistics: Issues and Perspectives,* edited by Yasir Suleiman, 43–55. New York: Routledge.

Abu-Lughod, Lila. 2002. "Do Muslim Women Really Need Saving? Anthropological Reflections on Cultural Relativism and its Others." *American Anthropologist* 104 (3): 783–790.

Abu-Lughod, Lila. 1986. *Veiled Sentiments: Honor and Poetry in a Bedouin Society,* 1st ed. Berkeley: University of California Press.

Agha, Asif. 2007. *Language and Social Relations.* Cambridge: Cambridge University Press.

Agha, Asif. 2005. "Voice, Footing, Enregisterment." *Journal of Linguistic Anthropology* 15 (1): 38–59. doi:10.1525/jlin.2005.15.1.38.

Albert, Steve. 2002. *"Just Tough Enough: Aggressive Talk and Outsider Status in a French Secondary School."* Paper presented at the annual American Anthropological Association meeting, New Orleans, November 22.

Alim, H. Samy. 2009. "Straight outta Compton, Straight *aus München:* Global Linguistic Flows, Identities, and the Politics of Language in a Global Hip Hop Nation." In *Global Linguistic Flows: Hip Hop Cultures, Youth Identities and the Politics of Language,* edited by Samy H. Alim, Awad Ibrahim and Alastair Pennycook, 1–24. London: Routledge.

Amit-Talai, Vered. 1995. "Conclusion: The 'Multi' Cultural of Youth." In *Youth Cultures: A Cross-Cultural Perspective,* edited by Vered Amit-Talai and Helena Wulff, 223–233. London: Routledge.

Anderson, Benedict. 1991. *Imagined Communities: Reflections on the Origin and Spread of Nationalism*. London: Verso.

Androutsopoulos, Jannis K. 2007. "Bilingualism in the Mass Media and on the Internet." In *Bilingualism: A Social Approach*, edited by Monica Heller, 207–232. Basingstoke: Palgrave.

Androutsopoulos, Jannis K., and Alexandra Georgakopoulou, eds. 2003. *Discourse Constructions of Youth Identities*. Amsterdam: John Benjamins Pub Co.

Arthur. 1996. *Ta Mère*. Paris: Flammarion.

Arthur. 1996. *Ta Mère 2, La réponse*. Paris: Flammarion.

Auer, Peter, and Inci Dirim. 2003. "Sociocultural Orientation, Urban Youth Styles and the Spontaneous Acquisition of Turkish by non-Turkish in Germany." In *Discourse Constructions of Youth Identities*, edited by Jannis K. Androutsopoulos and Alexandra Georgakopoulou, 223–246. Amsterdam: John Benjamins Pub Co.

Badran, Margot. 1995. *Feminists, Islam, and Nation: Gender and the Making of Modern Egypt*. Princeton: Princeton University Press.

Bailey, Benjamin. 2000. "The Language of Multiple Identities among Dominican Americans." *Journal of Linguistic Anthropology* 10 (2): 190–223. doi:10.1525/jlin.2000.10.2.190.

Bakhtin, Mikhail. 1984. *Rabelais and His World*. Translated by Hélène Iswolsky. Bloomington: Indiana University Press.

Bakhtin, Mikhail. 1981. "Discourse in the Novel." In *The Dialogic Imagination: Four Essays*, edited by Michael Holquist, 259–422. Translated by Caryl Emerson and Michael Holquist. Austin: University of Texas Press.

Balibar, Etienne. 1991. "Is There a 'Neo-Racism'?" In *Race, Nation, Class: Ambiguous Indentities*, edited by Etienne Balibar and Immanuel Wallerstein, 17–28. First English Language Edition. London: Verso.

Barrett, Rusty. 1999. "Indexing Polyphonous Identity in the Speech of African American Drag Queens." In *Reinventing Identities: The Gendered Self In Discourse*, edited by Mary Bucholtz, A. C. Liang, and Laurel A. Sutton, 131–331. New York: Oxford University Press.

Basier, Luc, and Christian Bachmann. 1984. "Le Verlan: Argot D'école ou Langue des Keums?" *Mots* 8 (1): 169–187. doi:10.3406/mots.1984.1145.

Basso, Keith H. 1979. *Portraits of "The Whiteman": Linguistic Play and Cultural Symbols Among the Western Apache*. Cambridge, UK: Cambridge University Press.

Bauman, Richard. 2004. *A World of Others' Words: Cross-Cultural Perspectives on Intertextuality*. Malden, MA: Blackwell Publishing.

Bauman, Richard. 1977. *Verbal Art as Performance*. Prospect Heights, IL: Waveland Press.

Bauman, Richard, and Charles L. Briggs. 1990. "Poetics and Performance as Critical Perspectives on Language and Social Life." *Annual Review of Anthropology* 19: 59–88.

Begag, Azouz. 2005. *Le Gone du Chaâba*. Paris: Editions du Seuil.

Begag, Azouz, and Reynald Rossini. 1999. *Du Bon Usage de la Distance Chez les Sauvageons*. Paris: Seuil.

Bell, Allan. 1984. "Language Style as Audience Design." *Language in Society* 13 (2): 145–204.

Bénabou, Roland, Francis Kramarz and Corinne Prost. 2004. "Zones d'Education Prioritaire: Quels Moyens pour Quels Résultats? Une Evaluation sur la Période 1982–1992." *Économie et Statistique*, 380: 3–34.

Ben Jelloun, Tahar. 1984. *Hospitalité Française*. Paris: Seuil.

Bensignor, François. 1993. "Le Raï, entre Oran, Marseille et Paris." *Hommes et Migrations* 1170: 25–29.

Bentahila, Abdelali, and Eirlys E. Davies. 2002. "Language Mixing in Rai Music: Localisation or Globalisation?" *Language and Communication* 22 (2): 187–207.

Beriss, David. 2004. *Black Skins, French Voices: Caribbean Ethnicity and Activism in Urban France*. Boulder: Westview Press.

Billiez, Jacqueline. 1985. "Les Jeunes Issus de l'Immigration Algérienne et Espagnole à Grenoble: Quelques Aspects Sociolinguistiques." *International Journal of the Sociology of Language* 54: 41–56. doi:10.1515/ijsl.1985.54.41.

Blatt, David. 1997. "Immigrant Politics in a Republican Nation." In *Post-Colonial Cultures in France*, edited by Alec G. Hargreaves and Mark McKinney, 40–58. London: Routledge.

Blin, Louis. 1990. *L'Algérie, du Sahara au Sahal*. Paris: L'Harmattan.

Blommaert, Jan. 2010. *The Sociolinguistics of Globalization*. New York: Cambridge University Press.

Bloul, Rachel. 1996. "Engendering Muslim Identities: Deterritorialization and the Ethnicization Process in France." In Making Muslim *Space in North America and Europe*, edited by Barbara Daly Metcalf, 234–250. Berkeley: University of California Press.

Bonnafous, Simone. 1991. *L'Immigration Prise aux Mots*. Paris: Editions Kimé.

Bordet, Joëlle. 1998. *Les "Jeunes De La Cité"*. Paris: Presses Universitaires de France.

Bouamama, Saïd. 1993. *De la Galère à la Citoyenneté: Les Jeunes, la Cité, la Société*. Paris: Desclée de Brouwer.

Boucherit, Aziza. 2008. "Continuité, Rupture et Construction Identitaires: Analyse de Discours d'Immigrés Maghrébins en France." *International Journal of the Sociology of Language* 190: 49–77.

Bourdieu, Pierre. 1987. *Distinction: A Social Critique of the Judgement of Taste. Translated by Richard Nice*. Cambridge, MA: Harvard University Press.

Bourdieu, Pierre et al. 1999. *The Weight of the World: Social Suffering in Contemporary Society. Translated by Priscilla Parkhurst Ferguson*. Stanford, CA: Stanford University Press.

Bourdieu, Pierre, and Loïc Wacquant. 1992. *An Invitation to Reflexive Sociology*. Chicago: University of Chicago.

Bowen, John. 2007. *Why the French Don't Like Headscarves: Islam, the State, and Public Space*. Princeton, NJ: Princeton University Press.

Boyer, Henri. 1997. "'Nouveau Français', 'Parler Jeune' ou 'Langue des Cités'? Remarques sur un Objet Linguistique Médiatiquement Identifié." *Langue Française* 114 (1): 6–15. doi:10.3406/lfr.1997.5379.

Boyer, Henri. 1994. "Le Jeune Tel Qu'on en Parle." *Langage et Société* 70: 85–91.

Briggs, Charles, and Richard Bauman. 1992. "Genre, Intertextuality, and Social Power." *Journal of Linguistic Anthropology* 2 (2): 131–172.

Bucholtz, Mary. 2011. *White Kids: Language, Race, and Styles of Youth Identity*. New York: Cambridge University Press.

Bucholtz, Mary. 2003. "Sociolinguistic Nostalgia and the Authentication of Identity." *Journal of Sociolinguistics* 7 (3): 398–416. doi:10.1111/1467-9481.00232.

Bucholtz, Mary. 2002. "Youth and Cultural Practice." *Annual Review of Anthropology* 31 (1): 525–552. doi:10.1146/annurev.anthro.31.040402.085443.

Bucholtz, Mary. 1999. "'Why Be Normal?': Language and Identity Practices in a Community of Nerd Girls." *Language in Society* 28 (2): 203–223.

Bucholtz, Mary, A. C. Liang, and Laurel A. Sutton, eds. 1999. *Reinventing Identities: The Gendered Self in Discourse*. New York: Oxford University Press.

Butler, Judith. 1990. *Gender Trouble: Feminism and the Subversion of Identity*. New York: Routledge.

Cameron, Deborah. 1997. "Performing Gender Identity: Young Men's Talk and the Construction of Heterosexual Masculinity." In *Language and Masculinity*, edited by Sally Johnson and Ulrike Hanna Meinhof, 47–64. Oxford, UK: Blackwell Publishing.

Cantwell, Robert. 1993. *Ethnomimesis: Folklife and the Representation of Culture*. Chapel Hill: University of North Carolina Press.

Certeau, Michel de. 1984. *The Practice of Everyday Life*. Berkeley: University of California Press.

Chapman, Herrick, and Laura L. Frader, eds. 2004. *Race in France: Interdisciplinary Perspectives on the Politics of Difference*. London: Berghahn Books.

Chun, Elaine. 2009. "Speaking Like Asian Immigrants: Intersections of Accommodation and Mocking at a U.S. High School." *Pragmatics* 12 (1): 17–38.

Chun, Elaine. 2005. "Taking the Mike: Performances of Everyday Identities and Ideologies at a U.S High School." *Proceedings of the Annual Symposium about Language and Society-Austin: Texas Linguistic Forum* 49: 39–49.

Coates, Jennifer. 1999. "Changing Femininities: The Talk of Teenage Girls." In *Reinventing Identities: The Gendered Self in Discourse*, edited by Mary Bucholtz, A. C. Liang, and Laurel A. Sutton, 123–139. New York: Oxford University Press.

Costa-Lascoux, Jacqueline. 1989. *De l'Immigré au Citoyen*. Paris: Documentation française.

Cutler, Cecilia A. 1999. "Yorkville Crossing: White Teens, Hip Hop, and African American English." *Journal of Sociolinguistics* 3 (4): 428–442.

Dabène, Louise. 1991. "Le Parler Bilingue Issus De L'immigration En France." In *Codeswitching as a Worldwide Phenomenon*, edited by Rodolfo Jacobson, 159–168. New York: Peter Lang Publishing.

Dabène, Louise, and Jacqueline Billiez. 1987. "Le Parler des Jeunes Issu de l'Immigration." In *France, Pays Multilingue*, edited by Geneviève Vermès and Josiane Boutet, 62–74. Paris: L'Harmattan.

Dabène, Olivier. 1990. "Les 'Beurs', Les 'Potes': Identités Culturelles et Conduites Politiques." *Politix* 3 (12): 38–46. doi:10.3406/polix.1990.1422.

Dannequin, Claudine. 1999. "Interactions Verbales et Construction de L'Humiliation Chez les Jeunes des Quartiers Défavorisés." *Mots* 60 (1): 76–92. doi:10.3406/mots.1999.2165.

DeRudder, Veronique. 1980. "La Tolérance S'arrête au Seuil." *Pluriel-Débat* (21): 3–13.

Dick, Hilary. 2010. "Imagined Lives and Modernist Chronotopes in Mexican Nonmigrant Discourse." *American Ethnologist* 37 (2): 275–290.

Douville, Olivier. 1985. "Parcours de Scolarisation d'Enfants et d'Adolescents Maghrébins en France." *Cahiers d'Anthropologie et Biométrie Humaine* 3 (3–4): 23–45.

Du Bois, W. E. B. (1903). *The Souls of Black Folk*. New York: Bantam Classic.

Duranti, Alessandro. 1997. "Indexical Speech across Samoan Communities." *American Anthropologist* 99: 342–354.

Duret, Pascal. 1996. *Anthropologie de la Fraternité dans les Cités*. Paris: Presses Universitaires de France.

Durham, Deborah. 2000. "Youth and the Social Imagination in Africa: Introduction to Parts 1 and 2." *Anthropological Quarterly* 73 (3): 113–120.

Eckert, Penelope. 2004. "The Meaning of Style." *Proceedings of the Annual Symposium about Language and Society-Austin: Texas Linguistic Forum* 47: 41–53.

Eckert, Penelope. 2000. *Linguistic Variation as Social Practice*. Malden, MA: Blackwell Publishing.

Eckert, Penelope. 1989. *Jocks and Burnouts: Social Categories and Identity in the High School*. New York: Teachers College Press.

Eckert, Penelope and Sally McConnell-Ginet. 1992. "Communities of Practice: Where Language, Gender, and Power All Live." In *Locating Power: Proceedings of the Second Berkley Women and Language Conference*, edited by Kira Hall, Mary Bucholtz, and Birch Moonwomon, 89–99. Berkley: Women and Language Group.

Essed, Philomena. 1991. *Understanding Everyday Racism: An Interdisciplinary Theory*. Thousand Oaks, CA: Sage Publications.

Fairclough, Norman. 2001. *Language and Power*, 2nd ed. White Plains, NY: Pearson ESL.

Feldblum, Miriam. 1993. "Paradoxes of Ethnic Politics: The Case of Franco-Maghrebis in France." *Ethnic and Racial Studies* 16 (1): 52–74. doi:10.1080/01419870.1993.9993772.

Fernando, Mayanthi L. 2014. *The Republic Unsettled: Muslim French and the Contradictions of Secularism*. Durham, NC: Duke University Press.

Fernea, Elizabeth, and Robert Fernea. 1995. "Symbolizing Roles: Behind the Veil." In *Dress and Identity*, edited by Mary Ellen Roach-Higgins, Joanne B. Eicher, and Kim K. P. Johnson, 285–292. New York: Fairchild Publications.

Foley, Douglas E. 1990. *Learning Capitalist Culture: Deep in the Heart of Tejas*. Philadelphia: University of Pennsylvania Press.

Gadet, Françoise. 1996. *Le français ordinaire*. Paris: Armand Colin.

Gal, Susan. 2005. "Language Ideologies Compared: Metaphors of Public/Private." *Journal of Linguistic Anthropology* 15 (1): 23–37.

Gal, Susan. 2002. "A Semiotics of the Public/Private Distinction." *Differences: A Journal of Feminist Cultural Studies* 13 (1): 77–95.

Gal, Susan and Judith Irvine. 2000. "Language Ideology and Linguistic Differentiation." In *Regimes of Language: Ideologies, Politics, and Identities*, edited by Paul V. Kroskrity, 35–83. Santa Fe, NM: School of American Research Press.

García-Sánchez, Inmaculada M. 2014. *Language and Muslim Immigrant Childhoods: The Politics of Belonging*. New York: Wiley-Blackwell.

Gates, Henry Louis, Jr. 1988. *The Signifying Monkey: A Theory of African-American Literary Criticism*. New York: Oxford University Press.

Geertz, Clifford. 1983. *Local Knowledge: Further Essays in Interpretive Anthropology*. New York: Basic Books.

Ghannam, Farha. 2002. *Remaking the Modern: Space, Relocation, and the Politics of Identity in a Global Cairo*. Berkeley: University of California Press.

Giampapa, Frances. 2001. "Hyphenated Identities: Italian–Canadian Youth and the Negotiation of Ethnic Identities in Toronto." *International Journal of Bilingualism* 5 (3): 279–315.

Gilroy, Paul. 1993. *The Black Atlantic: Modernity and Double-Consciousness*. Cambridge, MA: Harvard University Press.

Gilroy, Paul. 1991. *"There Ain't No Black in the Union Jack': The Cultural Politics of Race and Nation*. Chicago, IL: University of Chicago Press.

Goffman, Erving. 1982. *Interaction Ritual: Essays on Face-to-Face Behavior*. New York: Pantheon.

Goffman, Erving. 1981. *Forms of Talk*. Philadelphia: University of Pennsylvania Press.

Goffman, Erving. 1963. *Stigma: Notes on the Management of Spoiled Identity*. Englewood Cliffs, NJ: Prentice-Hall.

Goffman, Erving. 1959. *The Presentation of Self in Everyday Life*. New York: Anchor.

Goodman, Jane E. 2005. *Berber Culture on the World Stage: From Village to Video*. Bloomington: Indiana University Press.

Goodwin, Marjorie H. 1990. *He-Said-She-Said: Talk as Social Organization among Black Children*. Bloomington: Indiana University Press.

Goudaillier, Jean-Pierre. 2012. "Langues et Identités: l'Exemple du Français Contemporain des Cités." *Informations Sociales* (119): 74–80.

Goudaillier, Jean-Pierre. 1997. *Comment Tu Tchatches!: Dictionnaire du Français Contemporain des Cités*. Paris: Maisonneuve et Larose.

Grillo, R. D. 2006. *Ideologies and Institutions in Urban France: The Representation of Immigrants*. New York: Cambridge University Press.

Gross, Joan, David McMurray, and Ted Swedenburg. 1994. "Arab Noise and Ramadan Nights: Raï, Rap, and Franco-Maghrebi Identity." *Diaspora* 1 (3): 3–39.

Gumperz, John. 1982a. *Discourse strategies*. Cambridge: Cambridge University Press.

Gumperz, John. 1982b. *Language and Social Identity*. Cambridge: Cambridge University Press.

Guyotat, Régis. 1994. "M. Chirac: 'Il y a Overdose'." *Le Monde*, June 21.

Hall, Kira. 1997. "Go Suck on Your Husband's Sugarcane: Hijras and the Use of Sexual Insult." In *Queerly Phrased: Language, Gender, and Sexuality*, edited by Anna Livia and Kira Hall, 432–469. New York: Oxford University Press.

Hall, Stuart, Chas Critcher, Tony Jefferson, John N. Clarke, and Brian Roberts. 1978. *Policing the Crisis: Mugging, the State and Law and Order*. London: Palgrave Macmillan.

Hanks, William F. 1989. "Text and Textuality." *Annual Review of Anthropology* 18: 95–127.

Hargreaves, Alec, and Mark McKinney, Ed. 1997. *Post-Colonial Cultures in France*. New York: Routledge.

Hebdige, Dick. 1979. *Subculture, the Meaning of Style*. London: Methuen.

Heller, Monica. 1999. *Linguistic Minorities and Modernity: A Sociolinguistic Ethnography*. Essex: Longman.

Hewitt, Roger. 1986. *White Talk, Black Talk: Inter-Racial Friendship and Communication Amongst Adolescents*. New York: Cambridge University Press.

Hill, Jane H. 1998. "Language, Race, and White Public Space." *American Anthropologist* 100 (3): 680–689. doi:10.1525/aa.1998.100.3.680.

Hoffmann–Dilloway, Erika. 2008. "Metasemiotic Regimentation in the Standardization of Nepali Sign Language." *The Journal of Linguistic Anthropology* 18 (2): 192–213.

INED. 2008. National French Census. http://statistiques_flux_immigration.site. ined.fr/en/admissions/

INSEE. Fiches thématiques: Populations immigrées. 2012.

Irvine, Judith T. 2001. "Style" as Distinctiveness: The Culture and Ideology of Linguistic Differentiation." In *Style and Sociolinguistic Variation*, edited by Penelope Eckert and John R. Rickford, 21–43. New York: Cambridge University Press.

Irvine, Judith T. 1996. "Shadow Conversations: the Indeterminacy of Participant Roles." In *Natural Histories of Discourse*, edited by Michael Silverstein and Greg Urban, 131–159. Chicago, IL: University of Chicago Press.

Irvine, Judith T. 1992. "Insult and Responsibility: Verbal Abuse in a Wolof Village." In *Responsibility and Evidence in Oral Discourse*, edited by Jane Hill and Judith T. Irvine, 104–134. Cambridge: Cambridge University Press.

Jaspers, Jürgen. 2005. "Linguistic Sabotage in a Context of Monolingualism and Standardization." *Language and Communication* 25 (3): 279–298.

Jazouli, Adil. 1992. *Les Années Banlieues*. Paris: Seuil.

Kapchan, Deborah. 1996. *Gender on the Market: Moroccan Women and the Revoicing of Tradition*. Philadelphia: University of Pennsylvania Press.

Kearney, Michael. 1995. "The Local and the Global: The Anthropology of Globalization and Transnationalism. *Annual Review of Anthropology* 24: 547–565.

Keaton, Trica Danielle. 2006. *Muslim Girls and the Other France: Race, Identity Politics, and Social Exclusion*. Bloomington: Indiana University Press.

Koven, Michèle. 2013. "Antiracist, Modern Selves and Racist, Unmodern Others: Chronotopes of Modernity in Luso-Descendants' Race Talk." *Language and Communication* 33: 544–558.

Koven, Michèle. 2004. "Transnational Perspectives on Sociolinguistic Capital among Luso-Descendants in France and Portugal." *American Ethnologist* 31: 270–290.

Koven, Michèle. 2001. "Comparing Bilinguals' Quoted Performances of Self and Others in Tellings of the Same Experience in Two Languages." *Language in Society* 30 (4): 513–558.

Kyratzis, Amy. 2004. "Talk and Interaction among Children and the Co-Construction of Peer Groups and Peer Culture." *Annual Review of Anthropology* 33: 625–649.

Labov, William. 1972. *Sociolinguistic Patterns*. Philadelphia: University of Pennsylvania Press.

Laronde, Michel. 1988. "La 'Mouvance Beure': Émergence Médiatique." *The French Review* 61 (5): 684–692.

Lefkowitz, Natalie. 1991. *Talking Backwards, Looking Forwards: The French Language Game Verlan*. Tübingen, Germany: Gunter Narr Verlag.

LePage, Robert Brock, and Andrée Tabouret-Keller. 1985. *Acts of Identity: Creole-based Approaches to Language and Ethnicity*. Cambridge: Cambridge University Press.

Lepoutre, David. 1997. *Coeur De Banlieue: Codes, Rites et Langages*. Paris: Editions Odile Jacob.

Lévi-Strauss, Claude. 2012 (1955). *Tristes Tropiques*. Translated by Jonathan Cape. New York: Penguin Classics, reprint edition.

Levinson, Stephen C. 1983. *Pragmatics*. Cambridge, UK: Cambridge University Press.

Lippi-Green, Rosina. 1997. *English with an Accent: Language, Ideology, and Discrimination in the United States*. New York: Routledge.

Lo, Adrienne. 1999. "Codeswitching, Speech Community Membership, and the Construction of Ethnic Identity." *Journal of Sociolinguistics* 3 (4): 461–479. doi:10.1111/1467-9481.00091.

MacMaster, Neil. 1997. *Colonial Migrants and Racism: Algerians in France, 1900–62*. New York: Palgrave Macmillan.

Mahmood, Saba. 2005. *The Politics of Piety: the Islamic Revival and the Feminist Subject*. Princeton: Princeton University Press.

McElhinny, Bonnie, ed. 2007. *Words, Worlds, Material Girls: Language and Gender in a Global Economy*. New York: Mouton de Gruyter.

McElhinny, Bonnie. 1995. "Challenging Hegemonic Masculinities: Female and Male Police Officers Handling Domestic Violence." In *Gender Articulated: Language and the Socially Constructed Self*, edited by Kira Hall and Mary Bucholtz, 217–243. New York: Routledge.

McMurray, David. 1997. "La France Arabe: Franco-Arab Popular Culture." In *Post-Colonial Cultures in France*, edited by Alec Hargreaves and Mark McKinney, 26–39. London: Routledge.

Mendoza-Denton, Norma. 2008. *Homegirls: Language and Cultural Practice among Latina Youth Gangs*. Malden, MA: Blackwell Publishing.

Mendoza-Denton, Norma. 2001. "Style." In *Key Terms in Language and Culture*, edited by Alessandro Duranti, 235–237. Malden, MA: Blackwell Publishing.

Metcalf, Barbara Daly. 1996. "Introduction: Sacred Words, Sanctioned Practice, New Communities." In *Making Muslim Space in North America and Europe* edited by Barbara Daly Metcalf, 1–30. Berkeley: University of California Press.

Ministère du Travail, de l'Emploi, de la Formation Professionelle et du Dialogue Social. 2012. "Emploi et chômage des immigrés en 2011, 2012". 077. Paris: DARES Analyses.

Mitchell-Kernan, Claudia. 1971. "Language Behavior in a Black Urban Community. Monograph of the Language-Behavior Research Laboratory, No. 2." University of California Language-Behavior Research Laboratory.

Modan, Gabriella Gahlia. 2007. *Turf Wars: Discourse, Diversity, and the Politics of Place*. Malden, MA: Blackwell Publishing.

Moïse, Claudine. 2003. "Pratiques Langagières des Banlieues: Où Sont les Femmes?" *La Lettre de l'Enfance et de l'Adolescence* 51 (1): 47–54.

Morgan, Marcyliena. 1999. "No Woman, No Cry: Claiming African American Women's Place." In *Reinventing Identities: The Gendered Self in Discourse*, edited by Mary Bucholtz, 27–45. New York: Oxford University Press.

Morgan, Marcyliena. 1996. "Redefining 'Language in The Inner City': Adolescents, Media and Urban Space." *Proceedings of the Annual Symposium about Language and Society-Austin: Texas Linguistic Forum* 4: 14–26.

Muxel, Anne. 1988. "Les Attitudes Socio-politiques des Jeunes Issus de l'Immigration en Région Parisienne." *Revue Française de Science Politique* 38 (6): 925–940. doi:10.3406/rfsp.1988.411178.

Noiriel, Gérard. 2007. "L'Historien dans la Cité: Comment Concilier Histoire et Mémoire de l'Immigration?" *Museum International (Edition Française)* 59 (1–2): 13–17. doi:10.1111/j.1755-5825.2007.0102x.x.

Ochs, Elinor. 2012. "Experiencing Language." *Anthropological Theory* 12 (2): 142–160.

Ochs, Elinor. 1992. "Indexing Gender." In *Rethinking Context,* edited by Alessandro Duranti and Charles Goodwin, 335–358. Cambridge: Cambridge University Press.

Orellana, Marjorie Faulstich. 2009. *Translating Childhoods: Immigrant Youth, Language and Culture*. New Brunswick, NJ: Rutgers University Press.

Ortiz, Fernando. 1947. *Cuban Counterpoint: Tobacco and Sugar. Translated from the Spanish by Harriet de Onís*. New York: A. A. Knopf.

Ossman, Susan. 1994. *Picturing Casablanca: Portraits of Power in a Modern City*. Berkeley: University of California Press.

Pagliai, Valentina. 2010. "Conflict, Cooperation, and Facework in Contrasto Verbal Duels." *Journal of Linguistic Anthropology* 20 (1): 87–100.

Park, Joseph Sung-Yul. 2009. *The Local Construction of a Global Language: Language Ideologies of English in South Korea*. Berlin, Germany: Mouton De Gruyter.

Peirce, Charles. 1931–1958. Collected Papers, Vols 1–8. Cambridge, MA: Harvard University Press.

Pennycook, Alastair. 2003. "Global Englishes, Rip Slyme, and Performativity." *Journal of Sociolinguistics* 7 (4): 513–533. doi:10.1111/j.1467-9841.2003.00240.x.

Peristiany, John. 1976. "Introduction." In *Mediterranean Family Structures*, J. G. Peristiany, Ed., pp. 1–26. New York: Cambridge University Press.

Pichler, Pia. 2005. "The Effect of Social Class and Ethnicity on the Discursive Negotiation of Femininities in the Talk of British Bangladeshi Girls." In *Language Across Boundaries*, edited by Janet Cotterill and Anne E. Ife, 25–46. London: Continuum International Publishing Group.

Pierre-Adolphe, Philippe, M. Mamoud, and G.-O. Tzanos. 1995. *Le Dico de la Banlieue*. Paris: La Sirène.

Poinsot, Marie. 1991. "L'Intégration Politique des Jeunes Maghrébins: Deux Stratégies Associatives dans la Région Lilloise." *Revue Européenne des Migrations Internationales* 7 (3): 119–138.

Pratt, Mary Louise. 2008/1992. *Imperial Eyes: Travel Writing and Transculturation*. New York: Routledge.

Pujolar, Joan. 2001 *Gender, Heteroglossia and Power: A Sociolinguistic Study of Youth Culture*. Berlin: Mouton De Gruyter.

Rampton, Ben. 2006. *Language in Late Modernity: Interaction in an Urban School*. Cambridge: Cambridge University Press.

Rampton, Ben. 1995a. "Language Crossing and the Problematisation of Ethnicity and Socialisation." *Pragmatics* 5 (4): 485–513. http://elanguage.net/journals/index.php/pragmatics/article/viewArticle/474.

Rampton, Ben. 1995b. *Crossing: Language and Ethnicity Among Adolescents*. Boston: Addison Wesley Publishing Company.

Rampton, Ben and Constadina Charalambous. 2010. "Crossing: A Review of Research." *Working Papers in Urban Language and Literacies* 55.

Reyes, Angela. 2006. *Language, Identity, and Stereotypes among Southeast Asian American Youth: The Other Asian*. New York: Routledge.

Reynolds, Jennifer F. 2013a "(Be)laboring Childhoods in Postville, Iowa." *Anthropological Quarterly* 86 (3): 851–890.

Reynolds, Jennifer F. 2013b. "Refracting Articulations of Citizenship, Delicuencia and Vigilantism in Boys' Sociodramatic Play in Postwar Guatemala." *Language and Communication* 33 (4): 515–531.

Ridet, Philippe. 2005. "M. Sarkozy Durcit Son Discours sur les Banlieues." *Le Monde*, November 21.

Rosello, Mireille, and Richard Bjornson. 1993. "The 'Beur Nation': Toward a Theory of 'Departenance'." *Research in African Literatures* 24 (3): 13–24.

Roth-Gordon, Jennifer. 2009. "The Language That Came Down the Hill: Slang, Crime, and Citizenship in Rio de Janeiro." *American Anthropologist* 111 (1): 57–68.

Rouse, Roger. 1991. Mexican Migration and the Social Space of Postmodernism. *Diaspora* 1: 8–23.

Sayad, Abdelmalek, and Eliane Dupuy. 2008. *Un Nanterre Algérien, Terre De Bidonvilles*. Paris: Autrement.

Schade-Poulsen, Marc. 1999. *The Social Significance of Raï: Men and Popular Music in Algeria*. Austin: University of Texas Press.

Schain, Martin A. 1985. "Immigrants and Politics in France." In *The French Socialist Experiment*, edited by John S. Ambler, 166–190. Philadelphia: Institute for the Study of Human Issues.

Schilling-Estes, Natalie. 1998. "Investigating 'Self-Conscious' Speech: The Performance Register in Okracoke English." *Language in Society* 27: 53–83.

Scott, Joan Wallach. 2007. *The Politics of the Veil*. Princeton, NJ: Princeton University Press.

Seguin, Boris, and Frédéric Teillard. 1996. *Les Céfrans Parlent aux Français. Chronique de la Langue des Cités*. Paris: Seuil.

Selby, Jennifer A. 2012. *Questioning French Secularism: Gender Politics and Islam in a Parisian Suburb*. New York: Palgrave Macmillan.

Seux, Bernard. 1997. "Une Parlure Argotique De Collégiens." *Langue Française* 114 (1): 82–103. doi:10.3406/lfr.1997.5386.

Shankar, Shalini. 2008. *Desi Land: Teen Culture, Class, and Success in Silicon Valley*. Durham, NC: Duke University Press.

Sherzer, Joel. 2002. *Speech Play and Verbal Art*. Austin: University of Texas Press.

Sherzer, Joel. 1990. *Verbal Art in San Blas: Kuna Culture through its Discourse*. Cambridge: Cambridge University Press.

Sherzer, Joel. 1987. "A Discourse-Centered Approach to Language and Culture." *American Anthropologist* 89 (2): 295–309.

Shukla, Sandhya. 2001. "Locations for South Asian Diasporas." *Annual Review of Anthropology* 30: 551–572.

Shuman, Amy. 1986. *Storytelling Rights: The Uses of Oral and Written Texts by Urban Adolescents*. Cambridge: Cambridge University Press.

Sidnell, Jack. 2003. "Constructing and Managing Male-Exclusivity in Talk-In-Interaction." In *The Handbook of Language and Gender*, edited by Janet Holmes and Miriam Meyerhoff, 327–352. Oxford: Blackwell.

Silverman, Maxim. 1992. *Deconstructing the Nation: Immigration, Racism and Citizenship in Modern France*. New York: Routledge.

Silverman, Maxim. 1991. "North African Immigration and the French Political Imaginary." In *Race, Discourse and Power in France*, edited by Maxim Silverman, 98–110. Brookfield, VT: Avebury.

Silverstein, Michael. 1976. "Shifters, Linguistic Categories, and Cultural Description." In *Meaning in Anthropology*, edited by Keith H. Basso and Henry Selby, 11–56. Albuquerque: University of New Mexico Press.

Silverstein, Paul A. 2005. "Immigrant Racialization and the New Savage Slot: Race, Migration, and Immigration in the New Europe." *Annual Review of Anthropology* 34: 363–384.

Silverstein, Paul A. 2004. *Algeria in France: Transpolitics, Race, and Nation*. Bloomington: Indiana University Press.

Silverstein, Paul A., and Chantal Tetreault. 2006. "Postcolonial Urban Apartheid." *Quarterly for the Social Science Research Council (Items and issues)*: 8–15. Middletown, Conn.: Wesleyan University Press.

Singh, Rajendra, Jayant Lele, and Gita Martohardjono. 1988.. "Communication in a Multilingual Society: Some Missed Opportunities." *Language in Society* 17 (1): 43–59.

Skapoulli, Elena. 2004. "Gender Codes at Odds and the Linguistic Construction of a Hybrid Identity." *Journal of Language Identity and Education* 3 (4): 245–260.

Smitherman-Donaldson, Geneva, and Teun A. van Dijk, Eds. 1988. *Discourse and Discrimination*. Detroit: Wayne State University Press.

Swedenburg, Ted. 2001. *"Islamic Hip Hop versus Islamophobia: Aki Nawaz, Natacha Atlas, Akhenaton."* In *Global Noise: Rap and Hip Hop Outside the USA*, edited by Tony Mitchell, pp. 57–85. Middletown, Conn.: Wesleyan University Press.

Taleb Ibrahimi, Khaoula. 1985. "Analyse et Confrontation des Productions Langagières des Jeunes Algériens en Milieu d'Origine et en Milieu d'Accueil." In *Les Algériens en France: Genèse et Devenir d'une Migration*, edited by Jacqueline Costa-Lascoux et Emile Témime, 311–319. Paris: Éditions Publisud.

Terrio, Susan J. 2009. *Judging Mohammed: Juvenile Delinquency, Immigration and Exclusion at the Paris Palace of Justice*. Stanford, CA: Stanford University Press.

Terrio, Susan J. 1999. "Crucible of the Millennium?: The Clovis Affair in Contemporary France." *Comparative Studies in Society and History* 41 (3): 438–457.

Tetreault, Chantal. 2010. "Collaborative Conflicts: Teens Performing Aggression and Intimacy in a French Cité." *Journal of Linguistic Anthropology* 20 (1): 72–86.

Tetreault, Chantal. 1997. "Strategically Splitting the Self: Constructions of Responsibility in Talk about Immigration." *Proceedings of the Annual Symposium about Language and Society-Austin: Texas Linguistic Forum* 39: 71–80.

Tetreault, Chantal. 1992. "*Mémoire de Maîtrise.*" Master's thesis, University of Paris, Jussieu.

Thorne, Barrie. 1993. *Gender Play: Girls and Boys in School*. New Brunswick, NJ: Rutgers University Press.

Tlatli, Soraya. 1998. "L'Ambivalence Linguistique dans la Littérature Maghrébine d'Expression Française." *The French Review* 72 (2): 297–307.

Tribalat, Michèle. 2009. "Mariages 'Mixtes' et Immigration en France." *Espace, Populations, Sociétés* 2: 203–214.

Tribalat, Michèle. 1995. *Faire France: Une Grande Enquête sur les Immigrés et Leurs Enfants*. Paris: Editions La Découverte.

Urban, Greg. 1991. *A Discourse-Centered Approach to Culture: Native South American Myths and Rituals*. Austin: University of Texas Press.

Urciuoli, Bonnie. 1996. *Exposing Prejudice: Puerto Rican Experiences of Language, Race, and Class*. Boulder, CO: Westview Press.

Van Dijk, Teun. 1993. *Elite Discourse and Racism*. Thousand Oaks, CA: Sage Publications.

Van Dijk, Teun. 1987. *Communicating Racism: Ethnic Prejudice in Thought and Talk*. Newbury Park, CA: Sage Publications.

Vermeij, Lotte. 2004. "'Ya Know What I'm Sayin'?' The Double Meaning of Language Crossing Among Teenagers in the Netherlands." *International Journal of the Sociology of Language* 170: 141–168. doi:10.1515/ijsl.2004.2004.170.141.

Wagner, Lauren. 2008. "Pratiquer la Langue Pendant les Vacances: Les Compétences Communicatives et la Catégorisation des Françaises d'Origine Parentale Marocaine." *Migrations et Plurlinguisme en France: Cahiers de l'Observatoire des Pratiques Linguistiques* 2: 80–86.

Walters, Keith. 1999. "'Opening the Door of Paradise a Cubit': Educated Tunisian Women, Embodied Linguistic Practice and Theories of Language and Gender." In *Reinventing Identities: The Gendered Self in Discourse*, edited by Mary Bucholtz, A. C. Liang, and Laurel A. Sutton, 200–217. Oxford, UK: Oxford University Press.

Wihtol de Wenden, Catherine. 1988. *Les Immigrés et la Politique: Cent Cinquante Ans D'évolution.* Paris: Presses de la Fondation Nationale des Sciences Politiques.

Wihtol de Wenden, Catherine, and Zakya Daoud. 1993. *Banlieues: Intégration ou Explosion?* Courbevoie, France: Éditions Corlet-Éditions Arléa.

Williams, Brackette F. 1991. *Stains on My Name, War in My Veins: Guyana and the Politics of Cultural Struggle.* Durham, NC: Duke University Press Books.

Willis, Paul. 1977. *Learning to Labor: How Working Class Kids Get Working Class Jobs.* New York: Columbia University Press.

Woolard, Kathryn. 1998. "Simultaneity and Bivalency as Strategies in Bilingualism." *Journal of Linguistic Anthropology* 8: 3–29.

Zentella, Ana Celia. 1990. "Returned Migration, Language, and Identity: Puerto Rican Bilinguals in Dos Worlds/Two Mundos." *International Journal of the Sociology of Language* 84: 81–100.

Ziv, Avner. 1984. *Personality and Sense of Humor.* New York: Springer Publishing Co.

INDEX

Transcultural Teens: Performing Youth Identities in French Cités, First Edition. Chantal Tetreault.
© 2015 John Wiley & Sons, Inc. Published 2015 by John Wiley & Sons, Inc.

ritual/religious practice, 17, 37, 38,
    57, 90, 93, 96–9, 105, 109–112,
    114, 123, 128, 133, 136, 138–40,
    146–7, 153, 161
Muxel, Anne, 33

names, naming, 3–6, 51, 80, 108, 112,
    146–50, 154–70, 173, 177, 179,
    180, 188, 190, 192, 194–8
Nanterre, 10, 19, 25, 47, 52, 54, 122,
    126–8
narrative(s), 5, 18, 32, 79, 82–3, 90, 92,
    100, 102, 104, 108–11, 144,
    174, 195
newspapers, 11, 24, 31
nicknames, 81, 156
Noiriel, Gérard, 33

Ochs, Elinor, 16, 100
Orellana, Marjorie Faulstich, 33
Ortiz, Fernando, 15
Ossman, Susan, 134

Pagliai, Valentina, 48
panic
    moral, 39, 91–3, 111
    social, 21
Park, Joseph Sung-Yul, 32
Paris, 2, 3, 7, 20, 23, 25, 27, 28, 41–3,
    54–5, 98, 107, 126, 131, 179
participant roles, 174, 179, 182, 184
Peirce, Charles, 16
Pennycook, Alastair, 46, 170
performance, 4–6, 14–15, 18, 29, 33,
    45–6, 48, 50–51, 53–6, 59, 79, 81,
    83–4, 89, 101, 116, 123, 148,
    150–152, 155–7, 160–163, 165–7,
    169, 170, 172–3, 175–80, 182–90,
    192–4, 196, 198
performative, 81, 83, 157, 176, 197
Peristiany, John, 112
Pichler, Pia, 170
Pierre-Adolphe, Philippe, 173
Poinsot, Marie, 33

police, 3, 10, 11, 24, 37, 91, 108, 126
post-colonial, post-colonialism, 18–24,
    27, 198
power, 16, 17, 21, 40–41, 63, 67, 79, 81,
    89, 99, 105, 128, 134, 145, 147,
    163, 170, 180, 184, 188, 193, 194
Pratt, Mary Louise, 7
prévention, 41, 125, 127
protest, 3, 9, 22, 126
Pujolar, Joan, 18

racaille ("street toughs"), 5, 11, 37–9,
    56–7, 91–8, 100–113, 119, 120,
    141–2, 195
"race", 5, 7, 13, 35, 57, 59, 60, 63, 79,
    80, 83, 89
raï, 14, 32, 39
racialization, 7, 46, 67, 83, 91, 194
racism, 10, 12–13, 16, 18, 42, 46, 57,
    59–61, 67–8, 71, 73, 77–9, 190,
    193–4, 196, 198
radio, 32, 122
Rampton, Ben, 35, 46, 170, 172
recursivity, 118–19 *see also* fractal
    recursivity
register(s), 56, 172–6, 178, 182–6, 189,
    192–4
respect, 5, 56, 92–3, 97–102, 105,
    109–10, 112–18, 120–123, 125,
    129–30, 132, 154, 157, 160–163,
    165–7, 169–70
Reyes, Angela, 18, 170
Reynolds, Jennifer F., 32, 63, 170
Ridet, Philippe, 37, 91, 92
ritual, ritualized, 2, 14, 18, 25, 38, 45,
    49–50, 55, 96–7, 100, 123, 156,
    158, 176, 184–5
Rosello, Mireille, 33
Roth-Gordon, Jennifer, 56
Rouse, Roger, 32

Sayad, Abdelmalek, 19
Schade-Poulsen, Marc, 32
Schain, Martin A., 20